# NATIONAL
# LABOR
# MOVEMENTS
# IN THE POSTWAR WORLD

EDITED BY EVERETT M. KASSALOW

*Northwestern University Press*
*1963*

# Foreword

by Ralph N. Campbell

Foreign policy and international labor affairs occupy to-day much time of a very large and increasing number of union leaders, officers, and staff members. Many labor representatives are serving in some international capacity, either with the U. S. government, or with a union, and international affairs as a discussion topic appears now almost as a matter of course in major union and university labor education programs.

The following collection of papers presented during a two-year period at a seminar on Comparative Labor Movements sponsored by the National Institute of Labor Education, deals primarily with problems faced by the labor movements in the developing countries. We trust the papers will be helpful to labor education practitioners and other interested persons in discussions on the subject matter. The Seminar itself and the publication of the papers have been assisted by a grant from the Ford Foundation. The responsibility for the content, however, lies entirely with the individual authors.

# Contents

vii

# Introduction

Within the past decade there has been increasing interest in the problems of labor movements abroad. The manner in which these movements are born and evolve has become of major political importance to the entire non-Communist world. In both the industrialized and the developing countries the structure and the ideology of labor movements are being molded and influenced by new forces.

In western Europe, for example, the process of economic recovery and spectacular economic growth, as well as the impact of sweeping new technological changes, have raised new problems for the working population and the trade-union movements in these countries. The almost simultaneous post-World War II process of reconstruction and expansion imposed a series of new strains on many of the old union structures and attitudes. Traditional Socialist-linked policies and programs in many of the northern and western European countries were subjected to re-examination and change.

While these forces have been at work in Europe, the American labor movement, in the space of 25 years, has grown from a somewhat limited and market-sheltered type of structure of three or four million members to a large sprawling economic force of 17 million members. The very change in size of this movement has transformed it from a more limited pressure-type institution into one of the key national economic forces.

The impact of these great social and economic forces inevitably has led to serious re-examination and re-evaluation of traditional labor attitudes and institutions both in the United States and western Europe. This process of restudy has been intensified by the great increase in travel and exchange of trade-union people which has taken place between the United States and other countries.

These changes were barely under way in the West when a veritable chain of social explosions began to occur in the so-called colonial or under-developed countries. Here the combined forces of nationalism and rapid industrialization are producing a series of labor movements which appear to be following neither an American nor European pattern of evolution, although important aspects of labor experience in the West do appear to have relevance to "new country" unionism.

Complicating the process of union evolution in many of the developing countries has been the powerful competitive thrust of Communist labor tactics and Communist labor movements. While pressure from competitive Communist labor movements has been of great significance in a few of the Western countries in the postwar period, notably France and Italy, it certainly does not represent the same general danger that it does in the more fragile societies of the developing nations.

In recognition of the need to achieve better understanding of these developments, and to think through some of their policy implications for American unions, government and private associations, a group of specialists in international labor problems in Washington, D. C. established in 1959 a continuing seminar on comparative labor movements.

Members of the seminar have included trade-unionists, government international labor experts from the State and Labor departments, as well as the United States Information Agency, several academicians, and a few individuals from private associations. All seminar members have, however, participated in their own individual capacities, and not as representatives of any organizations. A grant to support the seminar was obtained from the Ford Foundation through the intervention of the National Institute of Labor Education.

The seminar's common frame of reference or starting point has been a primary interest in the institutional development of labor unions as such. This is somewhat in contrast with other groups and individuals who have been studying unions and industrial relations as one of the problems incident to economic and industrial development. While the seminar papers and discussions have concentrated upon unions and union institutions, these have also been related to political parties and institutions, and especially labor-oriented parties.

Generally the seminar sessions have been structured around a series of formal papers, most of which were contributed by regular seminar members. In a few instances experts from universities outside of Washington also were invited to submit papers and lead discussions for the seminar.

In addition to the formal sessions at which papers have been presented, the seminar has held a number of informal meetings with trade-union leaders and labor specialists from abroad. These "confrontations" have helped to sharpen some of the insights and concepts about labor movements abroad which have been developed within the seminar.

The most critical theme which has recurred in the seminar sessions has been the nature and character of trade-union forms, trade-union ideology, and trade-union relationships in the developing countries. In preparing this volume, it was decided to select those papers that had been presented to the seminar which in one fashion or another bore upon this problem. While some of the papers, for instance, deal with Western movements, they were included because of their relevance in terms of parallel or comparable experience to problems confronting new-country trade-union movements. It should be added that while all of the papers stand as pieces of professional research, they also include policy judgments about the current and potential course of various labor movements in the world today.

The papers of Arnold Steinbach and David Saposs deal with the evolution of the international labor movements, both on the ideological and day-to-day operating planes. Saposs' paper furnishes a useful historical background to present-day ideological currents in the trade-union world. Steinbach stresses the changes in traditional concepts and practices of present-day international trade-union organizations. The new international trade-union organizations, unlike their pre-World War II predecessors, cannot rely upon the older, Socialist ideology to keep their various affiliates cemented together. It has not proven easy to find a common bond of social and political consensus which can unite trade-union movements from such diverse backgrounds as the United States, Scandinavia, Kenya, Mexico, and India, to name just five countries.

George Lichtblau's paper presents a detailed survey and analysis of Communist labor tactics in colonial and ex-colonial nations. The economic role of unions in the less-developed countries is one that constantly challenges development planners and nationalist political leaders in the new countries, as well as U. S. aid administrators. Paul Fisher's paper sets forth some of the limits and possibilities of economic unionism in the framework of economic development.

While the papers of Bruce Millen and Val Lorwin deal with unions in relatively highly developed countries, the experience they relate has relevance for union development in the new countries. Millen's paper on the Norwegian union movement and the labor party shows the way in which these twin engines of the Norwegian labor movement relate to one another. It sheds much light, in the context of a specific country, of the way in which political party and union needs and interests can be coordinated and reconciled in the social, economic, and political spheres.

The party and the union have separate organizations and functions, but rather than producing serious conflict, this dual power structure actually enhances labor's strength and flexibility of its actions. Norway is an interesting "case history" of the successful integration of the working class in the social, economic, and political life of a modern industrial society.

The relationship of unions to politics and parties is one of the critical questions confronting the trade-unions in many of the newly emerging countries where the very concept of an autonomous role for the trade-unions often meets with great resistance. A better understanding of the experience of the Norwegian labor movement, and indeed of labor movements in a number of western European nations, should be of assistance to the unions in the new countries.

In contrast with the "successful" integration or development of the Norwegian labor movement is the case of French unionism which is dealt with by Val Lorwin. Lorwin analyzes the persistence of "leftism" in the life of the labor movement in France. By drawing a comparison between French and Belgian labor movements, he throws much light on the problem of the almost continuous sense of "alienation" of large parts of the French working class from its own society. This sense of alienation helped pave the way for the current strength of Communist labor forces in France. With better understanding of the sociological and historical reasons for the deviation of the French labor movement from the norm of western Europe, it may be possible to avoid some similar mistakes elsewhere.

Solomon Levine, Stephen Low, and Robert Alexander analyze the forces which are influencing the evolution of unions in key parts of Asia, Africa, and Latin America. In each of these cases the effort is made to move from the particular problems encountered in given countries in these areas to observations on the nature of union evolution in developing countries generally. In Levine's paper we have a study of a labor movement based in a society which is being industrialized without having undergone the classic social or political revolution. The Japanese labor movement offers a strange contrast between what is a rather conservative structure of company-centered industrial relations combined with a radical labor union political ideology which takes the form of support for a revolutionist Socialist party.

Stephen Low's paper points up the stresses and strains upon African unions in the political struggle against colonialism. His paper also provides useful insight into the role of the trade-union movement in the typical one-party states springing up in so many of the new African nations. Low helps dispel some of the usual Western-centered judgments on the nature and character of these single-party states, as he tries to show how unions function within these new states.

Robert Alexander's study of the political role of unions in Latin America, with special emphasis on Bolivia, shows the problems and dilemmas confronting a "revolutionary" trade-union movement ten years after the "close" of a successful political revolution. The changing role of trade-unionism as it confronts its "own" government and the problems of economic development are well-drawn by Alexander.

The concluding paper, which I prepared myself, indicates where the seminar has come to in its consideration of unions in the developing countries. I hasten to add, however, that while this concluding paper is in a sense a product of the seminar, it nonetheless represents only my own views and I am sure that other members would not frame their conclusions in precisely the same way.

Of course any attempt to write about trade-unionism in the developing countries becomes almost a venture in prophecy. In most instances, the history of trade-unionism in these areas is still very brief, and attempts at generalization can be dangerous. On the other hand, there already is evidence that too often in these new countries political leaders look upon trade-unions, as well as other voluntary or intermediate associations, in purely manipulative terms.

The seminar members have been quite aware that democracy and pluralism are difficult enough to establish or maintain, as Western history demonstrates, in industrializing societies, whether the state or market place controls the economy; but without a will for democracy on the part of the leaders of parties in trade-unions, its establishment is impossible. It is hoped that these papers will make a contribution toward a better understanding of some of the dangers as well as the opportunities for democratic political evolution and trade-union development in the newly-emerging countries.

In addition to those whose papers are included in the volume, it seems appropriate to single out for mention additional Seminar members who at various times have served on its informal steering committee. These include: Morris Weisz of the U. S. Department of Labor and American University; Mark Perlman of Johns Hopkins University; Henri Sokolove, U. S. Department of State; Rudy Faupl, International Association of Machinists AFL-CIO; Harry Pollak and Donald Slaiman of the AFL-CIO; William Gausmann, Labor Adviser, U. S. Information Agency; John

# INTRODUCTION

Herling, Washington labor journalist; and Oliver Peterson of American University. (Several of those who contributed to the papers of the volume also served on this committee.) Among the earliest members of the steering committee were Philip Kaiser of American University and Ben Stephansky of the U. S. Department of State, who have since been appointed to ambassadorial posts in Senegal and Bolivia, respectively.

James Hoover, Daniel Lazorchick and Miss Alice Shurcliff of the U. S. Department of Labor; Frederic Meyers of the University of California at Los Angeles; and Adolf Sturmthal of the University of Illinois also prepared papers for different meetings of the Seminar. Reasons of space as well as the need to achieve general subject uniformity made it impossible to include these papers in the volume.

On the international side, the Seminar has been fortunate in having had sessions led by trade-union officials from a number of other countries. These include: Franz Olah, President of the Austrian Trade-Union Federation (ÖGB); Louis Wright, General Secretary of the Amalgamated Weavers Association and member of the General Council of the British Trades-Union Congress; P. P. Narayanan, General Secretary of the National Union of Plantation Workers and President of ICFTU Asian Regional Organization; N. M. Perera, President of the *Lanka Sama Samaj Party* (LSSP) (Trotskyite) and president of several Ceylonese trade-unions; and James Akumu, General Secretary of the Mombasa Dock Workers Union in Kenya.

Finally, I should also like to mention the warm and continuing support of the National Institute of Labor Education, including its officers, Ralph N. Campbell, Lawrence Rogin, Frank P. Graham, Lorentz H. Adolfson, and Joseph Mire. NILE's financial and administrative assistance helped to make possible the Seminar and this publication. It has been my pleasure to serve as the Seminar's Director and Editor of the volume.

EVERETT M. KASSALOW

# PART I

# Ideological Conflicts in the International Labor Movement*

1

by David J. Saposs

## Introduction

"The International Labor Movement" is a generic term including all organizational manifestations on the international level, basing outlook and actions on worker-status and aspirations. As dynamic, living movements, the separate groups experienced changes influenced by domestic and international social, economic, and other cultural events which usually give rise to internal differences and external conflicts with rival elements. By this process of action and reaction the movement readapted itself to changing conditions that have recently eventuated in a completely revolutionary ideological metamorphosis.

The radical labor movements favoring independent political action based on a labor ideology, have come to accept the political party as the ideological pivotal unit. It initiates and propounds the philosophy. On the other hand, those movements that accept non-partisan political action, or are entirely opposed to participating in it, have concentrated all thinking and action in the Trade-Union movement.

While this analysis will concentrate on the ideological phases, it will also touch on the structural and procedural. These three functions are intertwined, acting and reacting upon each other.

Changes in the procedural approach generally result in later basic ideologic adaptations. Ideologic concepts often stimulate a fundamental procedural approach. Similarly, the structural nomenclature occasionally induces alterations both in ideology and procedure.

* Grants from the American Philosophical Society Johnson and Penrose Funds aided in the pursuit of a study upon which this essay is based.

3

# NATIONAL LABOR MOVEMENTS

*Early Ideologic Conflict*

Since this essay concerns itself with ideologic evolution, the treatment, of necessity, will be chronological. Modern, radical and labor thinking and organization appeared with the earliest evidences of divorce of industry and commerce from feudalism. Some of the philosophizing was inspired by a nostalgic yearning to perpetuate the existing handicraft and its concomitant local commercial system, or the status quo; that is, combat the development of industrialism. The more persistent and successful philosophies were conceived by postulating an ideal social order inspired by oppressive industrial conditions. The early labor movement thinking originated in Europe, and especially western Europe, and was transported by migrants to other geographic areas.

Since Europe was culturally and economically the most advanced, it is natural that the radical and labor thinking should emanate from this part of the world. As groups sprang up and as leaders and the more alert rank and file studied and reacted to conditions, the idea of international organization became an imperative. Following preliminary meetings of key individuals, what became known as the First International, was founded in 1864 and continued to 1876. The ideology, structure and procedure was based on the Communist Manifesto and other ideas expounded by Karl Marx, Friedrich Engels and their associates. Ideologically, it was proclaimed that the workers were doomed to remain at the mercy of ruthless capitalism, hence the system must be abolished through the inevitable class struggle and replaced by a Socialist order. Procedurally, this objective was to be attained through capturing the State, whereby the new society would be introduced and built by the dictatorship of the proletariat. The structure of the organization whereby the workers were to be mustered, prepared, and through which they were to function, in fulfilling their heroic mission, was to be highly centralized. All direction was to come from the International Headquarters. And, since the movement, organizationally, was in its infancy and not clearly departmentalized functionally, all types of worker organizations

4

and groups were included—trade-union, political, cooperative, propaganda.

(Parenthetically, it should be mentioned that future international organizations of workers were categorically organized according to specific functional lines. The most accepted practice provides for separate political, trade-union, cooperative, and educational internationals. In addition, the Socialists have discarded the centralization concept. Each of the internationals subscribing to their philosophy is now completely decentralized with the affiliated units enjoying absolute autonomy, although the political organization serves as the ideological fountain head. While the Communists have accepted the functionalized, departmentalized principle, they still adhere to the highly centralized control precept, with the political party controlling the other units. The Syndicalists and trade-unionists accept only one functional group and subscribe to trade autonomy.)

Hardly had the First International come into existence when it became apparent that it was composed of two principal and irreconcilable ideological groups. Led by the Russian intellectual, Michael Bakunin, the Anarchists took issue with the Socialists on the three salient features propounded by the latter, namely, ideology, structure, and procedure. This irreconcilable difference was inevitable. The Anarchists predicated their philosophy on a retrograding feudalism supplemented by a going and independent handicraft system. As the lineal descendants of the Guild System, the typical handicraftsman was an independent self-employed businessman, who had either obtained or accumulated sufficient funds from his earnings to purchase the necessary tools and raw material to enable him to work for himself. But the Anarchists were in revolt against the rigid controls inherited from feudalism. Theirs was more than an economic rebellion; it was a social revolt against the entire system. The Church and the State, with its police and army, were all united in perpetuating an order, which interfered with the independence of the individual. Not having the ballot or power to further their objectives by legitimate means, the Anarchists advocated terroristic, insurrectory, and other illegal action, including intimidation and assassination. Propaganda of the deed was their shiboleth. Private property as the root of the attendant evil, must be abolished and the existing system would be replaced by one based on individual free local communities, practicing mutual aid. Structurally, this is but a replica of the handicraft system of production and small-scale commercialism of the Guild System, and ownership of the land tilled by the peasants, with the feudalistic restraints and private ownership discarded and mutual aid and cooperation substituted therefor.

On the contrary, the Socialists, led by Karl Marx and his associates, predicated their philosophy on an emerging industrialism, with the production and commercial units growing in size and markets steadily, concomitantly extending their boundaries. Concurrently, the mainstay of the capitalists was the authoritarian State, ruled by absolute monarchies, sustained by powerful military support, abetted by the Catholic Church with its tremendous land holdings. The workers were "exploited" and maintained in a state of destitution, hence the class struggle. The issue was the material well-being of the masses which historically was subordinated to that of the privileged class, which owned the means of livelihood, hence, historic materialism. Since the Church sided with the ruling and property-controlling class, it was accused of covering up the materialistic struggle in order to protect private property and other interests of the privileged class. Hence, religion became the opium of the people. This explains why the Socialist movement, particularly in continental Europe, was anti-clerical, bordering on agnosticism and even atheism. In the United Kingdom, the situation was different. While the Anglican Church sided with the property classes, the Non-conformist religious group worked very closely with the workers. As a result, the British Labor movement as a whole did not assume an anti-clerical or anti-religious coloration.

Confronted by a system of growing capitalism, sustained by a strong State, terroristic methods were not regarded by the Socialists as meeting the situation. And, with the increase in size of business units and expansion of markets, attempting to perpetuate a system of small shops, and confining activities to localized communities, was hardly the way out. (The Socialists did not generally concern themselves with the land problem.) Hence, they advocated capturing the State by the workers and then expropriating the expropriators by socializing production and distribution. With the lack of universal manhood suffrage, the Socialists put considerable emphasis on the right to vote. (This tactic explains why so many of the continental European Socialist parties included in their titles the word "democratic"; for instance, German Social Democratic party.)

These differences between the Anarchists and Socialists were irreconcilable. As usually happens, with the leaders on both sides being strong-willed and highly proficient at polemics, the controversy raged at boiling point. From all available authentic data, it is clear that the Anarchists were in the ascendency, because of popular hankering for something resembling the Guild System. In order to save the First International, Marx highhandedly arranged to move the headquarters to New York. But the times for a Socialist International were not yet propitious, so that the organization which had hardly ceased being a paper organization, finally faded away. As contrasted with the sociologists' term of "cultural lag," Marx and Engels' prognostication was evidently a cultural advance or lead.

The economic status of continental western Europe at this time seemed to most radical thinkers to favor the diagnosis of the Anarchists. To be sure, England was becoming the workshop of the world, but the rest of Europe was still at this time in the handicraft and small business-unit stage. And, lacking universal manhood suffrage, the Anarchists' analysis and program seemed to fit the immediate situation more logically than that of the Socialists. The Socialists labored under an additional disadvantage: The two countries with relatively viable trade-union movements, were uninterested in the First International or in socialism. Had these union movements become associated with the First International, there is no question, judging from their hostile reaction to Anarchist efforts in their respective countries, that

7

they would have aligned themselves with the Socialists. In Britain and the United States, the respective trade-union movements were, in this transition period towards industrialism, also stirred by the revolutionary, economic, and social situation, but they were preoccupied with indigenous reform theories. The British leaders and thinkers among the workers were at first mostly intrigued by the Chartist movement, with its Land Reform program and demand for other reform legislation that would remove serious disabilities of workers and other non-property elements, including the vote. Next the larger-thinking proportion of British labor became absorbed in Robert Owen's Producers Cooperation program. This panacea aimed to emancipate wage earners by raising their status to that of self-employed.

In the United States, the dominant labor movement, as ultimately epitomized in the Knights of Labor, in common with the farmer and small businessman, also aspired to realizing the middle-class ideal of self-employment. This movement consisted primarily of indigenous workers, and leaders. With the introduction of modern transportation, a large proportion of these workers had been forced to leave rural areas where they plied their trade as handicraftsmen or small merchants. To attain or retain their ideal, they embarked on political action, since they had the ballot. Usually, they collaborated with small businessmen and farmers, reaching the political pinnacle in the Populist movement. They advocated free, public education so that their children would have equal opportunities with the better-to-do elements and would not have to be subjected to the shame of wearing uniforms that marked them as attending charity schools. As small businessmen who were likely to find themselves in financial straits, they also advocated the abolition of imprisonment for debt. (This demand laid the basis for future bankruptcy legislation.) And, as creditors, they favored cheap money in the form of greenbacks. To maintain the ideal of self-employment, they favored producers' cooperation, where an individual who could not raise the necessary capital to go into business for himself, could still avoid being a wage-earner by associating with a small number of like-

minded and similarly conditioned people, in forming a producers cooperative. In addition thereto, they advocated other
forms of legislation that would give the small property
owner, that is the self-employed handicraftsman and the
small merchant, as well as the aspiring wage earner, status
equal to that of the better-to-do.

Union activities were regarded as temporary and inci-
dental. A worker wanted a union so as to enable him to
prevent the private employer from deteriorating the skilled
trade, and to enable the worker to earn enough so that he
could lay some funds aside, and by this saving, become either
self-employed or a cooperator. Some elements—primarily
among the intellectuals and more sophisticated—favored
legislation that would prohibit corporations from doing business, thus removing a serious, competitive threat to the ideal
of self-employment. The legal profession was most successful
in securing such legislation. It is still generally illegal for
corporations to practice law.

To the recent immigrants, mostly of British and German
extraction, this ideal did not appeal. They had come to
realize that it was not feasible to halt industrial progress.
Appreciating that they were doomed to remain workers
permanently, they favored continuous and strong unions,
hence they organized separately but did not become sufficiently strong to exercise the influence they enjoyed later.
During this period, the indigenous workers, as represented in
the Knights of Labor, were the dominant group, and it was
their ideal which prevailed both on the industrial as well as
the political field.

*Conflict Broadens*

With the disappearance of the First International, a
vacuum was left insofar as International Labor movement
organization was concerned. Nevertheless, with advancing
industrialism, sentiment for international organization grew
among the scattered national movements, which increased in
size and improved in viability. The first to take the next step
were the Anarchists. Following the usual preliminaries, the
International Working People's Association was brought

9

into existence in 1881. Unofficially, it was referred to as the Black International, the color the Anarchists selected for their banner as signifying death to the existing order and its key personnel. In this period of primitive industrialism, it was not only a thorn in the side of the government, wherever it had a substantial following, but it also was a challenge to the Socialists and pure trade-unionists. It exercised considerable influence in France, Italy, Britain, Germany, and the Scandinavian countries. In the United States, where its following was mostly German, led by Johann Most, its trade-union units were a troublesome force in the important population and industrial centers. Finally, its terroristic methods, including attacks on key government and industrial leaders, coupled with changing conditions that revealed their strategy as ineffective and detrimental, led to its decline, reducing the Anarchist movement to an insignificant sect of self-adulation with free-love overtones.

Not far behind in initiating new organization, were the Socialists. In 1889, they founded what became known popularly as the Second International, officially designated, International Socialist Congresses. It continued to function into 1914, disintegrating with the advent of World War I. In a sense, the Second International was the first dual ideologic organization on the international horizon, in that it now competed with the Black International. However, since it traced its lineage to the First International, this observation becomes a moot question. In the beginning, the structure was undefined, in addition to political clubs and parties, unions, cooperatives and miscellaneous bodies were admitted. Some union groups like those in the United States and Great Britain, which were not Socialist in philosophy, also casually participated by sending delegates to the various congresses. Later, affiliation was limited to political parties. Procedurally, the original Socialist tenet of achieving the aim through political action, was once more emphasized.

In characteristic fashion, internal conflict developed with the opposition coming from two divergent sources. Admitting union affiliation in the early period made it possible for Syndicalists to become associated. There is a tendency to regard syndicalism as an advanced development of anarchism. Indeed, a hyphenated term is used to clinch this view by referring to Anarcho-Syndicalists. This is distinctly erroneous, although there are certain seeming similarities. In common with the Socialists, Syndicalists and Anarchists have the same objective, namely, the abolition of the capitalist system, or the system based on private property and enterprise, and replacing it by socialized society. With the Anarchists, the Syndicalists also agree that political action and other parliamentary procedures are to be condemned. But from there on, they differ radically. The Syndicalists, like the Socialists, predicated their philosophy on an advancing and powerful industrialism. Hence, instead of free, localized communities, the Syndicalists advocated the worker-expropriating industry, with each broad industrial division to be operated by a particular industrial union. The industrial unions were to be allied for general, commercial and social purposes. Similarly, the Syndicalists rejected, indeed scorned, as a disorganized and impractical procedure, exclusive reliance on terrorism and other forms of scattered violence, advocated and practiced by the Anarchists. They preferred disciplinary organizational tactics. Sabotage, to harass the capitalist on the job and in the factory, as well as to demonstrate worker power, was one of their tactical favorites. In the directed local, industrial, and ultimate general strike, the Syndicalists placed their hopes. In the United States the Industrial Workers of the World represented a close facsimile of syndicalism. It achieved notoriety mostly because of its leadership of dramatic strikes of semi-skilled and unskilled immigrant workers, employed in large scale industries in the North, and hillbilly and poor whites in the South. These workers were neglected by the AFL unions. Similarly, it operated among migratory and seasonal workers in the harvest fields of the Midwest and lumber camps of the northwest. Usually, the volatile disturbances, which attracted world attention, centered around quickie strikes and free-speech fights. The I.W.W. already lost its attraction before World War I. The war prosecutions contributed to reducing it to general impotence as a union. However, it has continued functioning as an insignificant propaganda group. In the rest of the world the Syndicalist movement lost ground more slowly. But it was in their decline following World War I that the Syndicalists were impelled to organize themselves internationally. In 1922, they founded the International Working Men's Association.

As is common in mass movements, the membership was not so keenly ideologically oriented as to distinguish between socialism and syndicalism. At least, a large proportion were mainly interested in militant and heroic action as well as flamboyant pronouncements. These features, the Syndicalists provided in superlative fashion. Events in the United States served to illustrate the contradiction. William D. (Big Bill) Heywood, the picturesque, massive, and dynamic leader of the I.W.W. was regularly elected, in referendum vote, to the Executive Board of the Socialist party in the United States. It took action of the Board to expel him because of his Syndicalist views.

*Revolutionists vs Revisionists*

A more profound difference arose within the Second International. Originally, it appeared as a divergence affecting procedure. Finally, it eventuated into a basic ideological controversy. Within the last two decades this difference resulted in a complete ideological transformation with an outright discarding of Marxism, from which socialism initially received its inspiration, and upon which philosophy it was based for slightly over a century.

Marxian socialism appeared with the issuance of the Communist Manifesto in 1849. Fifteen years later in 1864 it temporarily achieved organizational form on the international horizon and continued its stormy and insecure course for about 17 years, when it temporarily was disembowled. It was reactivated towards the end of 1889. From its inception it also was confronted with ideological disputes, first with the Anarchists, then with the Syndicalists. In both instances, the controversy was sufficiently distinctive so that it eventuated in a schism, whereby each group followed an independent course. The Socialists categorically divested themselves from those opposing groups. The difference to be considered now, emanated as a family quarrel, both sides devoutly proclaiming their unalterable adherence to Marxism and socialism. The difference became articulate toward the end of the nineteenth century. Originally they regarded their difference as tactical. As the controversy raged, they began to assert different interpretations of Marxism. Tomes, brochures, leaflets, were written to prove that each side had the correct interpretation. The Socialist press discussed the matter and it was intellectually and emotionally debated at conferences and meetings within the various countries, and on the international level. Considerable written space, time, and energy were consumed in debating the disagreements which might have been employed in carrying the message to the uninitiated.

The difference centered over program emphasis. One side was of the firm opinion that the revolutionary objective of abolishing capitalism should be featured. In popular terminology, the aim was to stress ultimate demands. This group became known as the Revolutionists, because they aspired to give preference to expediting attainment of the social revolution. However, this faction recognized that the revolution was to be achieved by peaceful means through education and parliamentary, that is, political action. The opposition advocated concentration on issues that would bring about current improvements in the welfare of the workers, such as limiting hours of labor, factory and social legislation, and taxation reform. (In later years, these measures were described as Social Reform legislation.) In popular terminology, this procedure became characterized as a placing of emphasis on immediate demands. The contention of this faction was that, in this manner, the way would be prepared for the ultimate introduction of socialism. In contrast to the Revolutionists, these were dubbed Revisionists. This group agreed with its rival that education and political action were the prime procedures for achieving the aims. In this sense they both disagreed procedurely with the Anarchists and Syndicalists. As the controversy became heated, vituperative language was introduced. In its mildest manifestations, the

Revolutionists sarcastically labeled the Revisionists as opportunists. In retaliation, the latter denounced the Revolutionists as Impossiblists. This division arose independently in various countries. In France the Revisionists group named itself Possiblists. In England, the Fabians antedated the continental revisionists elements with their Socialist philosophy of Gradualism. It also was non-Marxian and, therefore, early anticipated the current transformation of the Socialist movement.

Because the German movement was outstanding numerically, electorally, and intellectually, reflecting more the reaction to conditions on the European continent, it became the leader of the International Socialist movement. The two towering intellectual exponents of the divergent views were Germans. Karl Kautsky upheld the Revolutionist position. Eduard Bernstein, as ably, sustained the Revisionist side. Their writings were translated and widely circulated. Naturally, able individuals in their respective countries aligned themselves and propagated the doctrines. In the United States, the disagreement had caused a split in the Socialist movement. The vitriolic, inflexible, able, and erudite Deniel De Leon transformed the Socialist Labor party into a vehicle for Impossiblist concepts. Those who regarded the Opportunist approach as the more practicable withdrew, and under the brilliant leadership of Morris Hillquit and Victor L. Berger, both sophisticated and steeped in the lore of international socialism, its movement and its philosophy, organized with the aid of their accomplished associates, the rival Socialist party in 1901. Since the American Federation of Labor had repudiated socialism, the impetuous De Leon declared war against it by founding the "dual" Socialist Trades and Labor Alliance. The moderates in control of the substantial Socialist unions continued adherence to the AFL, with the idea of "boring from within" as a means of converting the AFL to socialism. In the other important countries, like Germany, Austria, the Socialists continued to work out their differences within the party. In Britain the Social Democratic Federation in England, and the Socialist Labor party in Scotland, served as the upholders of pure Marxism or revolutionism. The Independent Labour Party (ILP), on the other hand, supported the concept of revisionism with a non-Marxian coloration, as expounded by the Fabians. The British Labour party founded in 1906 only embraced socialism in 1918.

Simultaneously with the development of the Socialist Political movement, the trade-unions in the advanced industrial countries made sufficient progress to attain considerable strength and stability. In the Scandinavian countries, Germany, Austria, Holland, Belgium, and Luxembourg, the unions were nurtured by the socialist political branch. Gradually, as mass trade-union organizations guided by competent, practical leadership which rose from the ranks, became the chief influential force within the Socialist movement in their respective countries, they began to exercise extraordinary influence within the political branch, that is, the Socialist parties, with which they were affiliated. The same was true of the ILP in England, and the Socialist party in the United States, which received its substantial support from the strong Socialist unions affiliated with the AFL. Because of the nature of their responsibilities in collective bargaining and otherwise ministering to the day-to-day-problems of their members, with some notable exceptions, the leaders became Opportunist-oriented. Hence they supported the advocates of this precept within the Socialist and Labor parties. The dominant leaders of the Social Democratic party in Germany, as represented by Wilhelm L. Liebkncht and August Bebel, were, however, staunch Revolutionists and sensed that the trade-unions were the prime carriers of revisionism. They, therefore, manifested unfriendly feeling towards over-encouraging the unions in Germany. Thus, when Eduard Bernstein translated the pioneering and scholarly *Webb's History of Trade-Unionism (in England)*," into German in 1896, he was severely censured by the dominant group in the German Socialist movement. Nevertheless, as the German unions advanced in strength, they too threw in their lot with the Revisionists. Thus, toward the end of the second decade of the twentieth century, the Revisionists came into the ascendency of the German Socialist movement, likewise the

Socialist movements of all the important industrial countries accepted its Revisionist approach. Thereby the outlook of the International movement became completely transformed, with the Revolutionists finding themselves a slight minority opposition.

Differences in outlook between the Revolutionists and Revisionists ripened over fundamental doctrines. The intellectual Revisionists took to seriously criticizing what was until then regarded as uncontestable Marxian doctrines, at the same time emphasizing current social problems, which were also the concern of the trade-union leaders. The Opportunists simultaneously began to revise basic Marxian doctrine. Besides, desiring specific reforms, they needed support from other elements in society. But, the external criticism of Socialist revolutionary doctrines by those whose support they needed tended to isolate the Socialists. This desire for alliance with socially inclined liberals and social reformers only gave additional impetus to the Revisionists trend. Naturally, concessions were in order. With the growth of industry and general economic development, fundamental bourgeois precepts had become practically universally accepted. The bourgeois revolutions of the nineteenth century against absolute monarchism, were fought for the establishment of government by law, assuring the application of freedom and democratic procedure—that is due process, as against whimsical authoritarianism. Two pillars sustaining freedom and democracy were (1) guarantee of individual rights, and (2) guarantee of property rights. The Socialists, in contrast to the procedural tenets of illegality of the Anarchists and Syndicalists, appropriated the positive bourgeois concepts of freedom and democracy by favoring political action and the use of the State for achieving their aims. In subscribing to this position they were, undoubtedly, influenced by the failure of much of the bourgeois revolutionary efforts, as well as by the general public indignation at the resort to "direct action" or "propaganda of the deed" of their radical rivals, the Anarchists and Syndicalists. General public reaction to violence and insurrection had become an accepted view by now. All Socialists likewise accepted the concept of individual rights, but the revolutionary Socialists clung to the Marxian tenet of expropriating the expropriators, that is, confiscation of private property. It was this belief that isolated the revolutionary Socialists from the rest of society. Being interested in a practical approach, and seeking collaboration of liberals and social reformers, the Revisionists acknowledged this bourgeois principle by incorporating in their programs the provision that owners of private property would be compensated in the event of nationalization. This act was indeed a means of driving an irreconcilable wedge between the Revisionists and the Revolutionists.

Perhaps this drift away by the Revisionists from Marxism, would have then led them on to a more decisive clarification of their philosophy. However, the war clouds of the years immediately preceding World War I monopolized their thinking and the breaking out of World War I created a more pressing intellectual crisis in the International Socialist movement. Originally, the Socialists had been unalterably opposed to capitalist wars. However, after considerable negotiation and conferences, the Socialist movements of their respective belligerent European countries decided to support the war efforts of their governments. In siding with their particular countries, the Socialists had discarded the international precept of socialism, which was based on working-class solidarity as against the international bourgeoisie. When put to the test this concept failed to materialize. Since then, their international outlook began to be transformed. While the Socialists still have an international ideal, it is no longer regarded as exclusive or superseding the national interest of the working class. Two other cardinal principles regarded as irrevocable Socialist doctrine were also discarded during the War. Much attention and discussion were given in pre-World War I days to Socialists' participating in bourgeois governments. This practice was overwhelmingly condemned. There was even greater unanimity within the International Socialist movement for Socialist legislators to vote against military appropriations. Both these principles were ignored during the War. Some of the Socialist parties, particularly that of France, revived, temporarily, the idea of non-participation in bourgeois governments immediately following World War I. Likewise, there was mild inclination toward opposing military appropriations. By soon abandoning these principles in general, as well as accepting the bourgeois concept of individual and property rights, most Socialist movements accentuated the trend towards fundamental revision of Marxism and its final abandonment.

### Trade-Union Challenge to Socialists

Certain trade-union movements were aloof or challenged the Socialists and other radical groups. In continental Europe, the Christian unions, predominantly Catholic in outlook, entered the arena as rivals. Eliminating the Scandinavian countries, all the other continental European countries contained either a large, compact Catholic segment, or were predominantly Catholic in population. However, the Catholic hierarchy, on the whole, was unsympathetic to the organized efforts of the workers to promote and protect their interests under the emerging industrialism. This attitude left an open field for the radicals. As the radicals progressed and manifested an anti-clerical attitude, individuals first in the lower Church levels, became alarmed, and this attitude gradually penetrated to the hierarchy. They recognized that the Church must replace its negative position towards the workers by a positive and sympathetic program. The upshot was the issuance by Pope Leo XIII of the famous encyclical Rerum Novarum in 1891. This encyclical recognized that wage earners had certain rights which employers and the State must recognize. Among these was the right of workers to organize into unions. But, the workers must not join atheistic unions, but instead must organize Christian unions, and with the aid of the clergy such unions were founded. A sufficient number were functioning by 1908 to warrant the founding of the Christian International. This was the first mass international ideological dual trade-union movement. It was designed primarily to challenge the International Federation of Trade-Unions controlled by the Socialists, and indirectly the national and international Socialist political movement. In addition to the usual trade union program based on collective bargaining, the Christian unions, following the lead of Rerum Novarum, promulgated extensive social reform demands. In this sense, they differed from the pure and simple or business unionism of the AFL. The Canadian unions, as represented by the Canadian Trades and Labor Congress, and most of them affiliated with the AFL Internationals, while remaining aloof from socialism, nevertheless supported social reform measures. Therefore, they resembled more the Christian unions in subscribing to a social reform philosophy.

*Communist and Fascist Threat*

Toward the end of the War, various conferences were held about reviving the International Socialist movement. But a new star appeared in the international firmament as an outgrowth of the Bolshevik Revolution in Russia, concurrently affecting the International Labor movement. With the Communists impetuously demanding control and taking an uncompromising position, the conflict was indeed intensive and bitter. As usually happens, following a holocaust like a war, the population was impelled to look with sympathy at extreme movements. Revolution was in the air in the radical and liberal movements. The Communists received a sympathetic response. They made rapid headway. At first they tried to capture the Socialist movement, succeeding particularly in France and Italy. As the Socialists rallied, the Communists turned to dualism by founding separate parties and a new international which they characterized as the Third International. The conflict was bitter. As usual, a small group of sincere radicals attempted to reconcile the two contending groups. They became known as the Second-and-a-half International. In the end, the Second-and-a-half International abandoned the insoluble mediation task. Most of the leaders of this group returned to the Socialist fold. In the meantime, the Socialists restored their international organization, naming it the Socialist and Labor International.

Hardly having re-established itself, the Socialist movement, in common with other democratic elements, was forced to concern itself with another more pressing and immediately threatening menace, in the form of fascism. Early storm signals occurred in the early 1920's with Mussolini's march on Rome and the subsequent eradication of the Italian Labor movement and all other democratic manifestations. The Movement was more profoundly stirred when the German Nazis began to augment their strength. In the interim, the Dolfus Putch in Austria, which abolished the powerful movement of that country, created further concern. Shortly thereafter followed the shocking blow in Germany where the Movement, regarded as the guiding star in the international Socialist firmament, was completely destroyed with the Nazi advent to power. In the wake of these horrendous developments, the thinking and action of the Movement was primarily absorbed with the Fascist menace. Little time was left for ideological thinking or bickering, except that of conducting a rearguard action with the Communists. In the meantime, the Communists were readapting their strategy, promulgating a popular front ostensibly to combat fascism, but actually designed to capture or destroy the Socialist and liberal movements. Some of the Socialists fell into this trap which cost them dearly in the end. A small group within the Socialist International did raise a point of difference regarding strategy in fighting fascism, which to the dominant Socialist group too clearly resembled Communist policy and tactics. Led by the British Independent Labour party, which by now embraced revolutionary traits, and supported by like-minded groups from other countries, they chastised the leadership for its timidity, urging a militant and revolutionary procedure, but not delineating a method of promoting it. Had time permitted its elaboration, they might have resuscitated, with some amplification, the previous Revolutionist Socialist program. But time was rapidly marching on, precipitating the Second World War.

On the fringes of the Socialist movement and outside its congresses, individuals or small groups urged ideological adaptations. An underground group in Germany, calling itself the New Beginning, advocated "revitalizing" the Movement on militant revolutionary lines. While criticizing the Communists for their inflexibility, they advocated unity with them. Circulated through the Movement, chiefly in the western countries, The New Beginning literature attracted attention mostly among the younger intellectuals. Too preoccupied with counteracting the Fascist menace, the established leaders of the movement paid little heed to the preachings of such fringe elements.

From another direction came a proposal to scrap Marxism entirely replacing it by social reformism akin to welfare statism. Henri de Man, the Belgian intellectual, was the outstanding proponent of this ideologically revolutionary program. He wrote extensively and pointedly and talked articulately. But, this was a highly critical situation, with revolutionary thinking favored only by the fringe opposition elements. Consequently, the Revisionists remained in control without much effort.

The outbreak of the Second World War did not find the Socialists in the same quandary that engulfed them when the First World War was in the offing. This was a war against totalitarianism—Communist and Fascist. Whereas the Socialists participated in the First World War with heavy hearts, they now joined most enthusiastically in the "Holy War." When the Nazis turned on Soviet Russia, the Communists were welcomed as allies by all elements in society. While there were reservations on the part of some Socialists, the general intellectual thinking, most of it artificially stimulated, was to overlook the past treachery of the Communists and accept their profession of honest collaboration for the successful prosecution of a mutual objective. The Communists proclaimed devoutly, and were believed, as not having any ulterior motives. Following the war, the Communists were included as honest comrades-in-arms, as the non-Communist elements were unaware that the Communists had secretly manipulated activities, as was their wont, so that they emerged as the strongest organized radical force. It soon became clear to the Socialists, as it did to other democratic forces, that the Communists were still bent on subverting democracy, and concentrating on furthering Soviet Russia's imperialistic designs. The Socialists and other knowledgeable democratic elements began to dissociate themselves from the

Communists by staunchly and successfully resisting them. As a result, the Communists were gradually reduced to fringe oppositions in practically all Western-oriented countries, except Italy and France. Henceforth their chief successes have occurred in the less-developed regions.

## Discarding Marxism

By now, the Communists had pretty well monopolized Marxism, giving it an extreme totalitarian connotation. In the public mind, Marxism and communism not only became synonymous, but began to be associated with the Soviet Russian conspiratorial, imperialistic ambitions. Communism also began to connote infiltration, subversion, aggression, brutality, slave labor camps, denial of civil liberties and other anti-democratic and inhumane practices. It became imperative for the Socialists distinctly to dissociate themselves from this scourge, in order to continue functioning as a democratic social force. They thus, tacitly, began to discontinue describing themselves as Marxists and emphasizing the immediate and practical phases, that is, their social reform objectives. Similarly, collaboration with bourgeois parties in elections and in governments was no longer regarded as sacrilegious or contrary to Socialist ideology. Neither was voting for military appropriations regarded as violating basic Socialist tenets. They also began more positively to cater to other less-prosperous elements, such as the lower-middle class.

More fundamental social and economic developments pressed for a complete ideological transformation. As the Socialist Labor movement grew, particularly in Western-oriented countries, the attitude of the workers, the mainstay of the Socialist movement, toward the social and economic system began to be revised. As we have seen, the Revisionists or Opportunists dominated the thinking and activities of the Movement in pre-World War I days. The unions grew in strength and through collective bargaining the workers' living and working conditions improved materially and noticeably. Through their organizations they also attained status, such as participating in control of their jobs and a voice in directing their work. Simultaneously, through powerful political parties the workers became a vital social force in the community. In alliance with other liberal elements, and often with the support of conservative political elements who tried to check the growth of the Socialist political parties, social reform legislation was obtained that positively improved the lot of the workers. Hours of labor, minimum wages, housing, factory regulations, social security measures—all this type of legislation contributed to the welfare of the workers. Through their unions workers gained a considerable degree of job security, such as seniority, union participation in drafting and enforcing work rules and other related practices. The workers now had acquired vested interests and rights in society. In order to safeguard and even improve those hard-won and valuable conditions, they now became interested in the stability of capitalism, that is, the existing order. Any precipitate action would threaten those gains. This new interest induced a stronger attachment to their respective countries. They had a stake in the nation. They were enjoying status. This psychologic metamorphosis began with the turn of the century, growing in proportion as the unions and political parties gained strength, and as living and working conditions steadily and perceptibly improved. One form of evidence was the workers' adherence to revisionism. Another was the patriotic embrace of their countries in support of the First World War. The worker had risen successively from a poverty standard to that of a subsistence standard, then a comfortable standard, followed by a cultural standard, and it is now advancing to a middle-class standard thereby giving the worker a new status. Besides, in the course of time additional gains could reasonably be expected. He belongs. He is no longer a despised castaway. He is catered to. He is an important factor in society.

Reacting to these social, economic, and psychologic manifestations, the Socialists, now dominated by the Revisionists, began tacitly and markedly to deviate from Marxian doctrine and policy, although they still used Marxian terminology, and staunchly professed adherence to it. As this transition advanced, the Socialist movements of some countries, without any fanfare, discontinued advocating such important So-

23

cialist principles as nationalization. The Scandinavian Socialists were the first to by-pass it completely, and when
leaders were questioned, they explained that they did not
regard nationalization as a vital feature of socialism. They
were interested in social justice, which can be attained by
the exercise of legislative and administrative power. By
monetary, fiscal policy and taxation, this aim can also be
furthered. Emphasis is placed on planning, full employment,
housing, education, civil rights and democracy. For this purpose, it is vital that the Socialist movement attain political
power, either as a powerful opposition, or, preferably, as the
government. By relying exclusively on worker-support this
latter aim would be difficult to achieve. Consequently the
base must be broadened by a program that would appeal to
other social elements. A viable and powerful Trade-Union
movement also contributes towards achieving this objective.
Similarly, producers' and consumers' cooperation are essential and functional institutions in the fulfillment of this
objective.

More recently, the Socialist parties of a number of the
continental European countries have boldly revised their
programs in line with the trail-blazing position taken by the
Scandinavians. Notable among these are the Dutch, Austrian,
and German parties. They have openly and in print dis-
sociated themslves from Marxism and are now proponents
of welfare statism, including a mixed economy and a far
reaching social reform program. The Austrians want it understood that they are no longer a worker party but a general
citizens party. Even the German Social Democrats are concerned about maintaining private enterprise in those sectors
of the economy still competitive. Recently the Australian
Labour party has proclaimed that it is primarily interested in
the government developing the resources and industry in the
unsettled areas. It is willing to forgo nationalization where
private enterprise is now functioning successfully. And, since
the 1959 election reverses in Britain, the Labour party is discussing whether rationalization should no longer be featured
as a prime issue. During the last election, a strenuous effort
was made by some of the leaders, including among them the

more influential, to substitute for the term nationalization that of public enterprise. One well-informed journalist reported that at the July 1959 Congress of the Socialist International, the name of Karl Marx was mentioned only once. Another observed that the liveliest discussions centered over differences on issues of nationalistic interest. For example, the British opposed further nuclear tests, whereas the French delegates favored a continuation. Evidently the latter were actuated in their stand by the nationalistic ambition of France to maintain its position as a world power by also exploding a bomb in the Sahara Desert.

*Search for a New Program*

Notwithstanding these ideological policy adaptations, the Socialist parties in some European countries have lost ground in recent elections. To be sure, the losses, on the whole, have been marginal. In other countries these parties are standing still. It is clear that the Socialist working-class appeal has reached its saturation point. Indeed, this appeal has lost its force with certain sectors of the working class, as the slight losses in recent elections reveal. It would seem that the better paid and fully employed workers are beginning to reconsider their ideological orientation. It is also beginning to appear that the old Socialist appeal makes very little impression upon white-collar, technician, and professional workers, and in general the lower-middle class. At the 1951 Socialist International Congress, even some of the old-time leaders like Oscar Pollak, the highly sophisticated and able Austrian Socialist and journalist, now an elder statesman, sounded the call for a restudy of the Socialist program in order to broaden the appeal. Shortly thereafter, a committee of experts was created by the Socialist International for that purpose.

Not only must the Socialists divest themselves of the Marxist ideology, but they must devise a program based on the welfare state concept, that will have a practical, general appeal to the workers and most of the middle class, including the highly skilled workers, white-collar workers, technicians, and lower level professional elements that are increasing in numbers. They must outdo their bourgeois competitor parties, which have also embraced a limited form of welfare statism.

This impasse confronting the Socialists which has halted their progress, at least temporarily, cannot be charged to their change in ideology. Rather, it is traceable to the competition of the reformed bourgeois parties who even tolerate existing nationalized enterprises, by having grudgingly accepted a mixed economy as a permanent feature. Had the Socialists not transformed their ideology, their recent electoral losses would have been considerably greater. Their small gains or failure to make no material gains, in some countries, would have turned into losses. Within the Western-oriented countries the threat from the Left, inside the Socialist movement, or its Communist rival is insignificant. In the recent British election, the Leftists' parliamentary candidates were less successful than the others. Some of the outstanding Leftists in the Labour party were found dismally swamped when the election returns were canvassed. These losses were garnered not only by the Tories but also by the Liberals. Indeed, the election returns reveal that most of the gains made by the Liberals were taken from the Labour party.

Likewise, current elections in the Western-oriented countries indicate conclusively that the Communist opposition is diminishing to negligible proportions in most instances. This is a striking contrast when compared to their achievements in the immediate post-World War II period. With prosperity, built-in welfare programs and other provisions that cushion recessions, providing protection to the less fortunate from undue hardship, the extreme Left and for that matter, Right, should offer little prospect of serious rivalry and threat to the Socialists and other moderate democratic parties. Even in Italy and France, the Communists have reached their peak and they are likely to lose heavily should a serious, international crisis arise. Their strength rests primarily on discontent over current domestic issues. The larger majority of their followers are, like most workers, basically patriotic. In their quest for winning majority electoral support, or even sustaining their present vote-getting prowess, the Socialists can best advance their fortunes not by outdoing the Left opposition, but by out-bidding the bourgeois mixed economy, welfare state-oriented parties.

### Less Developed Regions

In the convulsive, less-developed areas of Asia, Africa, and Latin America, the ideological outlook of the labor and allied movement is naturally influenced by the particular socio-economic and special cultural situation of those regions. Affected by various localized conditions, the movements are assuming peculiar orientations. The people are still smarting from the yoke of colonialism, although is is rapidly receding, and most of the colonies have already attained independence. Race, tribalism, pigmentation, and having been, or still being, abused by the whites, perpetuates a smoldering hatred and suspicion. Only time can dispel this highly emotional resentment. Their economic problems are also different from those of the western countries. Whereas Western socialism was predicated on an emerging industrialism and grew to maturity along side a prosperous capitalism, with a relatively stable economy, the radicals, of the less developed countries, are projecting their programs on a functioning feudalism and a handicraft mode of industrial production, with small commercial enterprises. Their economies are based primarily on plantation culture and extractive industries, mostly foreign and absentee-owned, and operated by aliens of a different racial extraction and social status. Starvation, destitution, malignant ailments and poverty are the lot of the bulk of the population. With little indigenous private capital, these large-scale enterprises can only be wrested from private, concentrated ownership by nationalization and extensive land distribution. The land question, with which the Western Socialists lack familiarity, is the most pressing. These countries are also absorbed with modernizing small-scale, handicraft-type industry, mostly owned indigenously. For the highest success of these localized industries, an efficient distributon system is imperative. In many areas, irrigation is a must, so that agriculture may thrive. For these purposes cheap power, chiefly generated by water, is exceedingly essential.

These and other problems induced the Asian Socialist leaders to declare in 1954 for a separate movement named the Asian Socialist Conference. They assembled a gathering for this purpose. Present were leaders from the Socialist International, all of them were Europeans who occupied important posts in the movement and their respective national parliaments, parties and trade-union organizations. Led by the former British Labour Premier, Clement Attlee, this delegation tried to induce the Asian Socialists to affiliate their conference with the Socialist International. In this they failed. The general feeling among the Asian Socialists was that for historical and practical reasons they must organically remain independent and must be free to devise and promote a program based on the particular social and economic milieu in which they live and operate. They particularly felt that the western Socialists were not sufficiently familiar with Asian problems to help in their solution. However they made the concession that the respective Asian Socialist parties, if they so desired, could retain their affiliation with the Socialist International. Most have followed this course.

In Africa and Latin America the labor movements generally are also radically inclined. Most of them advocate a form of national socialism designed to cope with their particular socio-economic and political problems. Some lean towards the Communists, more manifest a predeliction toward the Western oriented labor movements. A few profess themselves as non-aligned. Because of their colonial heritage most of them pronounce themselves as autonomous in relation to the international trade-union movements. Independence is the watchword in building their movements, as it is in building their nations. Actually, they happily favor, in common with the large majority of their compatriots, aid from all sources without strings, as they term it.

The Communists, their allies and other leftist-inclined groups, encourage the separation. They feel that not only would this attitude weaken the Socialist International and moderate trade-union movements, but it gives the Communists a better chance to either influence the labor movements of the less-developed countries or perhaps take them over through their customary penetration maneuvers. For a time, it seemed that the Communists were succeeding. In the early stages most of these movements revealed anti-Western symptoms. Their neutralism tended to favor Communists. Recently, becoming more sensitive to Communist infiltration tactics which threatens their independence, and becoming alarmed at communist aggression and conquest in Tibet, India, Laos, and other areas, as well as the general chicanery of the Communists, most of them have definitely turned less anti-democratic and anti-Western. The Communists, perceiving these changes, are openly attacking the new organizations because they prove a considerable obstacle to Communist progress. Negatively, these developments at least serve a useful purpose. Indigenously led by persons of colored pigmentation, with a program featuring the problems of pressing concern to their people, like land reform, encouragement of small business, anticolonialism, having no organization or limited ties with Western movements, and advocating neutralism, they present an alternative to communism for those susceptible to a revolutionary radical appeal.

Realizing that communism, as such, is not popular, the Communists are most active, not as an open movement, but through their covert activities and organization, not only in labor, but also in student, political and nationalistic Communist-front organizations as a means of spreading Communist influence. Hence, they rely less in most countries on their Communist parties, or clearly labeled Communist dominated unions. Their intensive activities are directed at infiltrating other political parties. Likewise, having made appreciable headway through their World Federation of Trade-Unions, they maneuver and manipulate promoting so-called neutral and nationalistic trade-unions. In this manner they create confusion and division which makes it easier for them to fan anti-Western hate. It also enables them to check the influence of the non-Communist genuine International Confederation of Free Trade-Unions, thereby further benefiting the Communist cause. It is still too early to gauge what success they are having in subverting these nationalistic trade-unions and political organizations.

A movement like the recently founded African Trade-Union Confederation, unaffiliated to any world international, should serve a useful purpose in counteracting Communist influence and intrigue. It does not propose to isolate itself from world affairs, and it permits its affiliates to associate themselves with international trade-union organizations. Indeed some of its affiliates are now members of either the ICFTU or the International Federation of Christian Trade-Unions, both of which are Western-minded. The ATUC has endorsed a mild form of socialism, at the same time condemning communism and other forms of dictatorship. Growing in influence, the International Confederation of Free Trade-Unions, through its regional units and ably assisted by the 22 unaffiliated but closely cooperating International Trade Secretariats, is contributing to the rallying of the radical and labor forces in the less-developed countries. These trade-union organizations, originally Socialist-based, have since World War II also begun to subscribe to the welfare state concept. The African ICFTU, motivated by similar outlook to that of African Trade-Union Federation, secured complete autonomy at the last ICFTU convention in December, 1959. It asked for this arrangement in order to counteract the argument that it is dominated by the Western-minded International. The Latin American affiliate of the ICFTU (ORIT) is also doing yeoman work in encouraging and aiding non-Communist union organization. Most of these labor unions likewise subscribe to some form of socialism.

It would seem that the Communist world bloc is at present becoming engaged in a profound ideological controversy. In some respects it appears to resemble the one experienced by the Socialist movement in the struggle between the Revolutionists and Revisionists. From available accounts it would seem that the Chinese Communist faction is vehemently championing a more extreme philosophy, and a less moderate procedure, whereas the Russian Communists are strenuously advocating more cautious and gradual approach. From accounts of what transpired at the 1960 summit gathering of the leaders of Communist parties from 81 nations within and outside the iron and bamboo curtains there appears to be developing a division between the have and have not countries in that camp. On the whole, economically and industrially speaking, the Communist parties from these more advanced countries which were enjoying better living standards, sided with Soviet Russia. On the other hand, the parties from the lesser advanced countries threw in their lot with Communist China. Perhaps the difference was further clarified by Nikita Khrushchev in his near-marathon talk of seven hours at the opening session of the Central Committee of the Communist party, USSR, in March, 1962. He declared that his camp aspires and is building an affluent society, whereas the Chinese Communist group is concerned with an ascetic society.

*Summary*

In a global review, we find the present situation as follows. Three geographic areas have, with some exceptions, viable and highly effective labor movements. Two of these areas, in addition to possessing clearly defined and viable trade-union movements, also operate through distinctive and effective political parties, and functioning cooperative movements. This feature is characteristic of western Europe and the Australasian countries. In both regions, the dominant movements have either from their inception or for a long time subscribed to Socialist doctrines. More recently, these movements, while still designating themselves as Socialist have gradually changed their ideology as they grew to maturity under a similarly maturing capitalism. They are rapidly embracing a welfare state, mixed economy philosophy. In continental Europe and eastern Canada, cheifly the Province of Quebec, as well as other scattered regions, there exists a non-Communist rival trade-union movement which is Christian, or predominantly Catholic. It has, from the outset, favored extensive labor and social reform legislation, and otherwise courted government aid and intervention in promoting the welfare and interests of the workers. It, too, is therefore welfare state in outlook. It is politically closely related to the Christian or predominantly Catholic political parties in which it generally functions as the Left Wing. In Germany and Austria since the War, and largely on the insistence of the occupied powers, the trade-union movement is unified and officially politically non-partisan. Actually, the bulk of the leaders and membership are Socialist-oriented, with the minority being of the Catholic persuasion. The Communists in western Europe and the Australasian countries are steadily declining, and are becoming a negligible factor in most of the countries. Italy and France, lacking a high degree of social stability, stand out as notable but questionable exceptions.

In the third global area, namely the United States and Canada, the labor movements are based on exclusively trade-union organizations. Political activity, conducted on a non-partisan basis, is controlled and directed by the trade-union movement. Since New Deal days, the AFL began to discard its voluntarism, or laissez faire philosophy, shunning extensive political action, and opposing all forms of labor and social reform legislation that would positively contribute to improving working and living standards of the workers. It has relented in its negative attitude toward government intervention in social and economic affairs, and it too has accepted the welfare state philosophy. From its inception the CIO embraced the welfare state concepts. Thus the merged movement automatically continued to operate in accordance with this ideological outlook.

The Canadian trade-union movement, while closely linked to the United States movement, has been greatly influenced by the British movement from whence the early membership originated. It has, for a long time, favored government aid and is welfare state in outlook. Since the merger of the AFL and CIO in the United States, their counterparts, and including a few unaffiliated unions, have also merged forming the Canadian Labor Congress. Most of its affiliates, with the parent body blessing, have joined other groups in forming the New Democratic party which adopted a welfare state program. This arrangement also commits the dominant Canadian trade-union movement to independent political action. Its Catholic rival, operating mostly in French Canada, is affiliated with the Christian Trade-Union International and subscribes to its social philosophy. At present, the two Canadian rival trade-union groups are seriously negotiating merger. Thus, these three global areas, operating in highly stable economies and organizationally viable, now adhere to th going social philosophy, namely the welfare state, so does the International Confederation of Trade-Unions (ICFTU) and the 22 International Trade Secretariats. They all favor a welfare state capitalistic society with a mixed economy as opposed to laissez-faire capitalism, although most of them still aspire to attaining a new social order sometime in the dim and distant future.

But in the rest of the world the hectic state of affairs induces confused social thinking. Anti-colonialist hangover, Xenophobia and struggle against feudalism, superimposed upon extreme poverty, disease, and illiteracy, has generated an amorphous radicalism and hysteria that fosters flamboyant talk and advocacy of visionary objectives. Further complications have intervened, making it easier for Communist and other demagogic manipulators to add to the confusion. Outstanding political leaders, often in control of the government, have also become proponents of vague nationalist Socialist programs, simultaneously subscribing to a lopsided neutralism, whereby Communists are welcomed as honest collaborators. The labor movements, in common with the rest of society in these areas, are ephemeral and distorted. Disorder, bordering occasionally on chaos, are the prevailing modes of operation. Some of these countries are rising from this slough of despondency and concurrently, the labor movements are also beginning to assume a degree of coherence. Generally, with the aid of the Western-based labor movements, the prospect for attaining some firmness in these movements seems slightly favorable.

# Changing Concepts and Practices in the International Labor Movement

**2**

by Arnold L. Steinbach

## Introduction

When we speak today of international trade-union organizations and their differences, we are inclined to examine two exponents of diametrically different objectives—the International Confederation of Free Trade-Unions (ICFTU) as by far the largest organized representative of free labor, and the World Federation of Trade-Unions (WFTU) which, with comparatively small exceptions (5–10% of the total), represents captive labor.

These organizations have only one thing in common. They both claim to represent labor. Otherwise they have developed great differences in their structure, objectives, cohesion, and their interorganizational relations. It would be false, however, to limit the examination only to what these major mouthpieces of the two different philosophies are standing for or against, and how they perform their day-to-day activities.

To understand the character of these and similar organizations in the present world outside of the realm of ideology, it is necessary to approach the problems scientifically rather than emotionally. It is necessary to go back to the roots and to sketch the broad objectives of international organizations of workers, be they political or economic, ever since for the first time labor cracked the narrow bounds of the guilds and their professional relations with related guilds in other countries and reached beyond their countries' borders to organize on an international basis. Are the modern Internationals just successors to those formed a century ago—or are they something more than just successors?

# CHANGING CONCEPTS AND PRACTICES

This is the major theme of my paper. Almost all that I shall say in the paper may have been referred to by others, though not in a coordinated form. I hope that the "insiders," those in the middle of the stream of the international trade-union movement, will not mind the comments of an "outsider" since the "insider," pressured by day-to-day problems, never finds the time to check intimately the relationship of the structure of the organization to the dynamic changes in the role of labor within the society.

*Evolution of the Solidarity Concept*

The Industrial Revolution led to a concentration of the largely unskilled excess of agricultural labor around newly developed industrial plants. Suppression of the efforts of these masses to be heard and to present their grievances, and the resulting rebellion against a system which ignored their demands for human rights, were the stimuli for forming the earlier international organizations of labor. "International Solidarity of Labor" was the slogan under which labor united. Karl Marx annotated this cry for solidarity with the statement: "The workers have nothing to lose but their chains." It was this Solidarity Concept that led the Socialist labor movement, which developed in Europe in the second half of the nineteenth century, to choose the motto "Workers of All Countries Unite." The European worker, and in particular the continental worker to the extent he accepted the Socialist philosophy (and the great majority did), considered the State to be his enemy. His country was not his Fatherland. He learned that he had to fight the "privileged classes" if he wanted to obtain basic political rights. The International Solidarity Concept was accompanied by an international revolutionary spirit equal to the religious spirit which characterized the great sacrifices of the first Christians under the Roman Empire.

Within the last 100 years, "homeless" and "countryless" labor—through its national and international efforts, revolutionary and evolutionary—has been able to gain legal and economic recognition, not only in Europe, but also in other parts of the world. When talking about this international fight for recognition, I want to emphasize that I am excluding the United States, because, as I stated some years ago in a paper entitled "Basic Roots of Differences Between United States and European Trade-Unionism," * labor in the United States was fortunate in not having to fight for basic political and economic rights. Feudalism was dead when the battle for independence was won and the hypothetical philosophy which we inherited from Great Britain facilitated an evolutionary rather than a revolutionary process of adjustment.

With the political and economic emancipation of labor, the interdependence of labor in the various countries of Europe as well as in other industrialized parts of the world began to diminish. The worker began to be interested in the status of his country as related to other countries; in other words, he became interested in international trade, currency, export and import, and in the defense of his country. In inverse proportion to the growing interest in his own country, his feeling for international solidarity began to decrease until it finally became one of those dreams of youth a person likes to talk about but does not practice.

*The Decline of the Solidarity Concept*

For all practical purposes the Solidarity Concept as of today is dead in the international Socialist labor movement of Europe and it is nearly dead in most of the general international trade-union movements. It is still alive in those international labor movements which cater to specific industrial or craft groups and where workers are also united by specific interest common to all workers in these industries and crafts, such as industrial hazards, the same ups and downs in the fluctuations of the cycle, the same machines and the same callouses.

The history of international labor up to at least the Second

* Steinbach, Arnold L., "Basic Roots of Differences Between United States and European Trade-Unionism," reprinted from Proceedings of a Conference on Human Resources and Labor Relations in Underdeveloped Countries by the Institute of International Industrial and Labor Relations, Cornell University, 1954.

World War cannot be understood without studying the effects of the Solidarity Concept.

The Solidarity Concept was the life blood of international labor. It lead to strong centralistic tendencies, to the development of ideological foundations, and to a domination of the international labor movement by European doctrines. European labor was first exposed to the hazards of the Industrial Revolution and, as a result, was instrumental in forming international organizations of labor. Hand-in-hand with the change of the Solidarity Concept went a lessening of the inferiority complex of labor in given countries vis-à-vis the former "privileged classes." This had obviously certain significant effects on the status of the workers and their unions in relation to the government, the employers, and to other significant institutions of the society.

## The Dynamics of Labor

I remember a discussion I had some two years ago with an old friend, the late president of the Austrian Trade-Union Federation, Johann Boehm, a former bricklayer who later became one of the most influential personalities in the political and economic life of the Austrian Republic. He expressed this change in the status of the worker vis-à-vis the once hated "State" in the following words: "Most workers now resent being called proletarians." And continuing, he stated, "When some thirty years ago workers from a plant would come to me and say 'We want to strike,' the only thing we considered was 'Can we win the strike?' Today, we have to ask ourselves how would a strike effect the economy of the country, the competitive status of its industries, the currency, and so on." When we hear such stories, we take them for granted. We do not see that behind these stories there had been a terrific change in the structure of the whole labor movement which, obviously, must have affected its strategy and techniques. Unfortunately, present-day developments are too fast for us to observe. Before we have been able to translate the developments into formulae and action, new developments have overshadowed those which we are trying to analyze and interpret. As a result, all of us become, to a

certain extent, dogmatic in spite of all our beliefs in pragmatism. We do not learn from the mistakes which Karl Marx
made when he tried to put the newly developed industrial
worker into the economic equation as a constant and not as a
variable. We developed the dogma of bread and butter without ethics, forgetting that every form of ideology has developed good and bad, realistic and unrealistic features around
some ethical standards. Ideology as well as religion has an
ethical basis.

### The Development of a Rigid Trade-Union Concept

If we want to understand present problems and future
trends in the international trade union movement, we have
to examine another concept which has a comparatively short
history, and which apparently originated right with us in the
United States. In spite of our belief in pragmatism, it has
become a rigid dogma. We pragmatists like concepts even if
they have become dogmas. Once one concept is dead, we create another. The newer concept is the free trade-union concept. We did not follow Sam Gompers' advice "to cross the
bridge when we come to it." We decided on a final definition
of the term "free trade-union" irrespective of the changes
which may affect the relations between worker and employee
and between worker and government. Thus all the world has
to accept our dogma that a free trade-union must be independent and bargain collectively. Every other form of workers' organizations is totalitarian. And there we run into another concept. Can we define "independence"? Is there
anything in the world which is truly independent? Or do we
want to turn the clock back to "Manchester Liberalism"?

We developed the concept of "plant bargaining" *vs.* "industrial bargaining," and we abhorred legislation. Then we
saw strong forces coming to the fore favoring industrial bargaining and driving for legislation to help the unskilled workers. We are now both against and for political or government
action depending on how strong we are in the collective
bargaining sector. The same European Continental unions,
which because of circumstances preferred to fight for legislative action ahead of other methods, were able to organize

their trade-unions against strong opposition by the government, and in face of bitter fights with the employers. We, because of another set of circumstances rooted in our society and in spite of all our Philippics against legislation, enacted the Wagner Labor Relations Act, or in other words, needed government interference in order to organize the great masses of the workers in steel, automobile, rubber, and other industries employing unskilled labor.

I have to ask your forgiveness for broadening the subject field, but I felt that I would have indulged in superficialities if I had not called the attention of the reader to the fact that ICFTU vs. WFTU is only a minor, though important, issue in the major problem of finding the way out of obsolete and false concepts. This is a *conditio sine qua non* for the understanding of what is going on in the so-called free trade-union movements of both the developed and less-developed parts of the world. There are different relations between workers and employers, different relations between citizen and government, different educational levels, different religious and philosophical forms of the society, different methods in presenting justified and unjustified demands of the workers and the organizational forms through which such presentations are performed. If we analyze all this *sine ira et studio*, we may have to adjust our rigid definition of free trade-unions with its concept of inherent independence and collective bargaining, realizing that this concept was not so much based on a scientific and thorough-going study, but on a conglomeration of various timely slogans.

After World War II, labor began to revive its political and economic representation under the phantom of a solidarity concept which was dead but not yet buried. The WFTU, when it was formed in 1945, by-and-large accepted the constitution of the International Federation of Trade-Unions (IFTU) adding only one important item, the integration of the International Trade Secretariats into the structure of the WFTU. Everybody who at one time or another has been called upon to write a constitution, knows that the authors do a lot of copying, and there was copying when the constitution of the WFTU and later when that of the ICFTU was written. The constitutions of most of the international trade organizations have a certain similarity even if the operations deviate from what was once the objectives. However, under the influence of the American unions, the ICFTU constitution differed quite distinctly from statutes of previous international trade-union organizations. For the first time an international trade-union organization with strong Socialist participation, threw overboard the A B C's of its predecessors, such as class struggle, overthrow of the economic system, and centralization. By doing so *nolens-volens*, without giving it any thought, they put the International Solidarity Concept into storage. Some ten years later, various European Socialist political organizations followed suit by adjusting some of their basic doctrines on class struggle and overthrow of the economic system to the advancement of the status of the workers in the given countries.

The significant omission of the tenets of pre-World War II socialism by the drafters of the ICFTU Constitution is actually the root of most of the great differences which have developed since 1949 between the ICFTU and WFTU policies.

The class struggle as further refined by the Soviet concept of the dictatorship of the proletariat, representing only a minority, became the ideological dogma of the WFTU. Needless to say, this had definite advantages in the propaganda sector, particularly when directed to those countries where labor still had not been able to gain political or economic equality, or in other words, the less-developed countries. It was given the slogan "rebellion" as in 1949 in Asia, and under the slogan "liberation from colonial powers," it brought communism to power on the wave of nationalism. It led large groups of subsistence workers and farmers to heed the propaganda and to offer sacrifices up to life itself to achieve the promised Messianic future, with Soviet Russia and later Red China as an example of success.

In the ICFTU, on the other hand, there was no systematic approach to long- and short-term problems. There was no common ground in overthrowing or changing an existing order. This obviously led to divisions of mind as to the best approach to achieve the main objectives—that is, the improvement of the standard of living of the workers, and the establishment of political and economic equality. This division became even more serious in the light of the existence of a competing organization which promised everything to everybody under the slogan of "unity." This was a new term for the old catchword "solidarity," but appealed to the deepest emotions of mankind. The competition forced the ICFTU to battle in two directions—positively for the improvement of living standards and negatively against the diversionist movements of the WFTU. On the one hand, the Communist World Federation of Trade-Unions was trying to lure the free workers into their fold under familiar slogans of solidarity, and on the other hand, the ICFTU tried to gain its objectives as partners of a free society and through participation in this society by using democratic methods of procedure.

*Transformation of the Membership Concept in International Communist Labor*

In the following, I shall try to show the moving apart of the ICFTU and the WFTU in a few more specific examples taken from the structure and the composition of the two organizations.

Let us look at the membership. The ICFTU has spread its membership throughout the world. Unlike the old International Federation of Trade-Unions (IFTU), which officially went out of business in 1945, it is no longer a European organization with a foothold in the United States. Outside of the Iron and Bamboo Curtain areas, parts of the world taboo for any free trade-union organization, the major trade-unions in almost all parts of the globe are among its members. Outside of the Communist bloc, the WFTU, however, is limited by-and-large to a few countries—to France and Italy in Europe, and to Indonesia and India in Asia. Its very existence, however, has persuaded a number of strong free trade-unions in Asia and Latin America to remain "neutral." This so-called neutrality weakens the power of free labor before international forums.

The ICFTU has a rigid procedure in admitting members, though it permits those in less-developed areas to pay a reduced scale of affiliation fees. The WFTU, however, has recently developed something unique in the definition of membership. The Leipzig Congress of the WFTU in 1957 opened attendance to everybody who wanted to come; moreover, voting was not restricted to its members. Anybody who attended could vote, even delegates who called themselves observers, such as the Yugoslavian trade-unions and the International Confederation of Arab Trade-Unions. The Yugoslavians at least protested against being included in the roll call, but the observers from the UAR were called and voted. The same Leipzig Congress changed the constitution in order to make it easier for outsiders, that is to say non-members, to participate in the proceedings of the WFTU without knowing that they were used as stooges in the propaganda work of the WFTU.

What does this development mean? First, it means that the WFTU has ceased to be an organization of labor unions joining together for certain objectives and paying the bill to obtain these objectives. If anybody can come without paying, then somebody else has to pay the bill. In addition, if nobody is kept from participating, the organization must be quite sure that those participants cannot use the power of their votes to direct the organization into lines other than those of the leadership of the WFTU. Even to those who are "blind," it must become clear that the WFTU uses the congresses and other meetings for propagandistic purposes only, or to use a good colloquialism, for "window dressing." Those who are not members but like to participate with all costs paid have no opportunity to use the organization for their interests, but they will be used whether they like it or not.

No wonder that the proceedings of the WFTU are smooth and well-directed. There might even be organized speeches of dissension if it fits the propagandistic value of the meetings. No wonder that there is a great difference between the "staged" meetings of the WFTU and the "open" meetings of the ICFTU, and that some observers are shocked by the comparative lack of positive actions taken on the part of the ICFTU—an organization where the members still dare to express different opinions. If we agree that the Solidarity Concept in international labor is on the downward curve, such differences are understandable because each delegate thinks of his country first.

If we consider the change of international thinking and the death of the Solidarity Concept, then we can understand when an article which a distinguished observer of the ICFTU Congress wrote was titled (not by the author of the article) a "Do-Nothing" Congress. "Do-Something" presupposes joint interests. Obviously, there are joint interests which necessitate the existence of an international trade-union organization but there also may be divergent interests that cannot be solved by voting.

*Centralization vs. Decentralization in the Trade-Union Internationals*

Another item which we might look into is the degree of centralization and decentralization in the two organizations. The old international organizations, both in the political and trade-union field, were characterized by a high degree of centralization. The international organization represented the otherwise uniting ties of a nation; solidarity was the statute of the united workers' movement—the rigid ideological objectives were their laws. In addition, experiences in the first International, the battle between Marx and Bakunin, convinced the leadership that they could win only when marching under one flag. Still, the rigid centralization worked only by way of passing resolutions giving the guidelines for the affiliated groups. There was no way to enforce the resolutions except by appeal to solidarity. This was particularly true when the enforcement meant action against governments. Even the few international boycotts ordered by the international organization when its prestige was at its peak, fizzled out. Apart from all other considerations, centralization was paramount and would be policed as long as the organization was practically limited to civilized Europe. The

ICFTU, for the first time in the history of international labor, broke with the principle of centralization, and this under the decisive influence of the American delegation.

The Founding Congress of the ICFTU decided to bring the organization closer to the worker by establishing regional organizations. Such organizations were formed in Europe, Asia, Latin America and, more recently, in Africa. Their development and success did not live up to expectations. The ICFTU was torn between the old dogma of the dominance of the headquarters with its star performers on the one hand, and the pressing need for transferring the point of gravity to the outlying posts on the other hand. The headquarters' school pointed to the need for central guidance. The participating unions were in different stages of underdevelopment. They lacked trained leadership; there was no cohesion between the ICFTU affiliates within the regions, and except for Europe the regions did not have the financial strength which alone could back up their claim to autonomy and independence. Those top officials of the headquarters who had grown up in the doctrine of centralization found support for their point of view when the regional organizations were not able to exercise their responsibilities without advice and financial help from the headquarters or from some "big brother." The battle between centralization and decentralization in the ICFTU is still in full swing; but one thing is true—there has been a good try toward the right direction.

The WFTU, on the other hand, drifted to even stricter centralization after the split in 1949. Once the inhibitions dictated by the presence of unions from democratic countries had been removed, it proceeded in line with the forms of government under which the great majority of the WFTU affiliates was permitted to perform. Dictatorship at home, strong centralization at home, obviously translated itself into rigid centralization in the international arena. Thus, unlike the ICFTU, the WFTU did not experiment with the establishment of regional organizations; all power was in the headquarters. Even when the headquarters of the WFTU had to yield to separatist tendencies, such as in Red China, the offices created were given the name "liaison bureau." CTAL, which was a regional organization when it joined the WFTU in 1945, became a shadow regional bureau. But the fact that the WFTU had to yield in order to keep the decor, shows that there is a basic trend for decentralization, although the child may be given a more innocent name. There are other exceptions to the rule. Some future historian will perhaps shed light on what happened in Peking when the WFTU Liaison Bureau, formed in December, 1949, was put under the direction of a Westerner—the Australian Ernst Thornton. Some years later, the Westerner was deposed and replaced by a Red Chinese. Did the WFTU act voluntarily or under pressure when it lost its authoritarian control of part of Asia?

### The False Unity Concept in International Communist Labor

There is still another difference between the two Internationals—a rather negative one.

In line with the objectives of the WFTU to gain domination of labor throughout the world by hook or crook, the WFTU has usurped the familiar century-old slogan of international labor, the slogan of "unity." The Communists are experts in the science of expropriation. They have expropriated, and unfortunately we let them do it, institutions and ideals of free labor which had become sacred to many workers throughout the world. The Communists expropriated the red flag of the Socialists. They also expropriated the first of May. They hurt the feelings of democratic Socialist labor by adopting Marx as the saint of themselves only; and they have stolen the pride of labor, the feeling for solidarity. They now call it "unity." They would even dissolve weak Communist-dominated trade-unions in order to infiltrate free trade-unions under the slogan of "unity." Under this slogan, they developed front organizations and by doing so, and this hurts, they put the free trade-unions on the defense. It is rather tragic that the ICFTU cannot use the word "unity" in its organizational drive because it has become a permanent part of the WFTU, i.e., Communist vocabulary.

*Emergence of a New Solidarity Concept in the Developing Areas*

But even more, the WFTU is taking fast-advantage of the development of a new Solidarity Concept in the less-developed countries—the Solidarity Concept of the "have nots" *vs.* the "haves." The "haves" are western Europe and the United States, and the "have nots" include the Communist world. Thus, the fact that labor in the free world has been able to achieve a standard of living higher than that in the Iron and Bamboo Curtain countries is being used by the WFTU to speed new solidarity slogans—"Asia for Asians," "Africa for the Africans."

We all agree that the main battle is now fought in the lesser-developed countries where missionary work has to be done. There the WFTU has a distinct advantage because the social structure of the countries from which its major affiliates hail is close to that of the lesser-developed countries. Agriculture in Europe was freed before the Industrial Revolution started and became the backbone of modern conservatism. Organizations of agricultural workers played, at the time the "Bolshevik Revolution" started, a comparatively minor role in Europe, as well as in the United States. In Soviet Russia, the "Bolshevik" minority by "freeing" the peasant from Czarist oppression, established a dictatorship over the majority of an agricultural population. It did not actually free the agricultural segment of the population, but used it for doctrinal experiments and molded it into various forms of collectivism. As a result, the Soviet Russian Communists learned to understand the complex agricultural problems of today and, in particular, the needs and complaints of the agricultural sector, the agricultural worker, the tenant and the subsistence peasant. They had their program for Asia ready while the ICFTU organizers were still using methods geared to the organization of industrial workers. The Communist WFTU had all the experts and propagandists, whom they could send out as requested, but the ICFTU had only one Tom Bavin (General Secretary of the Intl. Federation of Plantation, Agricultural and Allied Workers). Thus, the difference in the social structure of the countries from which the major affiliates of the ICFTU and the WFTU came has been playing a great role in the expansion drive of the two Internationals. The ICFTU has still to overcome the historical advantages of the WFTU. At this point it is quite interesting to note that the only ICFTU affiliate which enjoys a great reputation amongst labor in the lesser-developed countries is Israel's Histadrut with its vast experience in agriculture cooperatives.

*Contrasting Structures Between ITS and WFTU Trade Departments*

In comparing the ICFTU and the WFTU, it is necessary to say a few words about a set of international organizations which of late has gained great publicity.

The International Trade Secretariats, which are not only autonomous but fully independent of the ICFTU, were able to resist integration into the WFTU during the critical postwar years. As we all know, the Communists in the WFTU felt that with the integration of the International Trade Secretariats they would be able to use free labor at will. After the 1949 split the WFTU formed about a dozen trade-union internationals (TUI's) and made them part and parcel of the WFTU. These organizations have to dance to Louis Saillant's "whistling." They have only as much freedom as the headquarters of the WFTU permits them to exercise. They are to perform in those areas where the WFTU has no access. Up to now, however, their efforts have been rather infinitesimal. Except for the teachers' and other intellectual or semi-intellectual groups, they have not been able to gain a strong foothold outside of their home territory. For some time it was felt that the Agricultural TUI was making considerable progress. To adjust its activities to the Asian social structure, it was organized in three sections—peasants, tenants, and workers. An Indonesian became head of the organization. Its expansion drive may have been stemmed by the activities of the ITS of Plantation Workers.

47

All of us are now tired of hearing about differences. Let us therefore, before I come to an end, spend some time on an interesting phenomenon.

### The African Phenomenon of Nationalism Comparing Communism in the Trade-Union Movement

After World War II, it was generally accepted that communism successfully uses nationalist uprisings to come to power. This was definitely true in Asia, where they gained strength on the wave of nationalism, which meant liberation from the "colonial" powers. Labor in various Asian countries, in Indonesia, the Philippines, Malaya, Korea, and Vietnam was used by the Communists to fight for independence under the flag of communism. Within the last few years, we learned that it is not wise to accept such a phenomenon as eternal truth. Another phenomenon surprised us in North and French West Africa where nationalism came to power on the wave of communism, or in other words, turned the Communist-dominated unions into strongholds of nationalism with anti-Communist aspects. In Tunis and in Morocco strong Communist unions were literally wiped out when labor joined the independence movement. What happened? Why did our predictions fail? In Asia there were no Communist unions when the Communists marched in. In the French parts of Africa the Communists had gained control over the workers after World War II when the existing local unions of French metropolitan Communists were the only ones who would, "illegally," admit native labor to membership with the government officials looking the other way. The same native members rebelled against the leadership of the minority of French Communists and that was the end of Communist domination of the trade-unions in North Africa.

In French West Africa and in French Equatorial Africa the Communist leadership of the labor unions was forced by rising nationalism to take the unions out of the WFTU and to resign its WFTU functions. Whether the Communists will be able to return by the back door is a question which only the future can answer.

# CHANGING CONCEPTS AND PRACTICES

*Possible Structural Changes of the ICFTU in the Future*

I have mentioned in the beginning that the international organizations are by and large still sticking to the forms of organization which were found most suitable some 100 years ago, that even the ICFTU has made only minor modifications in adjusting itself to the changes brought about by geographic expansion and emancipation of labor. Obviously, we all know how hard it is to fight against tradition. After all, dogmas are very often the result of strong habits. If rigid legislation of a country prevents necessary adjustments to structural changes, history reports revolutionary upheavals. The frictions and differences in the ICFTU which we are reading about are nothing else but a rebellion against a structure of the past which does not fit the needs of modern international labor. International labor is not any more a European affair; it has spread to various newly developed and underdeveloped areas of the world. Different philosophies and different stages of development of the society in these areas call for different kinds of activities; and the ICFTU may have to go much further than it did in 1949 when it tried to bring the worker closer to the headquarters. They may find that this was only patchwork.

No systematic study of the needs of a modern international organization of free labor has ever been done. Perhaps we do not know enough yet to do it. Some observers believe that what at one time was discussed at the Stockholm Congress of the ICFTU in 1953, might be the right way to a solution— to give the regional organizations not only an autonomy on paper but autonomy in fact, and to change at the same time the role of the headquarters to serve the regional organizations, servicing them in the field of education, in the field of representation before international agencies, in the advice on international economic problems, and in providing a reservoir of trouble shooters. Some experts may object by pointing out that the regional organizations do not have the personnel, the finances, nor the ability to do the job, which, at present, the well-staffed, though not too wealthy, ICFTU is unable to do. Here experience has shown that whenever there is a need for qualified people, they pop up from nowhere. There are in the underdeveloped countries a number of highly-qualified persons who at present stay aside, but may offer their knowledge and talents if the need arises. And finances? The European labor movement grew some 100 years ago by sacrifices in spite of persecution, jail, blacklisting and lack of finances. Has labor in the less-developed countries fewer of the ideals which were the strength of their European brothers? If the international movement is to succeed, it must have the courage to try.

# 3

# Communist Labor Tactics in the Colonial and Former Colonial Countries

by George Lichtblau

*Introduction: The World Federation of Trade-Unions and the Communist Offensive in the Underdeveloped Countries*

The significance of the World Federation of Trade-Unions (WFTU) derives from its role within the framework of the larger Soviet effort to affect the political climates in countries outside the Soviet orbits and especially in the underdeveloped and former colonial areas. Its main target, organized labor, is expected to play an important role in the political and social restructuring of the societies of these countries. This makes the WFTU by far the most substantial of the so-called Communist-front organizations. Like other fronts which address themselves to special target groups such as young people, students, professional groups, and women, it combines in its appeals special group-interests with general political objectives, such as anti-imperialism, peace, freedom of association, social welfare measures, anti-capitalism, nuclear disarmament, etc. On the basis of such common interests a bridge of solidarity is to be established by means of which attitudes favorable to the Soviet bloc and antagonistic to the Western powers are to be promoted.

Time and again the Communists boldly assert in their propaganda that the stronger the Socialist camp has become the more the imperialist powers have been forced into retreat and the more readily have the nationalist independence movements been able to win their objectives. To speed up this process the newly developing countries should therefore commit themselves to closer collaboration with the Sino-Soviet bloc. They can best do this not only by their foreign policy alignment but also by reorganizing their political and economic structures in accordance with the model of the "Socialist countries."

As a by-product of this drive, fronts like the WFTU and their national affiliates are supposed to contribute to the creation of political climates which are likely to facilitate alliances between nationalist and Communist groups. So far, however, the Soviet Union and the Communist fronts have subordinated their considerations for the local Communist movements to their larger international objectives. But as a result of the gradual changes of relations within the Communist movement following Khrushchev's de-Stalinization campaign, the demands for greater consideration of the interests of the national affiliates have become an increasingly important problem for the WFTU.

The Sino-Soviet conflict has, of late, greatly complicated the WFTU's guidance role by injecting the problem of polycentrism. The required adjustments of international Communist labor tactics of alliances, both at the national and international levels, to the changes of Soviet relations within the Bloc and toward the outside world become thus the main topic of this paper.

From the time of the departure of the non-Communist trade-unions from the WFTU in January 1949 until the end of the Stalin era, the organization remained primarily a propaganda organ proclaiming the authoritative international Communist line for the benefit of its affiliates. It promoted international solidarity demonstrations and contacts between Communist trade-unions from both within and without the Soviet bloc and collaborated with other front groups in order to reinforce each others' propaganda drives and to give the participants the illusion of vast movements and activities. Yet the WFTU remained throughout this period isolated, and hardly played a significant role even in influencing the policies of its affiliates since these were directed by the local Communist parties. At best it could dispense some patronage in the form of funds, publicity, appointments to one of its executive bodies, or invitations to travel.

Beginning in 1953 the WFTU assumed increasingly concrete functions, going considerably beyond the mere dispensation of propaganda and patronage, even though these continued among its major preoccupations. Such new activities as training and financial assistance, and even occasional policy guidance of affiliates were no more than traditional international trade-union tasks which may have been adopted at least in part in reaction to similar activities by the ICFTU and the International Trade Secretariats (ITS). However, by giving the WFTU a more substantive organizational character they also reflected the changing relations between the Soviet bloc and the outside world, especially with the nationalist and neutralist states and political movements in the former colonial countries. As a result of these changes the WFTU was gradually able to draw within its influence an increasing number of anti-Western nationalist trade-unions, even turning some away from the ICFTU. Hence, WFTU aid and patronage to these movements contributed greatly to the strengthening of contacts between their countries and the Soviet camp.

Paradoxically, despite the rapprochement between the new states and the Soviet bloc and the growing tolerance among the nationalist movements for the Communists in many areas, the Soviet emphasis on the state-to-state approach required that the local Communist political and labor movements be subordinated and, if necessary, sacrificed to the larger objectives of Soviet foreign policy, particularly in the Afro-Asian area. As a result the WFTU was for a time forced to play a rather self-effacing role, so that by the end of 1956 some observers were led to speculate on the possibility that it would yield to a new Afro-Asian neutralist international labor movement based on the "Spirit of Bandung." However, if the Russians ever entertained such a plan it was quickly abandoned, as was shown in 1957 by the preparatory drive for the convention of the Fourth World Trade-Union Congress which fully revealed the usefulness of the WFTU as an instrument of the Soviet drive among the former colonial countries.

The effectiveness of the Russian drive in the ex-colonial areas clearly reflected the increasingly anti-Western and pro-Soviet reaction of the so-called "neutralists" in the wake of the Suez crisis. Thus subsequent events readily overshadowed for the Afro-Asians the Stalinist past and even the realities of Hungary. This fortuitously aided the WFTU in carrying out the mandate of the 20th Congress of the CPSU of February 1959 to promote closer relations between the Soviet Bloc and the Afro-Asian nationalist movements.[1] Its ensuing alliance policy showed the remarkable tactical resourcefulness and flexibility of the Communists in the field of international trade-unionism. This same tactical ability must be credited with sustaining this campaign, notwithstanding occasional setbacks from the unfavorable reactions to either Soviet or Chinese Communist foreign policies. This policy was built largely on the basis of regional crises involving interest clashes between the nationalist-neutralist forces and the West.

Reacting to Suez, the Congo, Algeria, or Cuba, the WFTU quickly mobilized spectacular international support for the regional solidarity movements which such crises evoked. However, as experience has subsequently shown the Communists, such solidarity is difficult to sustain, nor is it possible for them to remain aloof from the intra-regional conflicts, since by now Soviet interests become invariably involved. This tendency has already at times affected the working alliances of the WFTU with the Asian, Arab, African, and Latin American neutralist trade-unions. But in view of the fact that the Soviet Union and/or Communist China can always be counted upon to evoke or exacerbate new crises, the WFTU is not likely to want for opportunities. Moreover, the clashes of interest between the Communists and the neutralists at this stage do not seem as profound as those with the West. Furthermore, any division among the regional forces tends to make the remaining allies of communism more dependent on them for support.

*The Postwar United Front*

At its inception in October 1945 the WFTU was able to attract twenty trade-unions from Africa and Asia, many of them founded during or immediately after the war. The

British Trade-Union Congress (TUC) convened a special colonial trade-union conference a few days before the preliminary World Trade-Union Conference opened in London in February 1945 in order to bring as many colonial and other Commonwealth trade-unions as possible into the new International. Not only did the TUC wish thereby to encourage these new trade-unions and to demonstrate the enlightened nature of British colonial and social policy, but it also expected to be able to use the WFTU as an instrument for affecting their development.[2] Elsewhere in the underdeveloped countries the very prospect of a new international labor movement with affiliates from all parts of the world and of all political hues encouraged Communist and nationalist leaders to form new trade-unions in order to obtain international recognition. Local Communist leaders were especially alert to this opportunity, as for instance in Egypt, where they organized several rival labor movements representing various party factions just prior to the founding of the WFTU to compete for recognition.[3]

The early post-war united-front period enabled the Communist leaders of the WFTU to make frequent use of their non-Communist colleagues' penchant for solidarity and the protection of trade-union rights. Thus they were able to bring the considerable initial prestige of the new International to bear on the promotion of mergers, or on the preservation of unity under conditions most likely to favor the Communists. Where pro-Western governments surpressed Communist political and trade-union movements, as in Greece and Iran, these WFTU leaders by invoking the issue of violated trade-union rights, obtained non-Communist support for branding such governments as undemocratic. Under other occasions they channeled the prestige and the financial support of the WFTU into the strengthening of local Communist-dominated affiliates, as in the case of the exiled Chinese Association of Labor.

Or again they helped Communist affiliates by using the powers of the Executive Committee (under a loose constitutional provision regarding the affiliation of more than one trade-union center from any one country) to challenge the trade-union *bona fides* or claims to "most representative" status of rivals. These last tactics were used with fleeting effectiveness in Syria,[4] Iran, Tunisia, and among the Arabs of Palestine,[5] thus leaving the non-Communist labor movements who were refused accreditation internationally isolated. As it turned out, these favored movements, international backing notwithstanding, were too weak and lacked sufficient disciplined following in the trade-unions to change their countries' political climate and to resist governmental curbs. Thus they benefited little from the WFTU endorsement.

While unity lasted, the non-Communist Western trade unions under the leadership of the TUC also sought to take advantage of the tactical restraints imposed on the Communists and to promote their own causes through the WFTU. Thus in the case of the Communist-dominated All-Burma Trade Union Congress the TUC imposed constitutional changes through the WFTU in the hope of transforming it from a political into a more bona fide labor movement. Similarly, the TUC barred the affiliation of the Pan Malayan Trade Union Federation for its failure to reform. In the case of the Philippine Congress of Labor Organizations (CLO), a Communist-dominated labor movement closely collaborating with the rebel Hukbalahap movement, affiliation was blocked in deference to the CIO which made it dependent on the unification of the Philippine labor movement, a measure which both the CIO and the AFL were promoting at the time.

During the period of the united front from above three factors tended to limit the effectiveness of the WFTU in Asia and Africa. First, the concern of the major colonial powers with preserving political tranquillity in their dependent territories was reflected in the policies of their leading trade-unions. Thus WFTU operations in colonial and Western-occupied countries were restricted by the combined efforts of the Western non-Communist unions from within that organization and by suspicious governments from without. This was especially true of the TUC.[6] Secondly, during the early postwar years the USSR showed little interest in challenging the West in the underdeveloped countries. And thirdly, there were the obstacles imposed by most governments of the independent countries in Africa, Asia, and the Middle East who were suppressing Communist political and trade-union activities.

Among the more notable failures of the WFTU were the Pan-African Trade-Union Conference at Dakar in April 1947, and the special missions to Greece, Iran, Tunisia, Korea, and Japan. Other efforts in these areas, such as a proposed mission to Palestine in 1947 and the holding of a Pan-Asian trade-union conference in India in 1948 were effectively blocked by the non-Communist members, while a mission to Vietnam was barred by the French Government. At the Dakar meeting, the WFTU deplored the lack of social security legislation and the adequate legal protection of workers in the colonial countries of Africa, and blamed the situation on imperialist exploitation. This approach angered the British TUC, which criticized the meeting as unconstructive and purely propagandistic,[7] and thereupon barred the holding of the proposed Asian meeting.

The WFTU missions to Greece, Iran, Tunisia, and Japan constituted efforts to unify the trade-union movements of these countries by using the prestige of the WFTU to help the Communists capture their leadership. In Korea as well as in Japan, the Communists sought also to use the WFTU mission to discredit the social and labor policies of the U. S. occupation authorities who as an antidote to the Communist victories in China were helping to revive the economic and political status of the conservative business and landed classes at the expense of the labor movement which they had hitherto favored. However, neither in Korea nor in Japan were the Communists able to promote unity or to obtain non-Communist endorsement of their critical statements.

By 1949, when most of the efforts on behalf of Communist unions in the colonial and former colonial countries of

Afrca and Asia had failed, even the Communist leadership of the WFTU had to admit that its main efforts had been restricted to propaganda.[8]

## The WFTU Campaign in the Afro-Asian Countries after the 1949 Split

By 1948 Soviet foreign policy had created conditions of international tension which made further cooperation between the Communist and non-Communist unions untenable. In line with the Cominform dictates of uncompromising hostility toward the non-Communists, the WFTU's Communist leadership became increasingly intransigent and in effect abandoned what remained of the united-front-from-above. Its hostility was directed as much against the nationalist unions of the underdeveloped countries as it was against those of the advanced nations. In South and Southeast Asia the combined impact of the Cominform line toward all non-Communists and the Communist victory in the Chinese civil war resulted in the outbreak of open rebellion. Consequently, the major non-Communist Asian trade-unions turned first to the AFL for aid in the formation of the Asian Federation of Labor, and later to the ICFTU for international support against the threat from their Communist rivals and against the security of the entire nationalist movement.

After the walk-out of the non-Communist unions at an Executive Committee meeting in Paris in January, 1949, the WFTU, faithfully following the dictates of Soviet foreign policy requirements, made a valiant but abortive effort to shift the focus of its attention to Africa and Asia. It immediately accepted as members several Asian and African trade-unions whose applications for affiliation had been held in abeyance for several years. Chief among those accepted were the *Union Generale Tunisienne du Travail* (UGTT) which was the nationalist rival of the Communist-dominated and WFTU-affiliated *Union des Syndicats des Travailleurs de Tunisie* (USTT). The UGTT's application for membership had been held in abeyance for several years because it had refused unification with the Communists.

Next to be accepted in the WFTU was the Communist-dominated Philippine CLO. The CLO, having failed to promote Philippine labor unity, split in late 1948 following the division of the Philippine Communist party on the issue of emphasis on political versus revolutionary activity.[9] The group accepted in January, 1949 was the orthodox Stalinist group supporting the Huk rebellion.

A third addition to the WFTU in its new shift toward Africa and Asia was the Japanese *Sanbetsu*, the Communist faction of *Zenroren* which signaled through its WFTU affiliation the abandonment of all efforts to unite the Japanese labor movement. At the time this last mentioned affiliation was hailed by the WFTU as a major victory, but actually it contributed only to the isolation and rapid decline of the Communist labor movement in Japan. The very forcing of the issue of WFTU affiliation by the Communists was the catalyst that precipitated the breakup of the national trade-union movement into several politically divergent segments.[10] A fourth member was the Pakistan Trade-Union Federation founded in January, 1948 as an offspring of the Communist All-India Trade-Union Congress (AITUC).

The largest increase of the WFTU's Asian membership, was produced by the emergence of the All-China Federation of Labor (later the All-China Federation of Trade-Unions) from a congress at Harbin in August, 1948. There the various anti-Kuomintang labor organizations had merged into one movement, which then claimed 2,830,000 members, but soon thereafter grew to become, next to the Soviet All Union Central Council of Trade-Unions (AUCCTU), the largest WFTU affiliate.[11]

Although the second World Congress of the WFTU at Milan in July, 1949 officially signaled the new Communist interest in the labor movements of the colonial and former colonial countries, it was its Asian and Australasian Trade-Union Conference in Peking in November, 1949 that provided a more dramatic demonstration of this new shift in emphasis. Here Mao Tse-tung's special formulation of Communist strategy in China was pronounced *de rigeur* throughout the "colonial and semi-colonial countries." Even though the armed struggle was declared the highest form of political action in deference to the civil war victory of the Communist Chinese, resort to it was to be made dependent on its chance of success, as in Indochina. However, regardless of whether a Communist movement resorted to armed rebellion or not, its great new task was to forge new political alliances in the anti-imperialist struggle of the national bourgeoisie, the peasantry, and the intelligentsia under the leadership of the working class and the Communist party. The new program assigned to the trade-unions the task of helping the Communist parties find allies in the cities, and beyond this to extend Communist influence into the countryside.

At the Peking Conference a permanent Asian and Australasian liaison bureau was established, and similar regional bureaus were proposed for Africa and the Near and Middle East. This Peking bureau, which was dissolved in April, 1958, operated mostly as a publishing and distribution center for WFTU propaganda, and seems to have played only a minor role as a contact center for the Soviet and Chinese Communists with Asian and Middle Eastern unions. Proposals for the other regional organizations failed to materialize.[12]

The WFTU also devoted some attention to the trade-union movements of Africa below the Sahara. By the end of 1950, a preparatory committee was set up in Paris for holding another Pan-African Trade-Union Conference in Duala, French Cameroons, in April, 1951.[13] However, in view of the Indochina crisis, these activities immediately aroused the suspicion of the French authorities and led to the outlawing of all direct WFTU activities in French West and Equatorial Africa in January, 1951 before the meeting could get underway. Similarly, efforts in the British Sudan to obtain the affiliation of the TUC-nurtured Sudanese trade-unions led also to the outlawing of WFTU activities in that territory the following year. An attempt to circumvent the prohibitions against the WFTU was made by the French CGT when it conducted an African Trade-Union Conference in Bamako, French Sudan in October, 1951, at which both CGT and non-CGT unions participated and at which coordinating committees of the participating unions from the various French Black African territories were established. The WFTU, although barred from participation, subsequently claimed credit for the initiative leading to the meeting.

In November, 1951, when the first signs of a thaw were beginning to appear in the Soviets' hostility toward the former colonial countries, the WFTU obediently fell in line by announcing at its Berlin General Council meeting that a new intensified effort would be made to reach the labor movements of Africa and Asia. As a first step in this direction, the General Secretary, Louis Saillant, established two special advisory committees in lieu of regional bureaus: one for African countries and one for the Middle East, as well as a Colonial Department attached to the Secretariat.[14] Furthermore, he proposed that, in order to overcome the open hostility of non-Communist unions to the WFTU, cooperation between affiliated and unaffiliated organizations be more effectively promoted through functional trade departments, paralleling the ITS of the free trade-unions.

The WFTU trade departments were expected to facilitate unity-of-action-from-below type of cooperation with dissident elements in the industrial branches of unaffiliated national centers.[15] In addition, they were to help coordinate activities of affiliated port and maritime workers seeking to harass Western arms and aid shipments not only to Europe, but also to the British in Malaya, to the French in Indochina, and to the UN forces in Korea. These actions by the WFTU affiliates were to be reinforced by efforts to enlist the support of non-Communist Asian unions in the name of their common anti-colonialism.

However, at this stage the functional internationals proved no more effective than the WFTU itself in their propaganda appeals for unity-of-action-from-below. By the WFTU's own admission, the efforts of the trade departments were hampered not only by the police and the employers, but by "a lack of political awareness of the workers" and the counteractivities of the anti-Communist International Transport Workers' Federation.[16]

*The Post-Stalin Era*

Even though the WFTU tried its best to impress the Afro-Asian labor movements after the non-Communist movements had broken off, its main preoccupation until 1953 remained with Europe, the center of the cold war. Only after Stalin's death in March of that year, the subsequent signing of the Korean armistice, and the change in policy of the USSR and Communist China toward the underdeveloped and former colonial countries, did the WFTU stand any chance of eliciting a favorable response from the Afro-Asian labor movements. Shedding its hostility toward the governments and nationalist movements of the former colonial countries, the WFTU quickly fell in line with the Sino-Soviet campaign to improve official relations with the governments of Asia and the Middle East by diplomacy, aid, and trade offers.

In response to this campaign, the attitudes of the Asian nationalist labor and political leaders toward the Communists also began to change. The Communists were gradually permitted to return to political life, if not openly, at least through front organizations. In Syria, for instance, where the Communist labor movement had been outlawed, some of its leaders emerged within the ranks of the nationalist unions [17] with the aid of the *Ba'atists* (Socialist Resurrectionists). With anti-westernism in many areas becoming the main rallying force of the nationalist-neutralist movements for checking discontent in the face of mounting social and economic problems, cooperation with the Communists became increasingly acceptable in view of the Communists' own anti-Western orientation.

In the international labor field the desire for greater detachment from the West manifested itself in the growing dissatisfaction of the Asian non-Communist labor movements with the ICFTU and its Asian Regional Organization, and conversely in their readiness to accept invitations to Peking and Moscow. A significant segment of these non-Communist movements showed itself ready to cooperate with the Communists, not only on limited local issues, but perhaps even more on foreign policy issues, such as demonstrations for peace and against military alliances and nuclear weapons tests. As the Communist movements of the former colonial countries eliminated the establishment of "peoples' democracies" from their immediate programs and committed themselves increasingly to the support of both the foreign and domestic policies of their governments, they found that the new atmosphere afforded them steadily increasing opportunities for united action both from above and from below.

Since 1953 a growing number of nationalist trade-union leaders of ICFTU affiliates have defied their international in order to vie for invitations to labor congresses and for honorific travel tours in Soviet bloc countries. Before long some were even accepting invitations to attend meetings openly sponsored by the WFTU. In 1952 the first ICFTU affiliate—the Indian *Hind Mazdoor Sabha* (HMS)—sent a delegate to the May Day celebration in Peking.[18] The following year saw for the first time since 1949 a non-Communist—or perhaps better, non-Stalinist—movement, a small left-wing organization from Indonesia,[19] affiliate with the WFTU, while several other Left Wing Nationalist movements from India, Indonesia, Japan, and Ceylon declared their readiness to cooperate with the Communist camp by attending the Seventh All-China Congress of Trade-Unions in Peking in May, 1953 [20] and by sending observers to the Third World Congress of the WFTU in Vienna, one of whose main official themes was the promotion of united trade-union action from below.

For the time being these manifestations of willingness to cooperate with the WFTU on the part of the non-Communist unions remained the exception. In most cases such participation represented demonstrations of united-action-from-below through the attendance of unauthorized delegations claiming to voice the real sentiment of a muzzled rank-and-file. However, these acts did mark the beginning of a new trend. The confidence of the WFTU in this trend was indicated by the actual opening of long-planned training and indoctrination facilities for promising young trade-unionists from the colonial and former colonial countries in Budapest and Prague.

The year 1953 revealed also new attempts on the part of the WFTU to broaden the appeal to the Afro-Asian trade-unions through its international trade departments. This time the special emphasis was given to the Agricultural and Forestry Workers' Trade-Union International. In connection with the Third World Congress in Vienna in October, 1953 a World Conference of Agricultural and Forestry Workers was held with the special purpose of appealing to the plantation unions of the colonial and underdeveloped countries and to orient them more favorably toward the Soviet bloc through WFTU propaganda.

This conference sought to impress the delegates and observers with the importance which the WFTU and the Communist movement attached to the organizing of agricultural workers and peasants. In a detailed program the trade-unions were called upon to take advantage of rural discontent to extend their influence from the plantation workers to the peasants in the villages, and to counteract the influence of the traditional village leaders such as land owners, village elders, and religious leaders who sought to preserve the status quo in order to continue the exploitation of these peasants and agricultural workers. Communist organizers were also to take advantage of spontaneous outbreaks of rural discontent and of the activities by political and cooperative movements. Contacts were to be maintained especially with seasonal agricultural workers, who for the short periods of their wage employment came within the purview of trade-union activities, but with whom contact is normally lost upon their return to their home villages.

The vehicles for appealing to peasants and seasonal agricultural workers were to be land reform programs, demands for higher wages and better housing, pointing up governmental responsibility for the failure to improve the standard of living, abolition of contract labor, and calls for health services, etc. One important facet of this organizing campaign was to be the collection of dues from the workers and peasants in order to create a vested interest among these people in their organization. The difficulties of collecting dues and of organizing anything but transitory political activities in rural areas of the underdeveloped countries, while freely admitted, were to test the mettle of those assigned to carry out the task.[21]

## The Bandung Spirit and the WFTU's "Forward Leap"

Since 1955, the WFTU policy toward the underdeveloped countries has largely evolved under the influence of the new spirit engendered by the Bandung Conference in April of that year and of the use which the Communist camp was able to make of it. It freely took advantage of such events as the formal ceasefire between East and West in Korea and Indochina; the spectacular visits of Khrushchev and Bulganin, and Chou En-lai to South and Southeast Asia in 1955; the steadily increasing bloc aid and trade campaign; Soviet arming of Egypt; the pronouncements of the 20th CPSU Congress in February, 1956 on the necessity of strengthening relations with the nations of what the Soviets then called the "Zone of Peace"; and the aftermath of the Suez crisis.

The attractiveness of this new WFTU policy was dramatically revealed by the extent of Afro-Asian collaboration with the international Communist labor movement at the WFTU Leipzig Congress in October, 1957, which was attended by 181 Afro-Asian delegates and observers from 19 affiliated and 18 unaffiliated organizations.[22] Among the latter, two were members of the ICFTU, one was affiliated with the functional non-Communist International Trade Secretariats, and one union was the major constituent of an organization that had just applied for membership in the ICFTU.[23] Not only was the attendance of persons from affiliated organizations impressive, but even more so was the number of non-Communist personalities who dignified the Congress by giving it their blessing. Among them was Sékou Touré, then Vice President and now President of Guinea who is also President [24] of the neutralist *Union Generale des Travailleurs d'Afrique Noire* (UGTAN). He sent a trusted lieutenant, Diallo Seydou, as a gesture of trade-union solidarity and the anti-colonialism of the WFTU.[25] Also prominent among the non-Communists in attendance were the members of the Executive Committee of the Egyptian-sponsored International Confederation of Arab Trade-Unions (ICATU) an organization which claims a statutory ban against WFTU affiliates. Even Jao Goulart then a vice president of Brazil was expected to attend as honorary chairman of the Sao Paolo WFTU Committee, but at the last moment did not go.

Since the Leipzig Congress contacts of neutralist and ICFTU affiliated Afro-Asian trade-unions with the WFTU have considerably increased. One of the most successful united-front enterprises for this purpose is the International Trade-Union Committee for Solidarity with the Algerian Workers and People which was born from a resolution adopted at this Congress.[26]

*Movement toward Unity*

In the prevailing favorable climate the WFTU sought to make its contribution to anti-Western solidarity by emphasizing the common interest of the Communist and nationalist unions in fighting imperialist exploitation and aggression. It even suggested that tactical unity of action should lead to the unification of the nationalist and Communist organizations. Unity of action and unification on the national level, in turn, were presented as paving the way for eventual unification of the WFTU and the ICFTU, or failing this, to bring about the dissociation of the Afro-Asian neutralist unions from the ICFTU. Furthermore, it was claimed that the economies of the former colonial countries were evolving, if not directly toward "socialism as we scientifically understand it" at least toward something akin to it, i.e., "State capitalism." [27] Therefore, this process must be supported through unity as a right step toward national emancipation from Western influence.

As part of the new "unity" campaign, the class struggle, by being equated with the anti-imperialist struggle, was to become "outer directed" toward the international scene about which the masses in effect can do nothing. This meant its elimination from the party and trade-union programs—and in some cases even of the trade-unions themselves—as a threat to the nationalist governments and the reduction of Communist trade-union activities to what might be called "sound business unionism."

Accordingly in 1956 the Communist campaign for national and international trade-union unity assumed a new dimension. The hitherto spurious appeals to the non-Communist unions and the ICFTU gave way in several African and Asian countries to actual mergers of Communist unions with their nationalist rivals, thus creating new pressures from below for more international cooperation on all levels. Surprisingly enough such mergers were promoted regardless of whether the Communists stood to gain organizational control of non-Communist unions or not. In several cases the mergers had to be sternly imposed with backing from abroad against heavy opposition of local party and trade-union cadres who saw their cause undermined by such a sacrifice to the remote interests of the Soviet Union. The WFTU contributed to these pressures by giving publicity to such "achievements of unity" and through publishing articles by the local leaders who conducted these unity moves, strongly criticizing those elements who tried to hold out against the liquidation of their organization. No doubt such articles reflected also behind the scene pressures for compliance.

## Communist Labor Tactics in Africa

To turn to specific cases, between 1956 and 1958, Communist unions in Tunisia, French West Africa, and Algeria have merged with or have been absorbed by non-Communist trade-union centers. The most striking case was that of the Tunisian WFTU-affiliated USTT which in September, 1956 after a special congress, following a Communist party resolution on trade-union unity, dissolved to merge its rank-and-file with the Neo-Destour controlled, ICFTU-affiliated UGTT, from which the Communist USTT leaders remained excluded.[28] At the time when the USTT disbanded it had about 6,000 members or about 15–20 per cent of the organized workers in the country. This act of local Communist self-negation was justified on "anti-imperialist" grounds, i.e., that working class unity would strengthen the determination of the Tunisian nationalists to transform "formal" independence from France into "real" independence—i.e., neutralism.

In the case of Algeria, the Communist *Union Generale des Syndicats Algeriens* (UGSA) dissolved itself at the end of 1957, following the participation of the *Union Generale du Travail Algerienne* (UGTA), an organization aligned with the *Front de Liberation Nationale* (FLN) and affiliated with the ICFTU, at the Leipzig WFTU Congress. The Algerian Communist party announced this decision in a declaration calling for trade-union unity and urging UGSA members to join their rival nationalist movement.[29] The UGTA, in turn, despite its continued affiliation with the ICFTU, has since then closely collaborated with the WFTU, particularly in the promotion of the International Trade-Union Committee for Solidarity with the Algerian Workers and People. It also has accepted money and training for its cadres from both the WFTU and individual Soviet bloc unions, especially from the East German *Freier Deutscher Gewerkschaftsbund* (FDGB). Collaboration with the WFTU and the Soviet bloc trade-unions have so influenced the ideological outlook of the UGTA that unless the FLN can reorient its trade-union movement after Algerian independence is achieved, it will remain committed to structuring the new Algeria after the pattern of Guinea, Ghana, and Cuba with the outside support of the more extreme neutralists and the Communists.[30]

Perhaps the most effective Communist unity maneuvers took place in former French West Africa. Here the Communist *Confederation Generale du Travail* (CGT) joined with autonomous non-Communist unions at Cotonou, Dahomey, to form in January, 1957 the neutralist and unaffiliated *Union Generale des Travailleurs d'Afrique Noire* (UGTAN). The new movement included the CGT, the *Confederation Generale des Travailleurs d'Afrique* (CGTA), a nationalist labor movement aligned with the *Rassemblement Democratique Africain* (RDA); and several other autonomous unions, mostly of railways workers and

68

teachers. As the price of unity—approved and acknowledged by the French CGT and the WFTU—the West African CGT leaders despite resistance from their own cadres yielded control of their segment of the new labor movement to the CGTA. The CGT broke its affiliation with the WFTU in deference to Sekou Touré, who as General Secretary of the CGTA became also General Secretary of the UGTAN, and surrendered to his drive to bring the entire nationalist and labor movement under his control.

Touré is a dedicated but eclectic Marxist who, both as leader of the RDA and of a dissident section of the French West African CGT, had severed earlier associations with the Communists. Although he has increasingly aligned himself with the Soviet bloc since 1957, it is unlikely that at the time he would have, or could have, given the Communists any assurances that in return for their support he would detach Guinea from France and the Western political system, and instead look to the Soviet bloc for his main support and inspiration in restructuring the political and economic system of his country.

Abdoulay Diallo, ex-CGT chief in the Sudan, former chairman of the CGT-Coordinating Committee for French West Africa, and ex-vice president of the WFTU, was virtually eliminated from the international activities of UGTAN. Although he was given a vice presidency of UGTAN, he no longer seems to have any real influence on the Guinean labor movement. A similar case was that of Cisse Alioune, another ex-CGT man, who at the UGTAN Unity Congress at Conakry in January, 1959 was nominally entrusted with UGTAN international relations. In effect, however, these were conducted by Diallo Seydou, a Touré man who became General Secretary for Organization, Press, and Education.[31]

To justify this tactical self-negation, Communist propaganda declared that the unification of the French West African movement would lead to a Pan-African trade-union movement spreading from the French to the British areas of the continent. Furthermore, such unification would undercut the efforts of the ICFTU to establish an effective regional organization and would help speed up the process of detaching colonial Africa from the metropolitan powers through the strengthening of the nationalist movements. The effectiveness of this move in strengthening Communist influence on the growing African labor movement was soon proven. Despite the fact that the international policy of the UGTAN does not appear to be under the control of the ex-CGT leaders, the movement has become increasingly committed to the WFTU. Not only has the UGTAN attended the Fourth World Trade-Union Congress of the WFTU in Leipzig in October 1957, but subsequently has become a regular participant in all major WFTU affairs, including the meetings of the functional trade departments of that organization. By 1958 it joined, as a provisional member, the Technical Profession Forestry Section of the Trade-Union International of Agricultural and Forestry Workers.[32]

In July, 1960 the UGTAN played host to the Third World Teachers' Conference in Conakry, arranged by the *Federation Internationale Syndicale de l'Enseigment* (FISE), the teachers' trade department of the WFTU, for which the Guinean teachers' union, a UGTAN affiliate, acted as co-sponsor and host. Touré personally welcomed the congress. Perhaps even more important for the Soviet drive toward influencing labor developments in Africa was the establishment of a UGTAN trade-union training school in Conakry with the financial and technical assistance of the WFTU and the East German FDGB, both of whom provide instructors.

With Guinea having become a base for the spreading of Soviet influence in Africa, the UGTAN was turned into an instrument for purveying this influence among trade-unions. This was well-illustrated at the January, 1959 UGTAN Unity Congress at Conakry, when that organization proclaimed its intent of becoming a Pan-African labor movement. To emphasize this point the Ghana Trade-Union Congress, then one of the key ICFTU organizations in Africa, declared itself affiliated with the UGTAN. Despite the stress on non-commitment and the attendance of both ICFTU and WFTU fraternal delegates, Touré in his report to the Congress on orientation and doctrine stated that the unique character of the African labor movement did not prevent the

UGTAN from aligning its sympathy with the forces represented by the WFTU.[33]

Since their association at Conakry the Ghana TUC and the UGTAN have welcomed every support, not the least of which came from the WFTU, for their efforts of establishing an all-African trade-union movement associated with the Ghana-controlled All-African Peoples' Movement and designed to crowd the ICFTU and Western trade-union influence from the continent. To dramatize this objective the Ghana TUC disaffiliated from the ICFTU in October, 1959 just prior to the establishment of the ICFTU's African Regional Organization (AFRO). At the same time it promoted jointly with the UGTAN and the WFTU, a split of the Trade-Union Congress of Nigeria over the issue of international alignment when that organization was about to affiliate with the ICFTU.[34] This made it more difficult for the ICFTU to find in the Nigerian labor movement an effective alternate base to the Ghana TUC for its operations in Africa below the Sahara. Not only was the labor movement now divided, but the Pan-African neutralists to whom the so-called "unaligned" wing—the Nigerian Trade Union Congress—looked for guidance, could charge the ICFTU with the "responsibility" for the split.

The impact of the Congo crisis in summer, 1960 on Pan-African nationalism further strengthened the sentiment for a new all-African labor movement at the expense of the ICFTU. As a result this movement, with the backing of the Ghana TUC, the UGTAN, the U.A.R.-controlled Pan Arab ICATU, the Algerian UGTA, and the *Union Marocaine du Travail* (UMT), as well as the WFTU, became so attractive to African nationalists that, earlier difficulties and rivalries notwithstanding, no leader of an African ICFTU affiliate dared to oppose it outright. Even the most prominently identified African ICFTU leader Tom Mboya, the General Secretary of the Kenya Federation of Labor, who had been one of the main targets of the African neutralists, felt compelled to associate himself with this movement at the expense of his ties with the ICFTU.

While, of course, this trend within the African labor and

political movement cannot be directly attributed to the WFTU and other Communist efforts in the field of labor, the African nationalists and neutralists themselves freely admit that under the influence of Soviet bloc foreign policy these activities and tactics have considerably affected not only the political attitudes but also the focus of trade-unionism developing in Africa. By providing training for trade-union cadres both in Africa and Europe,[35] fraternal exchanges, roving representatives, money, propaganda, and various other forms of aid, the WFTU together with its Soviet affiliates and the Italian and French Communist unions seek to transform not only the African labor movements but also the social and political institutions in which they operate so that they will resemble those of the Peoples' Democracies. Developments in Guinea, Ghana, and elsewhere already indicate that such changes may make the restoration of normal relations—be they commercial, political, or labor—between these countries and the Western nations increasingly difficult.[36]

This trend toward the detachment of African labor from Western contacts and influence was further reinforced by the ability of the WFTU and its affiliates to promote ever-increasing international contacts and associations of the neutralists both with other Communist fronts, such as the World Peace, Youth, and Student movements, and with the regional neutralist movements which have emerged in recent years often with Communist help. Among these are the Afro-Asians, the Pan Arabs, the Pan-Africans, and the Pro-Castro Latin Americans, who are induced to collaborate with the Communists over such issues as the Algerian independence struggle, the Suez or Congo crisis, the South African race riots, the Angola rebellion, etc.

Thus, despite the fact that the number of WFTU affiliates in Africa remains insignificant,[37] the association with and participation in the nationalist turmol of Africa makes it an important instrument for undermining the regional status quo. Consequently, the disintegration of the UGTAN outside Guinea as a result of the breaking up of French West Africa into separate states aligned in a pro-French and a pro-

Guinean power bloc, has, if anything, strengthened the ability of the WFTU as an outside force to intensify the appeal for a Pan-African labor movement. Even though the pro-French "Entente" states remain suspicious of the Ghana-Guinea front against them and try to keep their trade-unions independent of the UGTAN, both official and unofficial contacts between their unions and the UGTAN continue. Curbs and suppressions of unions in Niger, Congo (Brazzaville), Senegal, Cameroun, etc., only tend to increase further the appeal of the Communist drive.

## Communist Labor Tactics in Asia

In Asia the Communist unity tactics were carried out only in Japan, neither an underdeveloped nor a neutralist country. Here, the big Left Wing Socialist Sohyo, resenting what it considered the interference of the United States in Japanese internal affairs on the side of the conservative elements, has reacted very similarly to the labor movements of the underdeveloped countries against imperialist interference. As a result of the readiness of the Left Wing forces to form a united front, the Japanese Communist party directed its labor movement to dissolve itself in order to "unify the trade-unions in Japan under the policies of the WFTU." [38] Thereupon, the Communist-dominated *Sanbetsu*, consisting mostly of a small metal workers' union with a membership of about 10,–000, obediently voted at its October, 1957 congress to dissolve itself and to merge with the National Metal Workers' Union (Zenkoku Kinzoku), an organization of some 90,000 members affiliated with Sohyo.

The final dissolution of *Sanbetsu* which took place at an extraordinary congress, jointly with the Sohyo Metal Workers' Union in February 1958, was hailed in a message of congratulations from the WFTU.[39] The fortuitous timing of this move with the general leftward trend of Sohyo contributed considerably toward the bolstering of Communist influence in that organization. This consolidation of all the forces of the radical Left culminated later that year in a proclamation by Sohyo that it was ready to collaborate with the Communist party and other progressive forces on the same footing as with the Socialist party with which it was aligned.[40] Since then Sohyo and many of its affiliates—some even members of the ICFTU—have collaborated with the WFTU and Soviet bloc trade-unions on a similar basis as the UGTA and the UGTAN. Such close association has helped the WFTU and the Communist labor movements, especially of East Germany and Communist China, to be prominently identified with the anti-U.S. demonstrations in Japan and the protests against Japanese Government measures to check the militant demonstrations of Sohyo and other Left Wing movements.

In at least two other areas, i.e., India and the Sudan, there is considerable circumstantial evidence that the Communist trade-unions came under pressure from Moscow to follow the pattern of Tunisia and French West Africa and accept their own dissolution and absorption into non-Communist organizations subject to a large measure of government control. That some such plan was at least contemplated in India is indicated by the facts that S. A. Dange, General Secretary of the All-India Trade-Union Congress (AITUC), not only issued invitations to the Congress party-controlled Indian National Trade-Union Congress (INTUC) for negotiating a general trade-union merger, but also appointed a special seven-man unity committee; and, that he wrote a special article in the September, 1956 issue of *World Trade-Union Movement* in which he criticized the "Left Wing and purist elements" who objected to unity with the INTUC as a "betrayal of working class principles."

The probable sincerity of these appeals was reinforced by the fact that simultaneously similar Communist moves were actually being carried out in other countries.[41]

Nevertheless both the local and national Communist labor leadership appears to have effectively resisted the new unity pattern, and instead has become increasingly successful in expanding the AITUC, infiltrating rival organizations, and promoting unity of action from below and from above.[42] While unity is still professed to be the ultimate objective of the AITUC, the current emphasis is on both the strengthening of its own organization at the expense of its rivals, and on the effective reinforcement of the united front against the INTUC.

Since 1958 Indian Communist unity maneuvers consisted mostly of efforts to absorb relatively weak anti-INTUC unions; of establishing unaffiliated unions, such as the Bombay Girni Kamgar (textile) union in February, 1959 with a prominent non-Communist figurehead, but apparently under Communist control; and of AITUC affiliates as well as nominally unaffiliated but Communist run unions participating in unaligned national federations, such as the All-India Defense Employees' Federation [43] and the All-India Port and Dock Workers' Federation. However, in January, 1961 the Communist controlled Southern Railway Union merged with the larger Praja-Socialist controlled Southern Railway Employees' Union which is a member of the unaffiliated All-India Railwaymen's Federation in order to strengthen the united front against the INTUC-affiliated National Federation of Indian Railwaymen which enjoys the exclusive patronage of the Indian Government.[44]

The success of Communist labor tactics since 1957, combined with Communist political gains has evoked an increasingly antagonistic reaction on the part of the government and the non-Communist unions. This trend was reinforced by the national indignation against the activities of the Communists in Kerala, the brutal repression of the Tibetian revolt, and the Chinese Communist border incursions. It has also made impossible any participation of the non-Communist Indian labor movement in any Afro-Asian trade-union solidarity demonstrations. As a result relations of both the Praja Socialist *Hind Mazdoor Sabha* (HMS) and the INTUC with the ICFTU have noticeably improved and both unions have refused to enter into closer relations with the All-China Federation of Trade-Unions (ACFTU) or the Soviet trade-unions. However, such anti-Communist reactions have failed to bring the HMS and the INTUC closer together. On the contrary, the HMS has not hesitated to collaborate on specific trade-union issues with the AITUC and the Left Wing *United Trade-Union Congress* (UTUC).

In the Sudan where the trade-union movement had split in April, 1956 as a result of a general strike appeal by the Communist leadership of the Sudan Workers Trade-Union Federation (SWTUF), reunification moves were started early in 1957, when the non-Communist Sudan General Workers Trade-Union Federation (SGWTUF) was negotiating with the ICFTU regarding affiliation. The basis of unity negotiations was in part the result of common demonstrations against the Anglo-French-Israeli attack on Egypt and in support of the Algerian rebellion and in part the government's intended reduction of civil servants' cost of living allowances which both the Communist and non-Communist unions opposed and which was withdrawn under the threat of a general strike. At the time the Sudan Railway Workers' Trade-Union, the largest labor organization in the country, was controlled by a narrow non-Communist majority, which hoped that the promotion of unity under conditions of non-alignment could preserve the balance of power within the labor movement in their favor. The government, in turn, encouraged this unity movement in the expectation that this would enable the non-Communists to capture control of the entire Sudanese labor movement. As it turned out, however, the Communists gained control of the Railway Workers' Trade-Union. Consequently, the unity movement collapsed and the truncated SGWFTU was accepted as an affiliate by the ICFTU in March, 1958. In November, 1958 the government, unable to cope with the political and trade-union situation outlawed all unions and political parties.[45]

## The Tactical Dilemmas Beyond Unity

Since 1957 the merger and unity maneuvers of the Communist labor movements have undergone certain tactical changes under the impact of international developments, and especially changes in the relations within the international Communist movement as a result of the Sino-Soviet conflict. As has been shown, except in the case of Tunisia, the mergers, while sacrificing viable Communist labor movements, have increased Soviet bloc influence in the countries in which they have taken place. They also had the advantage that, together with outside Soviet support, they removed from the Communists the onus of opposition to absolute national unity, one of the prerequisites of the new style "democracy" of the ultranationalist movements.[46]

In India and the Sudan where a pluralistic governmental structure existed—in the Sudan this has since been displaced by a military dictatorship—Communist labor movements, being in the ascendancy, resisted Soviet pressures and refused to yield to the pro-governmental nationalist forces, particularly when it became clear that this would make neither the governments nor such unified unions under their control more inclined toward the type of political and economic structuring which would favor the Soviet bloc. In Indonesia and for a time in Iraq as long as the Communists dominated the labor scene with the approval and the encouragement of the government, they were not identified with the opposition and no reason for the abandonment of their labor movements existed.[47]

Elsewhere Communist trade-unions, instead of letting themselves be incorporated into national front movements, followed for the most part the more traditional tactics of united action with non-Communists. They resorted to mergers only under conditions which would leave them either in control of the united trade-union movements—as in the case of the *Confederation Generale Africaine du Travail* (CGAT) of former French Equatorial Africa, permit them to retain their Communist identity within the united movement—as for instance in Syria prior to its merger with Egypt, and/or strengthen the opposition labor movement—as in the case of the South Indian railway workers.[48] Thus in contrast to the 1957 tactics,[49] the WFTU affiliated Ceylon Trade-Union Federation (CTUF) refused at the end of 1960 to join a united-front labor movement with the unions aligned with the ruling *Sree Lanka Freedom Party* (SLFP) and the Trotzkyite *Lanka Sama Samaja Party*, despite the fact that the Communists, the Trotzkyites, and the SLFP had formed an electoral and parliamentary coalition supporting the SLFP government and that the three labor movements participated already in a Coordinating Committee of Trade-

Union Organizations.[50] Apparently, the Communists feared that in such a united trade-union movement they might be forced to yield control over their sector.

Although these tactical changes reflected an increasingly selective and differentiated approach to the nationalist movements of the Afro-Asian countries, with the exception of Japan, the Communist labor and political movements have not moved into outright opposition to the nationalist forces. Even in the face of considerable repression, as for instance in Iraq and to a lesser extent in India, they by and large supported both the domestic and foreign policies of their countries. Occasional eruptions of strikes and demonstrations were directed primarily against economic grievances. The restraint of these movements thus reflects their continuing subservience to the Soviet state-to-state political and economic offensive among the neutralists.

The U.S.S.R., on its part, has generally been careful to avoid any undue show of concern for the fates of national Communist parties or mass movements in the neutralist countries. However, when some of these states which were also recipients of Soviet aid showed their displeasure with Sino-Soviet bloc policies affecting their areas by repressing local Communist movements, the U.S.S.R. and its entire international Communist propaganda apparatus in turn, also began to reflect increasing irritation.

Criticisms of anti-Communist measures by neutralist governments had begun to appear in Soviet journals earlier, but it was not until the 21st Congress of the CPSU in January, 1959 that Khrushchev himself lent his authority to them. On that occasion he warned that the suppression of the "working class," i.e., of Communist movements, by nationalist governments would aggravate the internal contradictions between capital and labor in the developing countries. In the ensuing class struggle the U.S.S.R. would have to side with the "progressive forces." The implication was clear for all to read that the state-to-state relations need not be the only Soviet means of affecting the affairs of the neutralists. This statement reflected Soviet irritation with Nasser for his persecution of Egyptian and Syrian Communists in reaction to U.S.S.R. and local Communist support for Qassim's 1958 revolt in Iraq which had created an alternate nationalist power-center to Nasser among the Arabs. Nevertheless, the Soviet bloc has adhered to its state-to-state approach despite mounting Communist criticism of repressive policies against Communists and other "progressive" political and labor movements in Iraq, the U.A.R., the Sudan, India, and elsewhere among the neutralists. Thus it continued to give aid and political support to the Generals Nasser, Qassim, and Aboud and to Nehru regardless of the domestic or even specific foreign policies of the recipients.

### The Sino-Soviet Conflict, Polycentrism, and Soviet Control [51]

Despite the successes of Soviet foreign policy since Stalin's death, the proclamation of "different roads to socialism" at the 20th Congress of the CPSU in 1956 and the changing orientation of Communist movements both within and without the bloc toward the Kremlin inevitably led to a challenge of this policy by the Chinese Communist leadership in protest over what they considered a neglect of their national interests. These policy differences reportedly go back at least to 1957 when the U.S.S.R. first demonstrated its missile superiority over the U. S., and the Chinese demanded a more aggressive foreign policy for the bloc. However, in 1959 Chinese policy first began to interfere seriously with Soviet policy toward the neutralist states. At that time the Chinese after their bloody repression of the revolt in Tibet challenged both diplomatically and militarily the border claims of one of the key states within the neutralist camp.

In the controversy over the rights or wrongs of the Chinese-Indian border dispute, the Russians sided with India and by implication with the entire neutralist camp against a fellow Socialist country. The Chinese responded by challenging an increasing number of fundamental tenets of Soviet policy, such as peaceful coexistence and the avoidability of war with the imperialists. Instead they argued for Communist support of wars of liberation against the imperialist camp, and denounced Soviet proposals of diverting the savings from universal disarmament both in the Socialist and Capitalist camps to aiding the underdeveloped countries as reflecting complete blindness to the aggressive nature of capitalism. Even more serious from a propaganda point of view, they pressed the international Communist movement to restore the class struggle to its traditional place in the programs of the Communist parties of the underdeveloped countries. The "national bourgeoisie" was to be declared an unreliable ally in the struggle for complete independence, which might align itself again with the imperialists in the final struggle for complete independence and socialism. Therefore, in accordance with Mao's strategic formula for telescoping the transition from national liberation to socialism, the Communists should increase their efforts to seize the leadership of the national liberation struggle and unite all anti-imperialist groups behind them.

Such arguments challenged the carefully established basis of Soviet policy toward promoting an evergrowing "peace camp" consisting of friendly powers attracted by the spectacular growth of strength of the Socialist camp, which would lend their support to the Soviet bloc against any "imperialist maneuvers" to extend or consolidate the Western position in the underdeveloped countries. However, the Chinese Communist challenge was not merely directed to matters of tactics and foreign policy, but also hit at Soviet supremacy as the guiding ideological center, especially for the movements of the underdeveloped countries. The Chinese claimed that theirs was an alternate route to socialism built not on the foundation of high economic development leading to abundance as Marx had assumed, but on the restructuring of society on the basis of a militant egalitarianism imposed by such organizational devices as communes. Thus China claimed to be a more representative example for the underdeveloped countries than the already highly industrialized Soviet Union.

The Russians reacted initially merely to the ideological arguments of the Chinese, but tried to ignore, at least in public, their criticism of Soviet foreign policy. However, the failure of the "spirit of Camp David" and the collapse of the Summit Conference in May 1960 forced them to take up the challenge on all levels. The first open sparring on this issue occurred at the 11th General Council Meeting of the WFTU at Peking in June. In this connection the coincidence is striking that at this, the second, WFTU meeting in Peking the Chinese again sought to assert what they consider their rightful preeminence in guiding the tactics and orientation of the Communist political and labor movements in the underdeveloped countries. In November, 1949 at the Asian and Australasian Trade-Union Conference, the Chinese had sought endorsement of the universal applicability throughout the underdeveloped countries for the Maoist strategy of having the Communists break up nationalist united fronts and lead the dissidents into armed rebellion. At the time the appropriate Soviet deference to the Chinese was possible because Soviet interests in the newly-emerging countries were not affected. In 1960, however, although the Chinese did not press for anywhere near as drastic a change in Communist tactics, their demands now affected Soviet interests far more directly.

At the WFTU General Council meeting the Chinese Vice President of the WFTU, Liu Chang-sheng, in a most unprecedented manner openly voiced the whole catalogue of Chinese criticism of U.S.S.R. policy and Communist tactics. Furthermore, he and his fellow Chinese delegates insisted on discussing these matters also in the non-public meetings.[52] Both the Russians and the Europeans strongly defended the Soviet position, especially the correctness of "peaceful coexistence." Only the Indonesian delegate and a Japanese representing Sohyo as an observer sided openly with the Chinese. To reduce the impact of this now open controversy to a minimum, the Russians sought to find a compromise formula admitting that just wars resulting from liberation struggles must be supported by the Communists and that the national bourgeoisie may not always be a reliable ally in the anti-imperialist struggle. But while admitting the Chinese arguments, they rejected their blanket applicability, demanding instead a differentiated policy toward the underdeveloped countries and greater tactical leeway for their various Communist parties. Above all, they insisted on the endorsement of peaceful coexistence and the avoidability of major wars.[53] By this stratagem they hoped to reduce the effect of the Chinese challenge and at the same time to obtain greater freedom of action for themselves. Old loyalties and habits were counted on to preserve Russian hegemony in guiding the Communist camp, even though the Chinese were trying hard to undermine these relations by impressing their point of view on an increasing number of Communists and collaborating neutralists invited to China or being visited by Chinese fraternal delegations.

Following the Peking meeting, the Russians not only solicited declarations of continued loyalty from the Communist parties, but through the WFTU and the Soviet All Union Central Council of Trade-Unions (AUCCTU) tried also to obtain such assurances from the Communist trade-union leadership either by dispatching high level trade-union delegations, as for instance to Indonesia, or by inviting key leaders to the U.S.S.R., as for instance WFTU president Novella of the Italian *Confederazione Generale Italiana del Lavoro* (CGIL). They also consulted with the leadership of both Eastern and Western European Communist trade-unions in order to consolidate their guidance and control over the movement. However, as the reports and resolutions of the WFTU meeting presaged and as the December 6, 1960 statement of the 81 Communist parties which had met in Moscow clearly emphasized, the structure of the entire Communist movement both within and without the Sino-Soviet bloc is changing.

The Communist world is gradually moving away from the monolithic centrally manipulated movement that looked to Moscow for its guidance both as to tactics and ideological orthodoxy. Ever since Stalin's death the Communist movements have pressed for and obtained increasing independence of action—although within strict limits, as the case of Hungary has clearly shown. So far this has been especially true for the members of the Sino-Soviet bloc and for the Communist movements of western Europe. Under the impact of the Sino-Soviet dispute it is now also becoming true of the hitherto more marginal and expendable parties and labor movements of the underdeveloped countries.

Up to 1959 the Soviet Union had been able to detach its foreign policy interests from the local Communist movements in the Afro-Asian areas, while these movements could not similarly detach themselves from the interests of the U.S.S.R. Although this still holds true to a large extent in view of the preeminence of the U.S.S.R. in the Communist camp, nevertheless it now has been shown that differences over strategy and tactics can be accommodated within the Communist camp. Hence the possibility of shifting alingments within that camp over specific issues affecting the interests of local parties and unions will have to be taken into consideration since they may also affect the interests of more important movements. While this restructuring of the relations within the international Communist movement, as also reflected in the changing character of the WFTU, was probably a deliberate policy on the part of Khrushchev, the Chinese have pushed their challenge beyond what was tolerable for the Russians. Therefore the Russians demanded reaffirmations of loyalty from the parties and trade-unions, which they have by and large received.

The programs and pronouncements of most Communist parties and labor movements in the Afro-Asian area, especially those of India, Indonesia, Ceylon, Cyprus, and even of Iraq, reveal that they continue to give support to their neutralist governments. But that loyalty is no longer taken completely for granted. As the pronouncements of the WFTU since the Moscow meeting of the 81 parties have indicated, the main problem for the WFTU and the international working-class movement remains that of unity and guidance in the light of that statement issued at the Moscow meeting.[54]

## The Promotion of Regional Labor Solidarity Among the Neutralists

Communist efforts to help promote regional neutralist labor internationals with which the WFTU and its affiliates could collaborate were at first directed toward the establishment of an Asian and subsequently an Afro-Asian labor movement. The immediate idea for an Asian regional labor organization—politically uncommitted to either East or

West—was sparked not by the Communists but by the Asian Socialist Conference at Rangoon in March, 1954. At this conference plans were made to conduct a series of Asian trade-union seminars, mainly for the purpose of exchanging information. The Indian and Burmese delegates were for excluding WFTU members, while some Japanese representatives who were members of Sohyo, sought to promote an all-inclusive meeting to which the All-China Federation of Trade-Unions (ACFTU) also could be invited. The Japanese found little support from the Socialists, but enthusiastic response from the Chinese Communists who apparently had well-advanced plans along these lines themselves.

On the Communist side the initiative was taken by the Chinese who thereby sought to enhance their own influence among the neutralists. The first informal discussions were held on the occasion of the 1954 May Day celebration in Peking.[55] Later that year, during the October, 1954 celebrations of the Fifth Anniversary of the Chinese People's Republic, an all-Asian Trade-Union Representatives' Preliminary Conference was held in Peiping. Trade-union leaders of the unaligned Trade-Union Congress of Burma (TUCB), of Sohyo, th United Trade-Union Congress (UTUC) of India, and the INTUC were drawn into consultation regarding the holding of an Asian trade-union meeting, preferably in India. While Sohyo supported the proposal, the Indians and Burmese excused themselves from active cooperation, referring to the political situation at home, and stating their lack of authority.

Encouraged by the Bandung Conference of April, 1955, the ACFTU renewed its efforts to promote a meeting of similar scope among the Asian and African trade-unions through an improvised conference of their delegates attending the 1955 Peking May Day celebration. Seventy-one Afro-Asian trade-union organizations from 15 countries attended. The non-Communists included such ICFTU affiliates as the INTUC, the HMS, the All-Pakistan Confederation of Labor (APCOL), and the *Jam'iat* of Lebanon. For the first time the meeting brought together Communist and non-Communist unions from the same countries, including India, Burma, and

Japan. At this meeting the Chinese clumsily pressured the ICFTU affiliates and the TUC of Burma to take the initiative. When they refused, they found themselves harassed and most of the non-Communist Indians left in a huff. Not only was this incident widely publicized in India, but both the INTUC and the HMS have since then refused to send delegations to Peiping.[56] However, they have subsequently received fraternal delegates from the ACFTU and the Soviet AUCCTU at their congresses.

While the refusal of the Indian non-Communists to participate in the preliminary arrangements put a damper on the prospects of an early Afro-Asian labor conference, Sohyo and the Central Organization of Labor Unions of Indonesia (SOBSI) kept up the appeal. New steam was injected into the campaign in 1956 as a result of the founding of the International Confederation of Arab Trade-Unions (ICATU) by the Egyptians at Damascus in March of that year. This movement was established by the Nasser Government with the support of the WFTU in order to promote neutralism and Pan-Arab solidarity. By virtue of Egypt's growing influence in both African and Asian affairs and because of its appeal to the Arab labor movements of both continents, the ICATU became a keystone in the maneuvers toward promoting an Afro-Asian labor organization. This provided the basis for close collaboration with the WFTU, despite the fact that the ICATU proclaimed itself as "uncommitted" and refused to admit WFTU affiliates into its ranks.[57] In ironic contrast, however, it did accept the Lybian General Workers' Union, an ICFTU affiliate, to membership, but made clear its primarily anti-western orientation and its objective of blocking the ICFTU from operating among the Arab labor movements.[58] Thus it proved to be an extremely useful ally for attracting not only unaligned unions, but also for breaking down the solidarity of the IFCTU by inducing some of its affiliates to collaborate with the WFTU. The Suez crisis at the end of 1956 and the Algerian independence struggle— both Arab issues of great interest to the neutralists—further contributed toward strengthening these informal trade-union alignments. The success of the WFTU-ICATU symbiosis, which also symbolized the new relationship between the neutralists and the Soviet bloc, caused a sudden and great upsurge of the prestige of the WFTU among the Afro-Asians which was further bolstered when the newly established West African UGTAN joined the alliance. This was clearly demonstrated at the Leipzig Congress of the WFTU in October, 1957.

The appeal of the Afro-Asian trade-union solidarity movement continued to be reflected in the large attendance of African and Asian delegates at the Eighth ACFTU Congress at Peiping in December, 1957, which included not only those of the UGTAN and the ICATU, but also of the UMT of Morocco and of the Lybian General Workers' Union, both ICFTU affiliates. Again the Chinese tried to use this occasion to obtain commitments from their guests for the early holding of an Afro-Asian trade-union conference on neutral ground.[59] At about the same time the World Peace Council-sponsored [60] Afro-Asian Peoples' Solidarity Conference met in Cairo, also with many Communist and neutralist trade-union leaders in attendance. These people got together at a special meeting and adopted a resolution to hold an Afro-Asian labor meeting in 1958.[61]

Building on this successful competition of the Communist labor movements with the ICFTU unions among the "uncommitted" unions, the WFTU stepped up its "international trade-union unity" campaign. This campaign, which is a major propaganda weapon of the WFTU, consists of baiting the ICFTU for refusing to cooperate with the Communists and neutralists on the basis of their common profession of anti-colonialism and concern for the welfare of the workers of the underdeveloped countries. This refusal is represented by the WFTU as proof that the ICFTU leaders are betraying their professed principles and attributed to their overriding loyalty to the "imperialist" governments. By these charges the neutralists are supplied with ready justifications for turning to the WFTU and the Communist camp. The increasing cooperation of these neutralists with the WFTU against the ICFTU is then presented as the mark of acceptance of these charges.

In contrast to the successes of the WFTU, the once considerable prestige of the ICFTU among the trade-unions now committed to Afro-Asian neutralism began to wane. Even though it had taken the same position as the WFTU during the Suez crisis, on colonialism, and on the Algerian issue, its links with the trade-unions of Great Britain, France, and Israel could no longer make it as attractive to the Afro-Asians as the WFTU, which permitted the neutralists freewheeling collaboration without commitment.[62] The ICFTU tried to take the wind out of the sails of the neutralist and Communist sponsors of the Afro-Asian labor solidarity campaign by holding an Afro-Asian trade-union conference of its own in connection with its Tunis Congress in July, 1957. Yet this meeting served only to show up the defensiveness of the Western trade-union position in regard to the neutralists. Henceforth, the moral authority of the ICFTU could no longer keep its Asian and African affiliates from steadily increasing contacts with the WFTU, the ICATU, and the major Communist trade-unions, especially those of China, East Germany, and Russia.

Early in 1958 the effect of the close collaboration between the WFTU and its affiliates and the ICATU went so far as to lead to purges of those ICATU leaders considered as too pro-Western. However, the harmony between these two organizations continued only for another year during which the Afro-Asian labor campaign began to lose momentum. For a time bilateral and multilateral discussions continued, but the reluctance of the Indian and Burmese non-Communist unions to participate, the ensuing competition between Sohyo of Japan and the ICATU over sponsorship, and the controversy over Soviet and ACFTU inclusion in an uncommitted organization continued to bar agreement. To this was added the effect of Soviet-U.A.R. differences over Iraq starting in summer, 1958 which led by early 1959 to a marked estrangement of relations between the WFTU and the ICATU. As a result the ICATU announced at its Second Conference at Cairo in April, 1959 its determination to reduce all contacts with the Soviet bloc and in a reverse purge eliminated its pro-Communist leaders.

The new leaders of the International Confederation of Arab Trade-Unions best symbolized by Salijm Shita, the General Secretary of the ICFTU-affiliated Lybian General Workers' Union, who was picked as the new president, were to be less committed to collaboration with the Bloc and were to facilitate contacts with the AFL-CIO, the ICFTU, and other Western trade-union movements for the purpose of anti-Communist solidarity gestures. Indeed, such overtures were successfully made and resulted in an invitation issued to the ICATU to attend the ICFTU World Congress in Brussels in December 1959,[63] even though until a short time before the ICFTU had sharply criticized the ICATU as purely a U.A.R. propaganda instrument. Other signs of the new orientation were declarations at the ICATU conference that in order to reduce its collaboration with the Bloc it would also reduce its activities on behalf of the Afro-Asian and Pan African movements and concentrate instead on the promotion of Pan-Arab unity under the leadership of Nasser.

However, Arab unity on U.A.R. terms was no more readily acceptable to the other Arab labor and nationalist movements than to their governments, and the ICATU had not proven very effective in this respect outside its home ground. In contrast, the Algerian issue and anti-imperialism attracted not only Arab support from all quarters, be they pro-Nasser, pro-Qassim, or pro-Bourghiba, but also support from non-Arab African and Asian neutralists and even from Latin America. Consequently, continuation in the WFTU-ICATU-sponsored International Trade-Union Committee for Solidarity with the Algerian Workers and People proved irresistible. No less than five Afro-Asian ICFTU affiliates from Morocco, Lybia, Algeria, Ghana, and Aden participated in the Committee, or the same number, as the non-bloc Afro-Asian WFTU affiliates from India, Indonesia, Sudan, Cyprus, and Iraq. These were joined not only by the ICATU and its affiliates but also by such unaffiliated neutralist unions as the UGTAN, CUTCH of Chile, and Sohyo. According to the *World Trade-Union News* even the INTUC, the Congress party-aligned ICFTU affiliate from India sent supporting statements to the Committee. As a result of continued participation in this commttee, contacts with the WFTU, and Communist trade-unions from both the Soviet bloc and the Afro-Asian countries, have become inevitable for the ICATU. In effect they helped to give the ICATU a new lease on life at a time when it seemed to be fading as a result of the Iraqi crisis and the failure of the Afro-Asian trade-union solidarity campaign. Furthermore, the Algerian Solidarity movement again drew the ICATU against its declared intent into the larger anti-Western neutralist campaign, this time through its Pan-African aspect.

The first concrete steps toward the formation of an "uncommitted" Pan-African labor movement were taken at a special meeting under Moroccan trade-union auspices in Casablanca, in September, 1959. Here the ICATU, the UGTAN, the Algerian UGTA (ICFTU), and the Moroccan UMT (ICFTU) agreed to convene a Pan-African trade-union conference before the end of the year, combining all African and Arab trade-unions regardless of affiliation.[64] Both ICFTU and WFTU representatives were to be invited in accordance with the standard formula of unity of action which is designed primarily to embarrass the ICFTU whether it accepts such an invitation on the same footing as the WFTU or rejects it.

The anti-ICFTU intent of the new African labor solidarity movement was further revealed when shortly before the ICFTU convened its second African regional conference at Lagos, Nigeria in November, 1959, the Ghana TUC and the All-African Peoples' Conference hastily called for another preliminary Pan-African Labor Conference at Accra to draw delegations and international attention away from the Lagos meeting. The UGTAN, the UMT of Morocco, the Algerian UGTA, and the ICATU readily responded to this call and agreed to convene a founding congress in Casablanca in May, 1960. However, because of regional and political rivalries among the sponsoring groups; i.e., the Pan-Arab ICATU, the North Africans, and the West Africans, the meeting was postponed several times until it finally met one year later.

The key issue in which these regional rivalries found their expression was whether membership in the new All-African

Trade-Union Federation (AATUF) could be made compatible with maintaining, simultaneously, affiliation with "other internationals," which meant the ICFTU. In the ensuing squabbles the Egyptians seemed to lose interest in the movement, turning instead to cementing their relations with their fellow Arab trade-unions.[65]

By mid-summer, 1960, however, the eruption of the Congo crisis and the ensuing three-cornered contentions of the Soviets, the neutralists, and the Western powers over the future political alignment of the Congo and over the use of the UN toward this end drew the WFTU, the UGTAN, the ICATU, and the North African trade-unions into closer collaboration again. Furthermore, it enabled the WFTU and the UGTAN to increase their influence among the unions of Central and East Africa which largely had remained loyal to the ICFTU. This trend was also reinforced by the prospect that joint neutralist and Soviet agitation might speed up a favorable settlement of the Algerian issue. Thus both the Congo crisis and the Algerian independence struggle revived the prospect of agreement on the establishment of the AATUF.

The Moroccan UMT became the pivotal movement in the restoration of the informal alliance between the WFTU and the Black African, North African, and Arab trade-unions. The readiness of the UMT to play this role stemmed from the fact that it found itself harassed by an increasingly hostile government which sought to secure its tenure by curbing its Left Wing opposition and trade-union movement at home while moving toward a rapprochement with the Soviet Bloc and the neutralist powers. Thus the UMT cast about frantically for international labor support wherever it could in order to increase the political risks for its government of further repressions. In this key role the UMT acted as host for a meeting of the Secretariat of the International Trade-Union Committee for Solidarity with the Workers and People of Algeria in Casablanca in August, 1960. The participants, which included also a WFTU delegate, discussed not only Algerian matters, but also their common interests in African labor affairs. Furthermore, the Secretariat announced the decision to hold a fullfledged meeting of the Committee in Havana in October.

The Havana meeting was attended not only by most WFTU affiliates and the African and Middle Eastern neutralists as well as by the Japanese Sohyo, but also by a large contingent of pro-Communist and neutralist Latin American trade-unions. It demonstrated both Latin American support for the Algerian and African cause and the effectiveness of neutralist and Soviet bloc working relations in the international trade-union field.

After the Havana meeting the AATUF campaign received a further boost when its main target the ICFTU held its Third African Regional Conference in Tunis in order to marshal its own forces against hostile inroads on the ICFTU position in Africa. This meeting decided that all members of the African Regional Organization should participate in the AATUF in order to fight the demands of the Ghana-Guinea-U.A.R. bloc for disaffiliation from the ICFTU as condition of membership. The neutralists, in turn, followed this meeting with one of their own in Accra at the beginning of December, just prior to the opening of the First African Regional Conference of the ILO at Lagos, and with another at Lagos during the ILO Conference. Soviet, Chinese, and WFTU representatives who had come as observers to Lagos gave their full support and encouragement both to the formation of the AATUF and to the principle of non-alignment. Thus by the end of the year the Pan-African labor campaign was in full swing again.

Although the air of uncertainty and bickering continued to surround the plans for the convening of the AATUF founding congress, the African solidarity demonstrated by the governments of the U.A.R., Morocco, Algeria, Ghana, and Mali at the Casablanca Conference in January, 1961 and by the All-African Peoples' Conference in Cairo in March, 1961 further increased the pressure for holding the AATUF Founding Congress at Casablanca at the end of May. Neutralist acceptance of WFTU and Communist alignment with this movement was reflected in an article by Assad Ragih, Secretary General of the ICATU in a Cairo English language publication.[66] In it he credited the WFTU with the "first practical step" toward the creation of AATUF through the Algerian Solidarity Committee. The WFTU, in turn, announced at its 22nd Executive Committee meeting in East Berlin in February that it would be prominently associated with the establishment of the AATUF by turning the Algerian Solidarity Committee into a committee for the support of all workers and people of Africa.

The neutralist-WFTU alliance was again confirmed when the founding Congress of the AATUF finally took place at Casablanca from May 25–30, 1961. At this meeting the loyal ICFTU affiliates were out-maneuvered. Despite bitter debates and the efforts of the North African delegates to avoid a showdown on the issue of ICFTU affiliation, the meeting agreed that all AATUF members would have to break their ties with the ICFTU and the WFTU within ten months. In the final line-up the Lybian, Moroccan, and Algerian unions—all nominally ICFTU affiliates—supported the new AATUF charter which included the disaffiliation provision. Apparently the victory was possible because the loyal ICFTU affiliates under the leadership of the Tunisian UGTT had left the meeting in the evening of May 29, its official closing date, while the final vote on the charter was not taken until the following day.[67]

Thus this Pan-African labor meeting reflected anything but the unity of the African labor movements and its participants found themselves grouped along much the same lines as their governments. Subsequent announcements of both the neutralists and the loyal ICFTU affiliates presaged the possibility of the formation of two rival African trade-union camps.[68] Nevertheless, the neutralists were able to maintain their initiative and the final alignment of the African labor movements remains far from certain. Furthermore, the appeal of a non-committed Pan-Africanism is likely to force even the loyal ICFTU affiliates to constantly reappraise the political usefulness of their formal ties with the Western labor movement. In contrast, the loss to the WFTU of a few minor affiliates, operating mostly illegally, was a small price to pay in return for its ability to be closely associated with the Pan-African neutralist camp and its offensive against the ICFTU.[69]

## Summary and Conclusions

As has been shown in this paper, the divergence of attitudes and outlooks among the trade-unions engaged in international labor activities reflects international power politics in a neat microcosm. The participants in these activities are strongly committed to fixed positions in the East-West struggle—be they pro-Western, pro-Soviet, or neutralist—but they are often less inhibited than official spokesmen by considerations of complex international involvements. Therefore, their views tend to reflect more bluntly national and politico-ideological attitudes than are ordinarily revealed in international diplomatic forums, even in this age of diplomacy by propaganda.

This correlation between international labor affairs and power politics is particularly revealed by the study of the international Communist trade-union offensive which has been fully integrated into the Soviet competitive coexistence campaign. The objective of this campaign is to nullify all major political and economic efforts of the West by showing that the Soviet camp is rapidly moving ahead and outdoing its non-Communist rivals. Both the WFTU and its affiliated Communist trade-unions are constantly probing for new opportunities and issues on which to base spectacular unity-of-action demonstrations against the Western powers and their trade-unions. Toward this end the Communists have even shown their readiness to sacrifice their own movements. Despite the fact that neither the WFTU nor Communist labor movements are the prime movers in such affairs as the Afro-Asian or Pan-African labor intrigues, the association of the neutralist unions with the WFTU as the main antagonist of the ICFTU contributes to Western disquietude over the political and economic future of the former colonial areas.

As a result of its role in this campaign, the WFTU is no longer purely a propaganda instrument reinforcing the foreign policy orientations of the nationalist-neutralist trade-unions and their governments through international solidarity demonstrations. Political developments in Africa and Latin America now enable it and the labor organizations of the Soviet bloc countries to contribute tactical and technical guidance, training of cadres, and financial assistance to a growing number of labor movements, helping them thereby to transform their societies into socio-economic structures resembling those of the "peoples' democracies." Such social transformations are to speed up the detachment of the former colonial countries from the Western political and economic system, making normal political, economic, or labor relations with them increasingly difficult. The fact that such countries despite their pro-Soviet orientation would mostly not want to be integrated into the Soviet system, or even if they did, could not be—vide Cuba—is irrelevant for the immediate objectives of this campaign.

The WFTU claims that the international working class struggle will establish socialism everywhere and makes clear that Communists consider the self-styled "socialism" now prevalent throughout much of the underdeveloped areas as merely a transitional stage which the Communist labor and political movements must transform into "peoples' democracies," [70] but this is clearly beyond their ability in the absence of outside Communist attacks. The general depolarization of international relations both in the Soviet and Western camp will make this increasingly less likely. The inherent barriers to large-scale Communist takeovers of power in the underdeveloped countries, however, do not diminish the current success of the Sino-Soviet offensive, especially in Africa and Latin America, or the threat emanating therefrom to Western policy objectives toward these countries.

Even if most of South and East Asia and the Middle East provide today few opportunities for the Communists to affect political and economic developments through the trade-unions, spectacular issues like the U. S.–Japanese Security Treaty, West Irian and anti-colonialism, provide continuing opportunities for publicizing the presence of the WFTU in Asia. At the same time the probing continues on a lower level in the form of functional and regional meetings, such as the

Pacific Dock Workers Conference in Tokyo and a Pacific Fishery Workers' Conference in Vancouver, both in 1959; or in the form of fraternal contacts, scholarships, financial support and the distribution of propaganda material. Sohyo as an unaffliated and neutralist organization willingly serves as the instrument for these efforts.

As for more spectacular regional meetings such as the African or Latin American labor meetings, new crises involving both Soviet and Western interests are counted on to provide new opportunities. These will then enable the international Communist drive to proclaim its solidarity with all those countries and labor movements which side against the West. If the crisis is severe enough, new Guineas and Cubas may become hand maids to the Soviet offensive in their areas.

## NOTES

1. See Morris, Bernard S., "Recent Shifts in Communist Strategy," *Soviet Survey* (London), June–July, 1957.
2. Padmore, George, *Pan Africanism or Communism*, London 1956), pp. 154–155.
3. Laqueur, Walter Z., *Communism and Nationalism in the Middle East*, London (1956), pp. 52–53.
4. Laqueur, Walter Z., *op. cit.*, pp. 149–150.
5. For an account of the split in the Palestinian Arab labor movement at the end of World War II, see Anglo-American Committee of Inquiry, *A Survey of Palestine*, Vol. II, pp. 763–766.
6. Even the Communist dominated *Confederation Generale du Travail* (CGT) of France was interested at least until the end of 1947 in maintaining labor tranquillity in French colonial areas. In part this was linked to Soviet disinterest in the colonial issue at the time, and in part it reflected the key position of the French Communist party and the CGT in Europe, a position which the Communists did not wish to jeopardize by a militant anti-colonialist campaign which only would have aroused the French electorate against them.
7. See Trades-Union Congress, *79th Annual Report*, Southport (1947), p. 177.
8. Saillant, Louis, "Report on WFTU Activity to Assist the Trade-Unions of Asian and Australasian Countries, and on

the Tasks of the Conference," *World Trade Union Movement* (December, 1949), pp. 17–21.

9. For early efforts of John Schulter to unite the Philippine labor movement on behalf of the AFL and CIO, see *Manila Post*, January 5, 1947. On the split of the Communist party and the CLO see *Manila Chronicle*, December 30, 1948.

10. See *Report of Activity of the World Federation of Trade-Unions*, 15 October 1948–30 April 1949, presented to the IInd World Trade-Union Congress, Milan (29 June–10 July, 1949), pp. 446–453.

11. At the end of 1957, it claimed over 16,300,000 members.

12. On the role of the Peking Bureau see *World Trade-Union Movement* (December, 1949), pp. 8–22.

13. IIIe Congres Syndical Mondial, Vienne (10–21 Octobre, 1953), pp. 681–682, and *World Trade-Union Movement* (Septembre, 20, 1951), p. 12.

14. WFTU, *World Trade-Union Movement* (January 1–15, 1952), p. 2. Report of the 6th Meeting of the General Council of the WFTU (Berlin), November, 1951, p. 163.

15. Two attempts at a functional appeal on a regional basis were undertaken by the Transport and Maritime Department, one in Latin America in May, 1951 and the other in Africa in March, 1952. Another attempt was made by the Agricultural and Forestry Department in Latin America, also in May, 1951.

16. *World Trade-Union Movement* (May, 1950), p. 7.

17. Laqueur, W. *op. cit.*, p. 158.

18. The Asian unions tend to disclaim any political motivation behind their acceptance of invitations from Iron Curtain trade-unions. Yet both the Communists and the ICFTU are fully aware of the political implications of these trips, Asian disclaimers notwithstanding.

19. The movement in Indonesia bears the initials SOBRI (*Sentral Organisasi Buruh Republik Indonesia*) and is identified with the Partai Murba, which calls itself a revolutionary proletarian party.

20. *World Trade-Union Movement* (July 1–15, 1953), p. 5.

21. *The First World Conference of Agricultural and Forestry Workers and Working Peasants, Reports, Decisions, and Texts*, Vienna, Oct. 24–28, 1953.

22. *World Trade-Union News* (October, 1957), p. 24.

23. The two ICFTU affiliates were the Algerian UGTA and the Thai TNTUC. The International Trade Secretariats' affiliate was the National Railway Workers' Union of Japan, which had been one of the key anti-Communist organizations founding Sohyo. The fourth organization was the Su-

danese Railway Workers' Union, then the mainstay of the anti-Communist Sudanese General Workers' Trade-Union Federation (SGWTUF) which had just applied for ICFTU membership. Shortly after the WFTU Congress the Communists who had once controlled it recaptured the Railway Workers' Union.

24. At the time of the Leipzig Congress, Touré was UGTAN General Secretary.

25. Seydou, Diallo, 'IV!' e Congres Syndical Mondial Leipzig 4–14 Octobre, 1957," *Revue UGTAN, Mouvement Syndical Africain*, Special Unity Issue, 1959, p. 39.

26. *World Trade-Union News* (June 1–15, 1959), p. 4, and (October, 11–20), p. 2.

27. Dange, S. A., "Some Problems Facing the Trade-Union Movement in India," *World Trade-Union Movement* (September, 1956), pp. 7–12.

28. Khiari, Belhassen, "A Single Trade-Union Center in Sight," *World Trade-Union Movement* (August, 1956), and "A United Trade-Union Center," *World Trade-Union Movement* (October, 1956).

29. "Une Resolution du P. C. Algerien sur les problemes de l'union nationale dans la guerre pour l'independence," *Est & Ouest*, 1–15 Octobre, 1959.

30. Maachou, Abdelkader, "The Algerian Trade-Union Movement Prepares for the Future," *World Trade-Union Movement* (March, 1960), pp. 14–16.

31. For UGTAN background see Eliot Berg, "French West Africa" in Walter Galenson, *Labor and Economic Development;* also selected articles in *World Trade-Union Movement*, April, 1956, July, 1956, November, 1957, March, 1959, and *Abidjan Matin*, 14 September, 1956. Abdoulay Diallo, now Guinea representative in Ghana, however, has been active promoting the formation of the All-African Trade-Union Federation in his capacity as General Secretary of the Ghana-dominated All-African People's Conference.

32. Trade-Union International of Ag. and Forestry Workers, *Land & Work* (Nov.–Dec., 1958), p. 306.

33. Touré, Sékou, *Rapport D'orientation et de doctrine, Congres General de l'UGTAN, Conakry, 15–18,* Janvier, 1959, pp. 11–12, 57.

34. "Ghana Move Splits Unionists in Africa," *New York Times*, Oct. 30, 1959. For an account of the financial support given to the neutralist Nigerian Trade-Union Congress by the Ghana TUC and the WFTU, see the charge by Lawrence Borha, Gen. Secretary of the pro ICFTU TUC of Nigeria, that the Ghanaians had contributed

£2,000 and the WFTU£5,000 in an *ICFTU Information Bulletin* (No. 17), September 1, 1960.

35. Training schools exist in East Berlin, Leipzig, Prague, and Budapest, as well as in Rome and Paris. Courses vary in length from a few weeks to a year. The number of African trade-union cadres trained each year by the Communists is estimated at several hundred.

36. See Suret-Canale, Jean, "L'Afrique a l'heure de l'independance et la 'Communaute Renoveé," *Cahiers du Communisme* (No. 11), November, 1960, p. 1744. According to this article, the internal social conflict in the newly developing independent states of Black Africa will be of "secondary importance" representing "contradictions of a non-antagonistic character" which will leave little room for the colonialists "to exploit." The term "non-antagonistic contradictions" is usually applied in Communist parlance to social conflicts arising out of the process of transition to socialism *after* the seizure of power by the Communists.

37. The WFTU affiliates in Africa are for the most part small organizations, many of the former CGT unions. In several cases these unions operate clandestinely. Currently the WFTU claims as members the General Confederation of Cameroun Trade-Unions (CGKT), the Mauritius Trade-Union Federation, the outlawed Sudanese Workers Trade-Union Federation (SWTUF), the Malgasy USTM *aka* FISEMA, the Confederation of Independent Indigenous Trade-Unions of French Somaliland, and branches of the former CGAT (Equatorial Africa) in the Congo (Brazzaville) (currently outlawed), the Gabon, the Central African Republic, and the Chad. The Unions of the CGAT had refused to affiliate with the UGTAN and retained their affiliation with the WFTU at a unity congress in April, 1957.

38. Japanese Communist Party, Secretariat of the Central Committee, "The Progressive Dissolution of *Sanbetsu Kaigi* and the International Trade-Union Solidarity Movement," Notice No. 161, February 13, 1958. Cited by the Japanese Public Security Investigation Agency, in *Nihon Kyosanto no Genjo* (Current conditions of the Japanese Communist party), Chapter II, Labor Movement, March 1, 1960.

39. *World Trade-Union News*, February 1–15, 1958.

40. Subsequently relations between Sohyo and the JCP became somewhat strained, and in 1959 Sohyo reverted to its traditional alignment with the Socialist party. His estrangement went so far that prior to the 1960 elections, Sohyo Chairman Kaoru Ota and General Secretary Akira

Iway issued a statement denouncing the Japanese Communists for their "irresponsible attitude" in the demonstrations against the Japan–US Security treaty and in the Miike Colliery dispute. However, on the international level close collaboration with the Communist camp continues.

41. For a reference to the possibility of unilateral dissolution of the AITUC and other minority trade-unions in India for the sake of trade-union unity, see Clain, Roger, "25th Congress of the All-India Trade-Union Congress," *World Trade-Union Movement* (No. 2), February, 1958, p. 14.

42. For an argument in favor of the reversal of the unity trend see Dange, S. A., "Trade-Union Tasks," *New Age* (New Delhi), December, 1957, pp. 1–16.

43. *World Trade-Union News,* March 1–15, 1958, p. 5.

44. In June, 1961 the Working Committee of the All-India Railwaymen's Federation expelled the Southern Railway Employees' Union for having merged with the Communists.

45. *World Trade-Union Movement* (June, 1957), pp. 16–18, and (March, 1959), pp. 16–18. See also U.S. Department of Labor, *Directory of Labor Organizations, Africa* (February, 1958).

46. In Cuba, however, the Communists while supporting national unity, have been able to maintain their separate identity.

47. For a discussion of the change in the SOBSI constitution to take account of its changing status in support of the established order see Iskandar Tedjasukmana, *The Political Character of the Indonesian Trade Union Movement,* Cornell University, Ithaca 1958, p. 54.

48. These varying unity and united front tactics have also been resorted to throughout Latin America.

49. In 1957 the Ceylonese Communists in reaction to the new trade-union tactics had also tried to promote a united trade-union movement.

50. Despite this rejection of joining a united Ceylonese trade-union movement, the programs of both the CTUF and of the Ceylonese Communist party call for trade-union unity. See Keuneman, Pieter, "Success of the Policy of Unity," *World Marxist Review* (October, 1960), pp. 73–75. See also "United May Day is now Possible," *Forward* (Colombo), March 24, 1961.

51. See Zagoria, Donald S., "Sino-Soviet Friction in Underdeveloped Areas," *Problems of Communism,* Vol. X, No. 2 (March–April, 1961), p. 3. Mr. Zagoria cites here Halpern, A. M., *The Chinese Communist Line on Neutralism,* the RAND Corporation, July, 1960. See also Lowenthal, Rich-

ard, "The Sino-Soviet Dispute," *Commentary* (May, 1961), pp. 379–394.

52. See *Avanti*, Rome, June 19, 1960.
53. See World Federation of Trade-Unions, *11th Session of the General Council of the WFTU, Reports and Resolutions* (Peking), June, 1960.
54. See the address by Grishin, V., Chairman of the AUCC of Soviet Trade-Unions to the 22nd Executive Committee Meeting of the WFTU at East Berlin, February 2–4, 1961. *World Trade-Union Movement*, No. 3 (March 1961), pp. 8–10.
55. "Asian Trade-Unions Exchange Opinions," *World Trade-Union Movement* (June, 1954), pp. 31–32.
56. See *All-China News Agency*, May 20, 1955; and *Evening News of India*, May 18, 19, and 24, 1955.
57. Despite this prohibition the Sudanese SWTUF was admitted to membership in 1958 on the technical ground that since Sudanese law forbade WFTU affiliation, it was not a member although the SWTUF General Secretary Shafie Ahmed El Sheikh is a Vice President of the WFTU. Only when the SWFTU was outlawed in November, 1958 while ICATU-WFTU relations were already changing, was it dropped from membership.
58. In January, 1960 the Aden Trade-Union Congress was admitted as the second ICFTU affiliate to join the ICATU.
59. *The World Trade-Union Movement* (January 15, 1958), p. 15.
60. The World Peace Council is a Communist Front.
61. *The World Trade-Union Movement* (May, 1958), p. 37.
62. Formal affiliation of the nationalist-neutralist labor movements with the WFTU was considered neither attainable nor even desired at this stage, since they insisted on preserving the formal symbols of non-alignment with either East or West. Thus a constitutional amendment was adopted at the Leipzig Congress of the WFTU which provided that: "The World Trade-Union Congress shall be open to all trade-union organizations and their participation shall not imply their affiliation to the WFTU." See *Texts and Decisions of the Fourth World Trade-Union Congress* (Leipzig), 4–15 October, 1957, page 34, paragraph II of Article 4. By such moves the WFTU's ability to contribute to the process of detachment from the West was given an effective impetus. It readily increased the opportunities for closer collaboration with the neutralists and for open and behind the scene Communist support of their defiant demonstrations against the Western powers and the ICFTU.

63. The ICATU did not attend, but in 1960 its Arab Oil Workers' Federation did resume its membership in the International Federation of Petroleum Workers. See Windmuller, John P., "ICFTU After Ten Years: Problems and Prospects." *Industrial and Labor Relations Review*, Vol. 14, No. 2 (January, 1961), p. 262.

64. *International Bulletin of the Trade-Union and Working Class Press*, published by the WFTU, November 1, 1959.

65. In this respect the ICATU was fortuitously aided by its successful counter-boycott against U. S. shipping throughout the Arab world in May, 1960 in retaliation for the refusal of the International Longshoremen's Association to unload the U.A.R. ship *Cleopatra* in New York in protest against the harassment of U. S. seamen serving on ships which had violated the Arab boycott of Israeli shipping. Its newly gained prestige was reflected in the statement of Arab trade-union solidarity of June 18, 1960 at the 44th ILO Conference in Geneva by the ICATU, and the Moroccan, Algerian, Tunisian, Lybian, Iraqi, Egyptian, Syrian trade-unions. (For a full text of the statement see the WFTU's *International Bulletin of the Trade-Union and Working Class Press*, No. 8 (July 15–31, 1960), p. 2).

66. *The Arab Observer* (Cairo), January 1, 1961.

67. "Africans threaten 'war' in labor rift." *Dakar Matin* (May 31, 1961), and *The N. Y. Times* (June 6, 1961).

68. *Le Petit Matin*, Tunis, May 31, 1961.

69. In anticipation of its increasing role in African labor affairs, the WFTU has announced plans to start a new African radio broadcasting program and a new African trade-union journal, as well as the expansion of its technical and functional trade-union meetings in Africa.

70. See Zakaria, Ibrahim, "The Contribution of Trade-Unions to the Struggle Against Colonialism," *11th Session of the General Council of the WFTU Reports and Resolutions* (Peking), June, 1960, p. 92.

# 4 Unions in the Less-developed Countries: A Reappraisal of Their Economic Role

by Paul Fisher *

Until very recently, labor unions in less-developed countries were treated rather roughly in the literature on economic development. Unions were considered a hindrance to their development. Carried to the logical conclusion, this finding would justify the suppression or control of the labor movement. This paper challenges the seriousness of this allegation. Beyond this, it holds that unions perform nearly always a positive, and often an indispensable function in the economic development process.

*Consumption versus Capital Accumulation-Dilemma of Unionism*

In the absence of a generally accepted theory, the literature had to be content with the patient exploration of one or the other major obstacle in the path of economic progress. Capital formation was one of the very first problems which received attention,[1] and it is in this context that the union case was first considered. To attract and maintain members, the union has to find some ways of gratifying the worker's demand for more food, better clothing, more adequate housing, and the many new consumption goods of which he has become aware, and which he sometimes helps to produce. Right there the conflict arises; the union's demand for a higher real income for the workers endangers the economy's efforts to increase the rate of investment. Disregarding external assist-

* Agency for International Development. The views expressed in this paper are the author's, and not necessarily that of any U. S. Government agency.

ance, this requires suppressing, or at least preventing an increase in, the consumption level of the population.

From this premise the argument proceeds: Since domestic savings are in some cases, as in the U.S.S.R., the only, and in all cases the major source of investment, the propensities of the unions to increase consumption instead of savings must be curbed. Furthermore, "strike actions tend to decrease production and may make development investment less attractive to foreign investors, but strikes may be necessary to achieve economic objectives of the labor organizations, to build disciplined labor organizations, and to keep interests of the membership." [2] Since accelerated economic growth can neither tolerate real wage increases nor, one of the means of achieving this goal, the strike, the union is left with very little choice. It can either join the opposition, which in the free and uncommitted world means as a rule the Communist apparatus, turn into an instrument of the State or of the employers; or through appeal to the patriotic, long run interests of the members, accept a policy of wage restraint. The latter course which usually takes the form of a "national purpose union" which acts as "partner of the state in carrying out mutually-agreed-upon goals," [3] is even in the case of a very well-disciplined membership, as for instance in western Germany or the U. K., difficult to maintain over long periods of time. It is a hopeless undertaking in the less-developed countries in the face of rival Communist labor organizations which, undeterred by patriotic considerations, attract workers discontented by extravagant promises, and vigorous aggressive action.

Communist competition also makes attempts to deny unions the right to strike dangerous, if not hopeless. Professors Dunlop, Galenson, and Sturmthal are unanimous in objecting to Asoka Mehta's prescription for transforming the Indian labor unions into a harmless, or at least economically not very expensive, productionist mechanism. [4]

The government is confronted by an equally hard choice. Should unions be suppressed, as in Saudi Arabia or Iran? Should they be transformed into agencies of government, as in the Soviet Union, in Argentina under Peron, or in Ghana?

Or should their freedom of action be seriously restricted as, up to recently, in Turkey? Can the state rely upon union wage restraint? Is the long run economic and political insight of an interlocking government-party and union leadership strong enough to bring about a shift in the time preference [5] of the membership as in Tunisia or Israel? These problems also affect those Western governments and trade-unions which are eager to assist the less-developed countries to achieve greater viability.

None of these choices seem to offer a promise of lasting effect. Unions grow irresistibly, as a result of the industrialization process, re-enforced by the demonstrated effect of copying all institutions of the highly-developed industrial societies, and the desire for prestige which ILO (UN) membership confers. Unions are, as Galenson stated, "integral parts of the productive mechanism"; they perform an indispensable, positive function in the development process.

On the other hand, unions "derive their power from the defense of the (short-run economic) interests of their members . . . they cannot exist for long periods of time, as social welfare agencies, and even less as instruments of wage restraint." [6] Union involvement in the administration of such consumptionist governmental or managerial functions as social security, housing, medical facilities, vacation, and recreation is no substitute for gaining wage advantages. The processing of workers' grievances is important but no match for the glamorous wage . . . and other . . . promises of rival Communist leaders.

The dilemma is quite clear, the solution less so. As a matter of policy, John Dunlop once suggested [7] "not to have any trade-union, at least for a time, or to have a controlled union." Karl de Schweinitz [8] left us with a choice between permitting some measure of effective unionism and delaying economic growth, or suppressing democracy altogether for the sake of maximum development, and between permissive or totalitarian methods of dealing with labor unions. Walter Galenson, in his introduction to "Labor and Economic Development" speaks of a "balance" which "must be struck which both satisfies the requirements of the economic planner and the minimum demands of the industrial worker." [9] Sturmthal suggested the nature of such a compromise: Union leaders should delay the struggle for a wage increase, accept postponement of the effective date to give the economy time "for the initial investment push. . . ." Where this is not feasible, he identifies the delay in capital formation as "the price to be paid to avert a further deterioration of the prospect for economic growth" caused by political or social upheavals.[10]

He was also the first to raise the question whether the importance of the problem had not been exaggerated, whether the positive (productionist) role of the union had been fully taken into account,[11] and whether union pressure on wages was not also an instrument of economic development. These questions merit further investigation.

*How Serious is the Problem?*

The literature on this subject has attached two important qualifications to this question, which are sometimes overlooked.

A. The problem arises only in the early stages of industrialization [12] in the "transitional society" and the beginnings of the "take-off" period in the Rostowian [13] scheme when the necessity for domestic savings permits "little of the investment" to become "available for consumption if growth is to become cumulative and self-perpetuating," when there is "not yet a bargaining-margin of national income available." [14] In other words, the problem arises in this form only in those economies which stand in the beginning of their development, economies which, in many cases because of the enormous spurt in population [15] which accompanies this stage, have not yet reached a desirable level of growth. Translated in the usual quantitative expression of this problem, it pertains to countries where domestic capital-formation has not yet escaped the 5 per cent of the net GNP level and is still very far from reaching the 12, 18, or 20 per cent plus levels which are the harbinger of self-sustaining growth.[16] Where, hence, a satisfactory rate of growth is about to be achieved, as for instance in the foreseeable future in India and Brazil, the need for domestic savings will no longer require a reduction and may even permit a cautious increase of consumption.

B. A second point made—and somewhat obliterated—recognizes the possibility that (1) higher wages may increase productivity, and (2) that higher wages accompanying increases in productivity [17] are—although they do not represent the optimal development path [18]—compatible with an increase in the marginal rate of saving. As J. T. Dunlop [19] stated, however, "this is likely to be a narrow and difficult range of wage policy to find."

*Factors Which Minimize Union Pressures on Capital Accumulation*

Insufficient attention has been given to a number of other considerations which minimize the negative effect which union efforts to secure wage increases may exert on the capital-formation process:

A. With some notable exceptions unions in the less-developed countries are too weak to exert economic pressure on the employers. In many cases, political factionalism fragments the labor movement as a whole; the individual union groups operate quite ineffectually on the enterprise level; and weak and part-time leadership is unable to secure lasting economic benefits through negotiation with the employer who, in addition often turns out to be the government. For this and other reasons, unions seek relief through legislation and political influence upon the administration of labor issues. Further research is needed to estimate the effects of this device on the workers' income. The suspicion is however warranted that most of this legislation refers to relatively inexpensive fringe benefits, some of them representing only deferred and contingent claims, which if funded tend to depress the present consumption and provide a source of forced savings. Many other legislative measures are concerned with improved working conditions (safety, hours, etc.) and job-security issues, which do not affect significantly capital-formation; they rather tend to improve workers' productivity.

The few cases of minimum wage legislation in force are generally not advancing the wage level, but only codify existing wage rates for the benefit of the least-favored groups of workers. In all cases, it must be borne in mind that most of the labor laws remain unenforced. They represent more of an ideal goal, a social aim for the economy, than an actual practice.

B. In view of the relatively small proportion of the labor force in the less-developed countries which is affected by successful union efforts to raise the wage level, it would seem rash to credit labor unions necessarily with the ability to increase substantially the general consumption level. As recently reported,[20] only 5 per cent of the total population of tropical Africa are wage earners, only 10 per cent of them are union members. Wage gains eventually reached by one-half per cent of the population do not easily affect the total consumption level. There is no automatic transmission of the income gain made by the unionized government employee or clerical worker (who lives in a world apart, in a non-competing group), to the rest of the economy. Dual economies persist in less-developed countries. In many cases, in the midst of oversupply of unskilled labor, labor markets achieve by various devices aiming at the limiting of access, a degree of isolation which reserves wage gains for the privileged permanent members.[21]

C. Most union wage drives are devoted to restoring the worker's wage eroded by inflation. Less-developed countries can almost be divided in two groups: those financing economic development by inflation, and those more or less temporarily stabilizing the value of their currency through an austerity program, which all too often curbs inflation and development as well, creates unemployment and thereby prevents real wage gains. There are, of course, some important exceptions to this generalization, e.g., Israel. We should also disregard in this connection those countries where government control of labor unions through a variety of means prevents upward wage movement (Pakistan, Ghana, India, etc.). Most of Latin America offers, in contradistinction, examples of money wages catching up—as a rule by government action—and only after the inevitable time lag, with the inflated price level.

D. In these cases labor unions act in their clearly understood role as a defense mechanism. Protest against lowering the worker's income through inflation meets a clear need, and attracts membership. Of equal attraction, without increasing the general wage level, are union efforts to prevent a reduction of labor's share in the national income to the benefit of other, politically and economically more powerful sectors of the economy. Furthermore, as Albert O. Hirschman demonstrated,[22] economic development does not proceed at an even pace in all sectors, unbalanced growth being the rule. Unions often attempt, although not always successfully, to prevent the continued existence of developmental islands by seeking to spread wage gains to other industries. These, under this stimulation, may seek in turn to modernize their equipment and process. Such protective union action meets a basic desire for wage equalization which can be gratified with little effect upon the general consumption level.

Since the universal worker's desire for a secure job is particularly pronounced in the early stages of economic development, union efforts to prevent the shifting of the development risk from management to the workers by various —mostly legislative—job-security measures also respond to a basic membership need. Quite apart from the many sociological reasons which make job-security a central point of the worker's interest, the mere economic fact of a practically unlimited labor supply ready to compete for his job provides sufficient explanation for his support of a union which protects his livelihood.

*Union Actions May Encourage Membership Savings*

Union actions which reduce immediate consumption in return for deferred claims, and others which lead to the accumulation of social security funds, which many countries —in violation of its trust function—invest in the expansion of the economy have already been noted. There is still another significant fact to consider: By engaging in productive undertakings, unions invest membership savings in the development of the economy. In other words, they participate directly in capital formation. There is foremost the well-documented case of the industrial empire of the Histadruth.[23] In this category fall also the many producer, consumer, credit, and housing cooperatives which unions operate in all parts of the world.[24] Not all of them have met with the success of the Tunisian cooperatives; not all of them are voluntary, as for instance in the case of Egypt, where in return for a compulsory check-off, one-third of the union income must be invested in welfare measures including cooperative union housing; and the total amounts involved are not too significant. On the other hand the Israeli pattern seems to spread to some parts of Africa.

## The Positive Union Contribution to Economic Development

The foregoing discussion centered upon one major problem: Is the effect of union wage policy on capital-formation so deleterious, that unions must be prohibited, repressed, or subverted? For the reasons just reviewed, this problem does not appear quite so serious or unmanageable as to sustain these alternatives.

This problem loomed so large only because it arose in a period when lack of capital (hence the need for an accelerated rate of domestic savings and curbs on present or increased consumption) was considered the main strategic obstacle to economic development. Our understanding has, however, since progressed. More than a decade of observation and experience, particularly in foreign aid, revealed that capital is not the only strategic factor affecting the rate of economic progress. The absorptive capacity of the less-developed countries for all kinds of aid,[25] and the rate of economic development itself has been found dependent upon men, their skills and motivation, and their institutions. Furthermore, it has now become far clearer than before that economic development cannot proceed without a favorable economic, social and political climate.

It is in this—environmental—area that the major economic significance of the union lies.

The Unions' positive role in regularizing and aiding recruitment, commitment, discipline, and training of the labor force has been fully accepted.[26] Although these are primarily managerial responsibilities, the union's role is of strategic importance. Let us take discipline: "Once the bargain is made, there is an expressed or implied obligation to deliver labor at the agreed rate and to participate in the maintenance of labor discipline. In this unions may be more effective than employers, since they appeal largely to individual self-discipline in the interest of maintaining union strength.[27] Equally effective is the appeal to the national cause, where the union and the state are still tied in the memory of the united struggle for independence.

Less attention has been awarded to the role of the union as a source of the scarcest type of manpower, i.e., administrators, managers, supervisors, etc., both on the economic and political level. Organized labor fulfills this function in the not infrequent case where capable leaders are barred for a variety of causes from the regular avenues of access to management, but make their way in unions affiliated with a political party which gains domination. This union role is of particular importance in the pre-independence labor movements. Regardless of whether they were created, tolerated or repressed by the previous colonial administrations (Ghana, Kenya, India, etc.), unions represented in many cases one of the principal, and sometimes the only environment in which local leadership qualities could be developed and tested. After independence the graduates of these labor movements constitute a very significant part of the very limited supply of organizational, executive and administrative experience from which national economic and political leaders can be recruited. When, in addition, expatriate (colonial) administrators and managers are abruptly removed (Indonesia, Tunisia, etc.), union leaders, some of them with experience in union-financed enterprises, fill the gap. The Jagans, Tettegahs, Mboyas, Sekou Tourés, and Bourgibas find their counterpart in the new government-sponsored industries. Nor is this necessarily only a unique historical occurrence, a case of " political management." [28] Western experience would point to the possibility of a continuous flow of managerial talent from unions to management, facilitated by the professionalization of managerial and administrative personnel in both camps. To adapt the terminology of Professor Theodore Schultz, labor unions offer one additional location for the placing of the needed investment in human capital.[29]

*Union Contributions to Economic Change and Stability*

Finally, let us refer to two, at first seemingly contradictory, aspects of the union role in the less-developed universe, i.e., labor's contribution to economic change, and to economic stability.

*Economic Change*

One of the characteristics of the societal structure of the less-developed countries lies in the absence of a sizeable and politically independently powerful middle class. In general, the few wealthy families confront without a buffer the poor masses of urban and rural breadwinners. Since the agricultural workers are as a rule not independently organized, the labor unions, their numerical and economic weakness notwithstanding, fill a political vacuum. By default they assume a political importance which is in no way commensurate with their organizational strength. Where the "rich" select, as usual, a conservative label, labor symbolizes economic progress, reform and occasionally revolution. In this role labor assumes an unique importance. Its effectiveness depends upon, as a rule, the attitude of the only other powerful mass organization, the army with its civilian adjuncts, gendarmerie and police. In certain countries, the student attitude also plays a role, although this vocal group lacks permanency, hence political independent significance.

Labor's surprisingly persistent, albeit spurious, political power position is as a rule exercised in close relation with a political party standing for progress, reform (or revolt). To be chosen for the part, the party must be able to offer substantial hope for the realization of the worker's economic, social, and political aspirations. In addition, it must offer promise for the achievement of some of the popular political, i.e., national and economic, i.e., consumer interests, which find their mass support [30] in the union and their leaders.

It is particularly in the early stages of economic development, when the resistance of a traditional society has to be overcome, when the necessary institutional changes, as for instance an archaic land tenure system, an inequitable tax system, a reform of the educational system, etc., spell success or failure of all internal and externally assisted economic measures, that the union's "mass" support of the reform forces is indispensable. Where the body politic is in the hands of the vested interests of a minority, the mass (mob) demonstration, an extra-legal pressure on society, becomes the only available means to bring about a peaceful change.

For this role, the union is eminently equipped. Its basic attitude is directed to a change for the better, towards progress. At that stage it has no vested interest to protect. It can only gain by a change of the ground rules.

*Economic Stability*

The union's contribution to the establishment and maintenance of industrial peace in the workshop has been accepted by many writers. "There is a tendency for industrial conflict at the early stages of industrialization to consist of short-lived incidents and to involve fights, riots, demonstrations, directed action, violence, and mob action." [31] Such spontaneous expressions of discontent are the more disruptive and costly, as they occur without warning. By establishing a grievance procedure, the union gives direction to the protest, "channels it into constructive lines and away from futile anomie." [32] The handling of local grievances can indeed be called a "productionist activity." [33] It replaces chaos by order, and is essential to rational production.

However, the union's major contribution to economic stability is made on the national level. Without organization the workers' deep-felt social and political frustrations would express themselves in a series of attempts to seek a radical change, perhaps to overthrow a society, which in many less-developed countries denies them the basic rights of men, respect, status, equality, opportunity, and freedom. Social and political equality are only won in fight. This was the case in all industrial development processes, here and in Europe. Labor's social and political rights are not inherent to the highly stratified societies of Asia, to Latin culture or African tribalism. Social justice, an ill-definable term, more easily expressed as a catalogue of bitter complaints against real and imagined class discrimination, needs a spokesman. Unions fill this role. Unless dominated by revolutionary political parties, they press for remedial action. Through membership in the unions the worker gains a sense of participation in the basic economic decisions of the society which no other groups, unless they are similarly solely devoted to worker interests, can provide. When satisfied with the vicarious participation through the union, the worker will be ready to accept the social and political fundamentals of the society. Union experience fosters substitution of reform for revolt. Union membership with its implied offer of democratic expression contributes to that political and social stability which is one of the basic ingredients of the climate in which peaceful economic development can proceed.

## Conclusion

Unless dominated by forces opposing economic progress, the union makes a necessary, positive and often indispensable contribution to the economic, social and political development of the new industrial societies. It renders this unique service at little social cost. On economic grounds, support rather than control or suppression would appear to be the wiser policy.

## NOTES

1. Hald, Marjorie, *A Selected Bibliography on Economic Development and Foreign Aid*, Rand Corp., 1958. See in particular Lewis, W. A., *The Theory of Economic Growth*, 1955; Kindleberger, Charles P., *Economic Development* (1958), p. 35.

2. Dunlop, J. T., *Industrial Relations Systems*, New York, 1958, p. 338.
3. Millen, Bruce, "Speech to Industrial Relations Seminar," University of Wisconsin (February 15, 1961), mimeograph, p. 4.
4. Mehta, Asoka, "The Role of the Trade-Union in Underdeveloped Countries," *Problems of Economic Growth*, Conference under the Auspices of the Congress for Cultural Freedom, Tokyo, April 1–6, 1957, and his "The Mediating Role of the Trade-Union in Underdeveloped Countries," *Economic Development and Cultural Change* (Vol. VI, No. 1), October, 1957.
5. Dunlop, J. T., in "American Labor's Role in Less-Developed Countries," A *Report on a Conference Held at Cornell University* (October 12–17, 1958), p. 19.
6. Sturmthal, Adolf, "Unions and Economic Development," Economic Development and Cultural Change," Vol. VIII, No. 2 (January, 1960), p. 202.
7. See footnote 4, page 18.
8. Karl de Schweinitz, "Industrialization, Labor Controls and Democracy," *Economic Development and Cultural Change*, Vol. VII, No. 4, July, 1959.
9. Galenson, Walter, *Labor and Economic Development*, New York: p. 14.
10. See footnote 5, p. 204.
11. See also Galenson, *op. cit.*, p. 18: Labor unions "will inevitably impose some costs upon the community and reduce the practicable rate of investment. However, if properly handled, they perform the vital function of channeling worker protest into socially useful forms, and help prevent the subversion of democracy. The role of the statesman is to minimize the cost and maximize the positive attributes of Nascent Unionism."
12. Kerr, Clark, Dunlop, John, Harbison, Fred, and Myers, Charles, *Industrialism and Industrial Man* (Harvard), 1960, p. 226.
13. Rostow, W. W., in *The Economist* (August 15, 1959), p. 1.
14. Sturmthal, *ibid.*, pp. 199–201.
15. Leibenstein, Harvey, *Economic Backwardness and Economic Growth* (1957), pp. 170–175.
16. Kuznets, S., "International Differences in Capital Formation and Financing," *Capital Formation and Economic Growth* (Princeton), 1955, pp. 26, 27.
    Rostow, W. W., "The Take-off Into Self-Sustained Growth," *Economic Journal* (March, 1956), p. 36.
17. Sturmthal, p. 205, highlights the role of the union as a stimulus for greater productivity vis-a-vis monopolistic en-

terprise, which—as the result of the size of the market, tariff protection, the predominance of government as entrepreneur—are found frequently in the industrializing nations. Here trade unions substitute for a competitive market.

18. Kindleberger, *op. cit.*, p. 227.
19. Dunlop, p. 338.
20. Millen, Bruce H., speech delivered to Industrial Relations Seminar, University of Wisconsin, February 15, 1961 (mimeograph).
21. James, Ralph C, "Labor Mobility, Unemployment and Economic Change," J. P. E., December, 1959.
22. Hirschman, Albert O., *The Strategy of Economic Development* (New Haven), 1958. See also Streeter, P., "Unbalanced Growth," *Oxford Economic Papers*, June, 1959.
23. Plunkett, Margaret L., "The Histadruth: The General Federation of Jewish Labor in Israel," *ILRR*, January, 1958.
24. Ghosh, Subratesh, *Trade-Unionism in Undeveloped Countries* (Calcutta), 1960, p. 392, advocates in addition to "small savings schemes" also capital formation through "labor squads for road-building and other similar projects."
25. Aid includes, besides capital aid, also advice (technical assistance), etc. Absorptive capacity as used here is a wider concept than the ability of a country to repay and service hard currency loans.
26. Kindleberger, *op. cit.*, p. 227.
27. Galenson, *op. cit.*, p. 13.
28. Kerr, Dunlop, Harbison, and Myers, op. cit., ch. 6, p. 142.
29. Schultz, Theodore W., Presidential Address, "Investment in Human Capital," *American Economic Review* (1961), pp. 15–16.
30. This identification takes also place in the industrialized countries. "The collection of measures governing general tax and expenditures policy that is considered 'liberal'— in the twentieth century—is strongly and effectively backed by labor union lobbyists . . . unions provide an effective means of mobilizing the political power of low income groups," Melvin Reder, "Job Scarcity and the Nature of Union Power," *ILRR* (April, 1960), p. 361–62.
31. Kerr, Dunlop, Harbison and Myers, *ibid.*, p. 206.
32. Kindleberger, *op. cit.*, p. 227.
33. Galenson, *op. cit.*, p. 13.

# PART II

# The Relationship of the Norwegian Labor Party to the Trade-Unions

5

by Bruce Millen

*Norwegian Labor in Power since 1935*

The Norwegian Labor party has been in power twenty-five years without interruption, first as the dominant party in a coalition government and since World War II as the majority government. In 1957, at a time when political movements of long tenure in other parts of the world were suffering defeats, the Labor party increased its total vote by 1.6 per cent to 48.33 per cent of the total vote.[1] The period of Labor party control has seen the development of political stability, social order, economic progress and the flowering of the welfare state. In large measure the Labor party can claim credit for these developments.

I modify the credit due the Labor party for many of the accomplishments not because of any desire to tarnish its proud shield, but only to place its accomplishments in proper perspective. The Labor party did not invent welfareism as a social concept; there were strong egalitarian strains in the society that existed outside of the Labor party in the early 1900's. One fruit of this was the passage of national health insurance legislation in 1911 when the Labor party had only 11 seats in the *Storting* (Parliament). The concession laws, passed at the turn of the century, by which state control over natural resources was assured, could easily be interpreted as the first step toward socialism. These facts are mentioned in passing to suggest that the concept of the welfare state and state control of resource allocation represent a continuum to which the Labor party gave shape and substance. The favorable international economic developments of the postwar period must also be mentioned as an important factor in the

119

success in attaining the social and political goals of the Labor government.

The Labor party has captured and strengthened its hold on the electorate since 1935 through the unique accomplishment of bridging the gap between small farmers, fishermen, and industrial workers. The first victories of the Labor party in the early 1900's were scored in the small fishing villages high above the Arctic Circle, and this capacity to win support from both major groups continues into the present. In the municipal elections of 1955, the Labor party won 42 per cent of the votes cast in the rural districts as opposed to 44 per cent in the urban areas. The number of urban voters is roughly over 60 per cent of the voters classified as rural so that one can visualize the necessity of developing programs that have an appeal to the rural voter.

*Trade-Union Movement, Center of Labor Power*

Accommodation by the Labor party to the farm-labor link does not alter the important fact that the Norwegian trade-union movement plays the dominant role in the complex of organizations and individuals which make up a broad gauged political movement which appeals to intellectuals, professional men, small businessmen, and young people, in addition to the masses of farmers, fishermen, and workers. The union movement is comprised of 45 national unions affiliated to the *Landsorganisasjonen i Norge,* or, as it is commonly known, the LO. There were 542,081 union members belonging to LO affiliates as of August 31, 1958. The largest affiliate is the Norwegian Union of Iron and Metal Workers with 63,000 members; the smallest is the Norwegian Watchmakers' Union with 108 members. There are approximately 5,000 local unions chartered by national unions. With the exception of 1952 and 1958, membership has increased every year since the Second World War. The figures on union membership represent slightly more than one-third of the total labor force, and a fraction over 50 per cent of the potentially organizable work force.

Like American unions, LO affiliates have difficulty in organizing white collar workers, but some success has been registered. Municipal employees, for example, are at least 80 per cent organized. Some 65,000 of the State's 115,000 employees are members of LO unions, while another 20,000 belong to independent unions.[2] The relatively high percentage of organization in the ranks of state employees is in part due to the 100 per cent union membership of the 20,000 railway workers on the state-owned system.

The weakest spot in the organization of white-collar workers is among clerical employees in industry and commerce. The shift in labor force composition wherein white-collar workers are increasing relative to blue-collar workers is taking place rapidly in Norway, though not as fast as in the United States. The white-collar man is taking on added political significance and his vote must be captured in large numbers if the labor movement is to dominate the political scene in the future.

*Industrial Unionism in Norway*

The bulk of Norwegian union members (75–80 per cent) belong to a dozen industrial unions which are the pattern-setters, and from which one gains an image of the union movement. The remainder are members of small craft unions which have successfully resisted a basic policy decision taken in 1923 to shift from a craft structure to an industrial-type structure. The decision in favor of industrial unionism was passed by the LO Convention of that year after a dozen years of agitation and factional activity stemming from the growing strength of radicalism and syndicalism in the ranks of both the Labor party and the trade-unions.

The LO and its affiliates form the single most powerful organization in Norway. Trade-union power reaches out to make its influence felt in the economic, political and social fields in an immediate and direct fashion, as contrasted to the often indirect impact of policies followed by unions in the United States. The locus of power in Norway lies in the LO which leads a tightly-knit movement. If the trade-unions were to exert their full strength in accordance with the traditional goals of "economic unionism," irreparable harm would be done to the economy as well as to political and social institutions. This monolithic power is tempered through association with a political movement composed of heterogeneous elements whose goals are broader and differentiated.

Norwegian trade-unions rose to their present positions of power in much the same manner as have those in the United States. They contested with employers at the plant gates and on the picket lines. The present-day position of strength is based in large measure on contracts which provide security and justice to the individual union member. The extent of invasion of so-called management prerogatives is about on a par with the situation in the United States, although outside of the construction and printing trades the "work rule" mentality is not as pronounced.

Norwegian unions have in addition "interfered" with management rights in the aggregate through their strong political influence. Furthermore, the LO pays lip-service to the idea of co-determination, although individual officials are frank to admit they are concerned about disturbing the "two sides of the table" collective bargaining procedures now in use. The Norwegian Employers' Association (*Norsk Arbeidsgiverforening*, NAF) and the LO amended the basic contract in 1957 to require consultation between the shop stewards and the plant board of directors at least once each year, although management still retains the right of final decision under the amended contract. Presumably for internal union political reasons, this amendment was referred to by the press and by the unions as dealing with co-determination.[3]

The unions, by virtue of their strong economic and political position, are represented at every level and in every phase of Norwegian life. One is particularly impressed with this fact when visiting the small towns throughout the country. In Oslo, union representation is realized through participation of national union leaders and professional staff members. In the field one comes upon the unpaid local union officers sitting as members of the town council, the school board, the community-owned cinema, the hospital board, etc. Functions such as these are an integral part of union activity with the result that every aspect of social and community life bears the mark of trade-union influence. Quite understandably the status position of union leadership is high as compared to that enjoyed by United States union leaders. It is equally understandable that the Norwegian should conceive of his role as being essentially different from that of his American brother. The Norwegian is fully conscious and proud that he, in coordination with others in the labor movement, is molding society in a fashion to his own liking.

The self-confidence and security engendered by the possession of power in the society on the part of the trade-unions has given rise to an interpretation of the trade-union function radically different from that to which we as Americans are accustomed. The highly centralized structure, under which the LO exerts a tremendous influence on the pattern of collective bargaining makes it possible for the union movement to participate in framing and implementing national economic policy. This demands that the LO exercise control over its affiliates so that these national goals, which include a generally upward standard of living and full employment, are realized.

Given this outlook it is not surprising that the union leaders in exile at the end of the war voluntarily worked out with employers provisions regarding wages, working conditions and legislation to be operative on the return of the government to Norway. Included in the package was a provision, enacted into law in 1946, for compulsory arbitration. To this day the establishment of compulsory wage boards is common, and decisions handed down by such boards have been respected. Thus, a feature of Norwegian legislation which had been tried by non-labor governments in 1915 and twice during the twenties, each time to be broken by the refusal of the unions and the workers to obey the law, has won acceptance by a union movement which shares power with other components within the Labor party. Strikes do occur, one million man days were lost in 1956, but the ground rules are different from those with which we are familiar. More will be said on this subject at a later point in this chapter.

*Party-Union Relationships*

The brief descriptive material about the Labor party and the trade-unions leads into an assessment of the relationship between the two organizations. In this connection, it is important to recognize that there is no formal link between the two. The trade-unions were in large measure spawned by the Labor party and the formation of the LO in 1899–1912 years after the Labor party was formed—was a product of encouragement by the political organization. Nevertheless, due to the fact that many workers and union leaders of the period were connected with the Liberal party, no formal link with the Labor party was feasible. The issue of trade-union independence was debated again in the 1925 LO Congress and a third time in 1949. At this time, as a reaction to the German attempt to capture the union movement during the occupation, the constitution was amended to include a statement that one of the aims of the LO is, "to work for the maintenance and freedom of the trade-union movement."

The organizational independence of the two organizations does not prevent the closest working relationship to exist, one in which the trade-unions accept leadership by the Labor party of the entire labor movement. Most Norwegian union leaders conceive it to be the function of the unions to fit their specific goals within the broad framework of a policy designed to advance the interests of the labor movement, and in the main, this viewpoint is supported by the union membership. A reservation must be made to the effect, however, that the Labor party is not free to follow a course of action destructive of the worker's position in society or his living standards.

The type of relationship which does exist between the political party and the trade-unions is summed up in a speech made by Trygve Bratteli, Vice Chairman of the Labor party, to the 1957 LO Convention. Speaking on behalf of the Labor party, as well as guests from other organizations within the labor movement, he stated:

The organizations which are represented here are a good expression of the breadth of the Norwegian labor movement, and the good, open cooperation which exists between these organizations contributes to create the milieu and the climate which gives us the possibilities of a progressive policy. There is a steady attempt to sow suspicion and to construct a situation of opposition between these two organizations [the LO and the Labor party]. Certain circles are in line for something favorable to them, if they succeed in this [maneuver]. I am, however, pleased that the trade-unions have had a horizon which has been wider than that which is concerned with . . . wage negotiations. It is clear this is the main task, but it is not enough. The significance of a strong, united and free trade-union cannot be overestimated. It is fundamental to a democratic society. We hear often that the LO is directed from the government. But just as often it is said that it is this organization [the LO] which in reality decides all that is done by the Party and by the government. The actual situation is that these two organizations through tradition, and mature consideration, have divided the labor tasks between themselves. This our opposition clearly cannot understand.[4]

*Party and Unions, Organizational Independence and Functional Unity*

An attempt will now be made to describe how the Labor party and the LO, organizationally independent, but functionally united, work together in the attainment of their objectives. One of the main points of contact between the Labor party and the LO is the committee on cooperation (*samarbeidskomiteen*) composed of the chief officers of both groups. This committee came into being in 1927 after the merger between the Labor party and the Social Democratic party. The committee meets almost every month to discuss problems and programs.

The trade-unions are heavily represented on the Central Committee of the Labor party with five seats out of a total of fifteen. The president of the LO, Konrad Nordahl, is supported on the Central Committee by the president of the important Seamen's Union, the president of the Forestry Workers Union, the president of the powerful Union of Building Workers and a representative of the textile union.

In 1957 the LO president adopted a new tactic in the postwar period, one that he had eschewed previously. He stood as a candidate for the *Storting* and at the same time demanded that local Labor party units include trade-unionists on the election lists. The reason for the move can only be surmised, but it is logical to assume the decision was made in order to counter what the trade-unions considered to be the excessive power of the farm interests within the Labor party *Storting* delegation. The success of this tactic has added to the ability of the trade-unions to exert influence at strategic points in the political structure.

The joint administration of the apparatus of the labor movement is equally important to the factor of strong union representation at the policy-making level. This cooperation is carried on exclusively through the means of joint representation on the executive bodies of the operating units. The Workers' Educational Association (*Arbeidernes Opplysningsforbund*) is financed and operated as a function of the entire labor movement, but the dominant elements are the LO and the Labor party. The executive board is composed of five top officials from the Party and five from the union movement. The caliber of the representation gives insight into the important role played by the WEA.[5]

The Norwegian Labor Press Association (*Norsk Arbeiderpresse A/S*) is a second instrument of key importance in supporting the labor movement. The Labor party and the LO each hold an equal share of the stock in this holding company which gives support to the labor press chain of 44 newspapers, 28 of which are dailies. The executive board is again composed of top officials of the Labor party and the unions. The 44 newspapers are owned jointly by the local party units and the local trade-union organizations.[6]

So it goes. Each operation carried on becomes a function of both the Labor party and the unions—at the national, district, and local level. The task of running the First of May celebrations provides one last example. The LO and the Party issue a joint manifesto which sets the theme to be emphasized. Normally, both trade-union and political (including foreign policy) questions are highlighted in the message. Speakers drawn from the ranks of the trade-unions and the Party are assigned to hundreds of areas around the country. In each locality a joint committee of the political and union organizations sponsor and administer the parade and demonstration. Political slogans and trade-union demand find expression side by side in the demonstration which symbolizes the unity of the working class in the broadest sense of the word.

## Union Funds Finance Entire Labor Movement

Trade-unions pay the major share of the costs involved in operating the manifold activities of the labor movement. The total list of organizations to which the LO and the individual national unions give support, either through membership in, or through direct subsidy, would in itself fill a printed page. Trade-union funds lubricate the machinery of the entire labor movement.

There is no law in Norway which prohibits the use of union funds derived from membership dues in political campaigns. The unions, therefore, constitute one of the most important sources of campaign money to the Labor party. The LO and the national unions make direct grants to the Party, while many local unions vote funds to be used at the district level. Announcement of these donations frequently appears in the press as routine news, although care is exercised not to reveal the aggregate amount by maintaining secrecy on the amount contributed by the Federation.

The organizational support given to the Labor party by the unions during election campaigns represents a contribution of greater significance than any financial help. The trade-unions become a gigantic political machine dedicated to victory at the polls.

The 1957 campaign started in May with the passage of a resolution asking all workers to support the Labor party in the October elections, and for all organizations affiliated with the LO to work actively for this objective. Two weeks later the Labor party Convention endorsed the primary aims of union policy, namely, a shorter work week and pensions for industrial workers. The stage was then set for an all-out campaign conducted from union headquarters. Every union meeting until the election bore a political stamp, the monthly union journals devoted fifty to sixty per cent of their space to political coverage. Union officials traveled the length of the country drumming up support for Labor party candidates. In Oslo, a special labor committee, not satisfied with attendance at local union meetings, moved the campaign to the plant gates. Special literature written by the trade-unions, in place of that printed by the Labor party, was circulated, and among other devices, every shop steward in Oslo received a personal letter from President Nordahl urging him to turn out the vote.

### Union Influence on Party Policy

Stress has been placed up to this point in illustrating two things, one the contribution made by the trade-unions to the support of the political organization, and two the key position occupied by the unions in the policy-making and administrative operation of the structure. This points up the fact that the unions operate within the Labor party from a position of strength. Policies advocated by the Labor Government which drove the union leaders to sulking in their tents would spell disaster to continued control over the levers of power by the labor forces.

The relationship between unions and Party remains strong because of the willingness of both organizations to compromise during the process of the informal bargaining, which takes place with each passing day on matters big and small, in order to harmonize differences within the structure. Tempers are lost; power plays are made. The continuous adaptation to internal pressures within the labor movement as a whole goes on as it must in any successful coalition of forces. The cement which binds is compounded out of ideology and practicality. No one person or group "takes a walk" because the term "labor movement" is one of depth which compels a high degree of sacrifice of individual interests to the whole.

It is necessary to introduce a few additional comments about the Norwegian Labor party in order to give a broader frame of reference to the subject. The Labor party is power-oriented. It has held national political power for 25 years and will not relinquish it in the pursuit of abstract or doctrinaire goals.

Most of its leaders to this day have been men who have worked with their hands and who have belonged to trade-unions. The list of Party chairmen from the period 1887 to 1958 reveals that only three have been professional men; the remaining thirteen began their careers as workingmen. At least five (in addition to the five union representatives mentioned earlier) of the members of the Central Committee, including the chairman of the Party, who is also the prime minister, were trade-unionists. The small size of the society and the relatively simple social structure insures that the responsible members of the Labor party and the government do not drift away from intimate association with the trade-unions and the workers.[7]

The intellectual, too, has played an important part within the Labor party, and to him much credit is due for many of the far-reaching advances that mark Norwegian social policy. Outstanding intellectuals serve in important capacities within the trade-unions and many occupy top positions in the government bureaucracy; from these positions they wield considerable influence. More important still are those intellectuals who have risen to the pinnacle of the structure as policy makers. Men such as Foreign Minister Lange, who is a member of the Party Central Committee, former Minister of Finance Brofoss, and the Minister of Commerce, Skaug, to name only a few, have created policies which have won acceptance by the entire labor movement. But men of this stripe have been practical men with a sense of political reality. Lange, for example, has published standard works in the labor field, and in 1939 was the director of the trade-union training center near Oslo. He is considered an outstanding interpreter of domestic political and trade-union currents. To project plans at the risk of losing votes has no more appeal for the intellectual than to other elements in the Labor party leadership. In addition, his plans must face the test of practicability and be subject to the internal bargaining process in order to win acceptance. The internal cohesiveness of the labor movement is a priority of the highest order.

The maintenance of unity within the labor movement is not self-generating, neither as it pertains to union leadership nor to union membership even though there are many, many factors working in favor of cohesion. There are approximately 100,000 union members of a total of 540,000 who are members of the Labor party through the collective affiliation of their local unions. Party activity is by no means limited to the locals which have affiliated, but lack of affiliation does indicate less than 100 per cent loyalty. The Labor party must work at the task of retaining the loyalty of the workers, and this demands concessions to the unions. There are divisive elements, notably the Communist party. Some local unions contribute to the campaign chest of the C.P. and others make political donations to both the Communist party and the Labor party. There is also need to fight the apathy of trade-union members, for in Norway, as elsewhere, workers form a large percentage of those who do not vote.

Parenthetically, the Communists have been driven out of all national union offices and from the National Council of the LO, but through their foothold in many local unions they can sometimes influence national union policies in regard to wages and contract conditions. Naturally, the Communists are the most aggressive in attacking the moderate wage policies of the LO. The Communist Party is sustained by the hope that the LO leaders will misjudge rank and file sentiment and set off a major revolt. Each year, however, has seen a reduction in Communist strength within the unions and in the political sphere. Communist votes in political elections have sunk from 176,000 in the elections of 1945 to 60,000 in 1957.

### Norwegian Labor and Nationalization

A good illustration of the pragmatic approach of the Labor party is furnished by the attitude toward nationalization. The LO Constitution makes direct favorable reference to this issue in its statement of aims and objectives. A similar goad to nationalization is contained in the constitutions of many of the national unions. These slogans of yesteryear, however, have little application to the present; the emphasis is placed instead on the question, will it work in the light of present-day conditions?

The Norwegian State today operates the railroads, the telephone and telegraph system, and the radio network. Through the concession laws it controls the natural resources such as waterfall and mines, although there are many instances where private concerns have been given the right to operate. About 15 per cent of total production facilities are held by state and municipal enterprises. In 1954 the State owned outright only 26 concerns, including two major aluminum firms and one steel mill developed since the war. It was the principal shareholder in 11 others and a minority stockholder in an additional 46.[8] The primary area of public investment since 1945 has been in state and municipal hydroelectric development. From this, one can see there is considerable room for private investment.

The Labor party is not planning nationalization of the private sector in the years ahead for eminently practical reasons. The Secretary-General of the Labor party explained it as follows to the writer:

We are convinced that nationalization should not be pushed for its own sake, but only when it brings definite advantages to the people. Any other view would be politically intolerable . . . We have a majority of only three seats in the Storting, only 48 per cent of the popular vote. The Labor party must take into consideration that every second year there are elections to be won. In order to win elections we must also take into consideration that our per cent of the total vote represented a coalition of workers, small farmers, and fishermen. The first Socialists to be elected to the Storting were elected by fishermen in the North. Some of the areas of labor strength are predominantly farming and logging areas. The fishermen and farmers definitely do not join or support the Labor party in order to see a program of nationalization realized. The farmers want to have their own land, and the fishermen their own boats. Furthermore, we are now in a state of development where the white-collar workers equal in numbers the industrial workers. We would hardly attract the vote of the white-collar workers on the basis of a policy of large-scale nationalization.[9]

This same theme is expressed by an official study group appointed by the Labor party in 1956. The report of this committee is published under the title *Sosialiseringsspørsma-*

*alet.* The report states: "The demand for freedom is central to our basic idea, and this means freedom for all, for the worker and for the capitalist . . . Socialization can contribute to carrying us to some of our objectives, but at the same time make it more difficult to attain others." [10] The committee concludes that nationalization must be highly selective if it is to be utilized as a technique in the future.

Interestingly enough, the majority of the 11-member committee was composed of so-called intellectuals. This is simply one more indication that continued interest in nationalization is centered among some local trade-union groups and, to a limited extent, among the younger members of the Socailst Youth movement. There were 17 resolutions dealing with the question of nationalization, forwarded by local unions through their national unions, considered by the 1957 LO Convention. The greatest emphasis in these resolutions was placed on the take-over of banking and insurance companies. The Convention passed a meaningless resolution, presumably waiting for a new policy to be adopted by the Labor party. Most, but not all, of the resolutions emanated from local unions in which Communist influence is evident.

*Strikes and Party-Union Relationships*

There is one other area of the Labor party-trade-union relationship to which attention might be directed profitably in order to gain a deeper understanding. This concerns the right to strike in an abstract sense as contrasted to the limitation on this right on numerous specific occasions in the past 13 years. This development has led many observers to be concerned as to the future of free collective bargaining institutions. Walter Galenson, for one, indirectly raises the specter of a Sovietized movement acting as no more than an administrative organ of the state.[11] Perhaps the development of the "shadow government" type of relationship between the Labor party and the Labor government, superficially not unlike the Soviet model, gives currency to such ideas.

The Party-government relationship would pose a threat to internal democracy in a society less dedicated to democratic procedures than is the Norwegian. Mark Leiserson provides an important illustration of the basic desire to protect the trade-union function. He states: "One of the most significant features of the postwar Norwegian economy—the deliberate demobilization of direct government regulations—has been closely connected with the desire to maintain autonomous collective bargaining institutions." [12]

The attitude within the labor movement regarding the right to strike is a mixed one. The trade-unions have accepted curbs on this right voluntarily, but there is a deep feeling among trade-union members and leaders that the right itself cannot be abrogated. Some of the strikes which have been permitted display that, at times, the basic right is given wider interpretation than in the United States. A ten-day strike of Oslo police in early 1958, while labeled "illegal" by the authorities, did not meet with the near hysteria that such an event would create in the United States. The police union called off the strike only after community and government pressures combined led to a willingness on the part of the independent union to accept a meaningless face-saving device which ended the strike.

The five-day walkout of 15,000 employees of the city of Oslo in the spring of 1958 provides another example that society as a whole still treats the right to strike as inherent to the democratic process. [13] This strike, in addition to shutting down all community services, stopped about 60 per cent of the transportation facilities. The strike was ended through the intervention of LO officials who worked out a satisfactory formula for the settlement of a dispute which had dragged on over a year.

There are many people in Norway both in the Labor party and out who express the hope that some day the strike weapon will become outmoded as being too wasteful in modern society. Prime Minister Gerhardsen gave expression to this point of view in a speech delivered January 1, 1957. He stated:

In Norway we ought to have come to a point where conflicts . . . should be solved without work stoppages or stoppages in distribution by sellers. A struggle of this degree is a two-edged sword which often strikes innocent third parties, and should be laid aside. Last year we lost a million man-days from strikes . . . It is such experiences which raises the question of finding other forms for the solution of economic disputes which have become locked fast.[14]

Private reaction in trade-union circles to this section of the Prime Minister's speech was less than enthusiastic although no public statements were released. LO president, Nordahl, gave indirect answer to the Prime Minister at the LO convention five months later in a major address. He stated:

> . . . I will only say definitely the LO's principal standpoint in this country, as in other countries, is that the right to strike is one of the rights which belongs to a democratic society, but it is with this right as with other rights—there are certain limitations—It is the organization's task to seek that one does not use the strike weapon in such a manner that the society, regardless of who governs, finds it necessary to apply a prohibition against strikes . . .[15]

Nordahl's statement quoted above expresses the basic union attitude; certain rights are inherent, but indiscriminate application can harm the trade-unions and society at large. A move on the part of the Government to abrogate the right of strike would meet with such opposition from the trade-unions that it would rip the labor movement asunder. The oft-quoted statement of Martin Tranmael, made many years ago, to the effect that trade-unions will be necessary within a Socialist state as "administrative divisions of society" has little validity under present-day circumstances. There is a general realization that within the type of mixed economy foreseen by present day Socialists in Norway, unions have a function far beyond that of mere administrators.

The right to strike will be retained even though it will be used sparingly under existing circumstances. The unions can "forego the full use of their economic power in order to maintain their status in respect to other tools of power which they have found so useful, particularly political power." [16] The threat of strike, however, still represents a potent bargaining weapon when dealing with employers, and in the bargaining that is integral to the functioning of a complex within the broad outlines of the Norwegian labor movement.

## Conclusions

Norwegian unionism has never been so "political" as to exclude the function of pure and simple unionism. This has been part of the "division of tasks" mentioned by Labor party Vice Chairman Bratelli in the previous section. The union movement is based on hard-core principles, insured by enforceable labor agreements. The trade-unions have been able to affect a transference of union loyalty into political loyalty in proportion to their ability to secure benefits for the worker on the job by a combination of economic and political methods. Operating in a country of limited resources and limited capital, and coming to power in a country already culturally mature but economically underdeveloped, the logic of the situation demanded political solutions to many of the economic insecurities faced by the workers. The national pooling of resources in order to finance social benefits, combined with the use of the tax mechanism to change income distribution, has produced a high level of security for all.

The unions have embraced a course of action different from that of unions in the United States. This does not invalidate the fulfillment of goals common to trade-unions everywhere, nor does it detract from the psychological enrichment of the worker gained through his participation in the governing of community and nation. The creative impulses generated through the medium of the labor movement is one of the most telling elements of the Norwegian story.

The functional unity of the union movement with a political movement has not resulted in a withering away of the trade-unions or domination by intellectuals intent on pursuing doctrinaire goals. The unions have accepted the leadership of the Labor party in the attainment of long-range objectives and, in so doing, have modified what have been considered some of the traditional operating methods of a union movement. Despite this, the basic interests of the union movement have been insured due to its strength and due to the strategic position it occupies at the policy-making level within the Labor party.

The most significant development within the labor movement in postwar history is related to the partial shift of the collective bargaining process to a point within the framework of the Labor party structure where union wage policy is subject to the downward pressure of the Labor Government. This would seem to make the task of the Norwegian Employers' Association considerably lighter, but even so, the NAF faces a heavy responsibility. A large residue of wage consciousness continues to motivate the Norwegian worker; the press for monetary concessions is a constant both in season and out. It might even be argued, considering the wage rise of the past decade attributable to union negotiations and the "wage drift," that Government pressure had done little more than eliminate the sharp points from union wage pressures.

The subtle nature of the procedural relationships between the unions and the political party demands great skill, infinite patience, and above all, integrity on the part of political leaders and trade-union officials alike. The duality of responsibility on the part of all concerned imposes obligations not normally faced by American union leaders.

This same note of integrity is also a characteristic of the relations between the unions and the representatives of employers. The mutual and genuine respect demonstrated between the union movement and the employers' association stands as testimony to a generation of honorable dealing. This has been accomplished with no loss in the representative function of the respective organizations. The extremes of passion and intemperance which mark the industrial relations scene in the United States have been removed, and a high degree of rational conduct has been substituted. No little credit for the constructive nature of present-day unionism in Norway should be given to the honesty of purpose of the *Norsk Arbeidsgiverforening*, the Norwegian Employers Association. By the same token, it might be said that some of the more baleful aspects of union operations in the United States is traceable to the methods by which American employers have fought the growth of unions.

One facet of the integrity so typical to the conduct of affairs within the Norwegian union movement is the compelling will to maintain democratic standards. Jack Barbash ascribes the "will to democracy" as being the most powerful determinant of whether or not unions function as democratic organizations.[17] The finest constitution and a loose intraorganizational discipline is no protection against those who do not place intrinsic worth in the concept of democracy.

Norwegians are born to democracy. They interpret the concept as containing a force compelling internal discipline in organizational behavior, not simply as offering protection for a potential revolt against established leadership. Norwegians as a group have faith in their institutions; union members in particular have faith in their organization and consider the union movement to be the embodiment of the democratic spirit. They see no threat to individual freedom in granting extensive powers to parent units in the structure.[18]

The labor movement is conscious of the fact it is charting a new course and is alert to possible dangers. There is continuing discussion on methods and forms which can be utilized to maintain the vigor of the union function. It was in part this reason which prompted a change in organizational form in 1953; under a resolution passed at the 1953 LO convention county district trades councils were abolished in favor of town and area councils in order to promote more participation at the local level. The search for a more complete democracy accounts for the intensification of the efforts by the Workers' Educational Association to expand its activities. It also accounts for the avid interest in ideas generated from abroad. In the final analysis, the creative striving for a more perfect democracy insures the continuation of a vigorous and vital trade-union movement which can serve as a source of inspiration to labor movements in other parts of the world.

Jumping now to some more general observations, one can conclude that the trade-unions of Scandinavia, for the Norwegian experience is quite similar to what has taken place in Denmark and Sweden, have followed a concept of organizational behavior to which we can apply the title "nation-building" or "national purpose" unionism. Israel's Histadrut, in a more self-conscious way, perhaps because the unions existed prior to the State itself, is even more marked by this characteristic. Study of the Mexican scene yields evidence of similar overtones in the development of the trade-unions of that country—although in this instance the traditional trade-union function has never developed fully.

In each instance the trade-unions apparently have been integrated into a national movement spreading horizontally across several interest groups—and during this process have come to identify broad national interests as legitimate objects of union concern. Under such circumstances the trade-unions have played a highly creative role, one in which the energies and sense of participation of the masses are enrolled, thereby giving added impetus to the drive for economic development and a stable social structure.

The danger to the trade-union movements in the emerging countries of becoming agents of the state, or at the least captives of the dominant political party, is an ever present one as can be seen on every hand. The record written by American trade-unions offers slight guidance under the circumstances to political and/or union leaders in many of the new countries. Perhaps, it would make more sense to explore the possibilities of projecting the image and the underlying social philosophies inherent in "national purpose" unionism whereby unions become a partner in the new national experiments.

I lay stress on the fact that I am not suggesting a wholesale transfer of institutions. Any transfer would be more psychological than real. The objective of the investigation suggested here is to determine if there are not certain intangibles—social and ethical motivations—which have won acceptance in the three referenced countries which can form a platform from which some of the newer countries can operate and by which an appropriate "division of tasks" can be made. The very fact that the countries in development lack experience, lack leadership, lack a democratic tradition makes it imperative to provide base—points which will provide an inspiration and guidance in the difficult years ahead.

## NOTES

1. Shortly after this paper was completed, the 1961 parliamentary election resulted in a small decline in the Labor party vote. A new Socialist Peoples party to the left of the Labor party won two seats in the parliament. Labor continues to govern the country but its task will not be more complicated. This is true even though the total labor vote, taking both the "socialist" parties, did not decline in the last election.

2. Independent unions have no strength among production workers. There are a good many thousands of white-collar workers, including government employees, nurses, etc., who do belong to independent unions. The most important of these belong to a confederation, *Funksjonaerenes Sentralorganisasjon* (FSO). The FSO listed its total membership at 35,950 as of December 31, 1956. See Statistisk Aarbok for Norge, 1957, Table 269, for complete list.

3. It is interesting to note that a majority report of a special *Storting* committee, established in 1918, recommended the formation of plant councils composed of management, salaried workers, and production workers in plants with more than ten employees. The councils were to have full management control. The *Storting* instead passed temporary legislation in 1920 establishing "advisory committees" with authority only to discuss plant problems. In 1924 there were 179 such committees functioning. The committees were not important after this date. See Petersen, Erling, *Norsk Arbeidsgiverforening* 1900–1950, official history of NAF (Oslo, Norway: 1950), p. 338 ff.

4. Speech by Trygve Bratteli, Vice Chairman of the Labor party, to 1957 LO Convention. *Protokoll Over Kongressen*, p. 26.

5. The part played by the WEA in sustaining the vitality of the labor movement cannot be underestimated. It has made an important contribution to present day labor control of Norway through locating and training leaders. Moreover, by exposing trade-union and political leaders to similar ideological stimuli much of the basis of potential conflict is harmonized. In a one-year period the WEA held 2,476 lectures, courses, and study groups attended by 35,168 people.

Of the participants 13,072 were union members. The unions also run courses under their own sponsorship. Record of WEA activity is contained in the 1957–58 report of the *Arbeidernes Opplysningsforbund* reprinted in *Fri Fagbevegelse* (December, 1958), pp. 376–77.

6. A small fraction of the individual's union dues is dedicated to the support of the labor press. It is estimated that approximately one out of three families in Norway reads a labor paper. During election campaigns this figure is increased to about one out of two through the medium of gratis short-term subscriptions. The conservative press coverage is wider but it does not provide as clear or as disciplined a political message. Editorial policies of the individual labor papers vary in their treatment of many issues, but on major questions there is unanimity.

7. To give one example: Prime Minister Gerhardsen devotes hundreds of hours each year to attendance at trade-union conventions where he takes note of issues important to the delegates. He is available to every person at the convention for private conversation. Fraternal delegates from other countries often expressed to the writer their amazement that one and all have such free access to high government officials.

8. *Sosialiseringsspørsmaalet, Kontakt, issue No. 5 and 6, Det Norske Arbeiderpartiet,* Oslo (1957), p. 31.

9. Private conversation with Haakon Lie, Secretary General, Norwegian Labor party, 1958.

10. *Sosialiseringsspørsmaalet,* pp. 6–7.

11. Galenson, Walter, *Labor in Norway,* Cambridge, Mass., Harvard Univ. Press (1949), p. 339.

12. Leiserson, Mark, *Wages and Economic Control in Norway, 1945–1957,* Cambridge, Mass.: Harvard Univ. Press (1959), p. 58.

13. This strike was a good demonstration of many of the built-in conflicts of interest within the labor movement. The city administration, naturally, opposed the strike as did the national government. The LO and the national union involved opposed taking strike action, but when negotiations broke down these two organs gave official sanction to a strike. A personal friend of the writer is an employee of the City Hall and an officer in the local union. She is also a member of the City Council as a representative of the Labor Party. She was, nevertheless, active in the strike. One highly placed government official, a former cabinet minister, who still retains union membership in the City Hall local union, is reported to have called the local union to volunteer a contribution to the strike fund.

14. Speech delivered New Year's Day 1957 by Prime Minister Gerhardsen, who is also Chairman of the Labor party, over the Norwegian Broadcasting System. Reported in Arbeiderbladet, January 2, 1957.
15. Speech of Konrad Nordahl before 1957 LO Convention reported in *Protokoll Over Kongressen*, p. 157.
16. Sturmthal, Adolf—*Unity and Diversity in European Labor*; Chicago, Ill., the Free Press (1953), p. 206.
17. Barbash, Jack, Informal speech before faculty and students of the University of Wisconsin Industrial Relations Research Center on February 18, 1959, Madison, Wis.
18. The writer, during his residence in Norway, sought evidence to show whether or not the restrictions imposed on local and national unions by virtue of the highly centralized structure of the union movement was regarded by union members as an infringement on democracy. In conversations held under the most informal circumstances with hundreds of local union officers and ordinary members, only one complaint was heard. The charge of undemocratic procedure was raised in a bitter argument, which took place in the hotel room of the writer, between a Communist chairman of a local trades council and a LO district secretary over the selection of delegates to a convention. The Communist daily newspaper, *Friheten*, attacks LO policies on all occasions, but not the procedures under which policy is framed.

# 6 Labor Organizations and Politics in Belgium and France *

by Val R. Lorwin

Walking along the quais of the Seine on a sunny Paris afternoon in August 1950, I came across Paul Finet, likewise walking alone (although not claiming to be doing research). I asked the likable and level-headed secretary-general of the Belgian General Federation of Labor (as he was then) about his impressions of the French unions.

"The same as always," he said. "Politics, politics, too much politics." As I already had this idea, I welcomed it as wisdom. "But," I had to go on to ask, "didn't you last month have a general strike in Belgium which forced King Leopold III off the throne?" The question was only slightly malicious; the answer not even slightly hesitant. "Ah, yes, we Socialists called a general strike. But that was quite different, you know." I resolved that if I ever finished my book on the French labor movement, I should try to understand, as my friend assumed I did, the differences between France and Belgium.

A year in Belgium (1957–1958) helped me to begin to understand Belgium—and to understand France (and the United States) better. Comparing the labor organizations of two countries is doing what comes naturally, as anyone who has been a "visiting fireman" or entertained "visiting firemen" knows. But it is a type of comparison which has been too little attempted in an explicit and somewhat systematic manner. Such comparison not only helps the under-

* I gratefully acknowledge the help of the Committee on Comparative Politics of the Social Science Research Council, which made possible a year's research in Belgium, the earlier aid of the Inter-University Study of Labor Problems in Economic Development, which made possible much of my research on France, and the recent aid of the Graduate School of the University of Oregon in my continuing work on the political system of Belgium.

standing of each of the countries being compared, but may also offer a few modest blocks for the building of the more impressive structures of theory, at least middle-range theory, of labor and political behavior.

On France almost everybody is an expert. In part this is because of what the English novelist Ford Madox Ford once called the desire of every Anglo-Saxon to reform the French economic system. There is a great deal of literature on the French movement, even in English. Therefore I shall not describe the French movement, except for purposes of contrast with the Belgian. I shall spend most of my time on the Belgian movement, about which all too little has been written in French and Flemish, and almost nothing in English, and whose history and characteristics are not as well known, even in Belgium, as they deserve to be.

*Structure of Unionism*

Belgium is one of the few countries (Holland and Switzerland are the two others) where unions are strong despite the division of organized labor into several rival movements. Much of Belgian economic and social organization, and its political life, are based on the three "spiritual families"— Catholic, Socialist, and Liberal. Each spiritual family has a network of political party, trade unions, consumer cooperatives, friendly societies (to use the agreeable English term for the mutual insurance or fraternal benefit societies), and other special interest groupings.

The unions, like those of France, first became a mass movement after World War I. They had their ups and downs between the wars, but with far less extreme swings than the French unions. Since World War II, the Belgian unions have grown greatly in number, bargaining power, and recognition in the national community.

Here is some idea of the numerical importance of the various branches of the Belgian trade-union movement as of now: At the end of the 1950's, membership stood at some 700,000 each for the Socialist Belgian General Federation of Labor (the Fédération Générale du Travail de Belgique or FGTB) and the Confederation of Catholic Trade-Unions (the Confédération des Syndicats Chrétiens or CSC). The FGTB had considerably more following among the workers in basic manufacturing industries and in the larger plants; the CSC more among white-collar employees and textiles and in dispersed small enterprises, notably the building trades. The influence of the FGTB was greater among unorganized workers that was that of the CSC.

The Liberal unions and small autonomous union groups brought the total to about 1,500,000 for some 2,500,000 wage and salary earners. This was not very far behind the number of union members France might count, for five times as many wage and salary earners. (But who would even try to count members in France, where the very concept of union membership is so hazy?) The ratio of membership to potential in Belgium, in unions whose membership is almost entirely voluntary, is almost twice that of the United States, with the compulsions unions may legally apply.

The Belgian unions, unlike the French, are centralized in structure. Unionists are, by and large, disciplined in behavior: dues payment, acceptance of union decisions, strike action. The national union is the basic unit of structure. There is, however, a vital regional differentiation within each national union, as within every form of organized national life in Belgium, between the Flemish and the Walloons. The Flemish (who speak a Germanic tongue called Flemish or Dutch) live north of the old linguistic frontier which runs west to east across the nation just south of Brussels. The Walloons (who speak French) live in the southern provinces. Only in and around Brussels do the two ethnic-cultural groups mix. Otherwise they are almost two separate nationalities. Organizational life in Flanders resembles that of the Netherlands; life in Wallonia is akin to that of Northern France.[1]

The Flemish have tighter organizations and a stronger sense of discipline than the Walloons, within each of the labor movements, Socialist and Catholic. For example, the Flemish unions and friendly societies collect their members' dues (jointly) at their homes; the Walloons do not. Each organization must maintain a formal or informal balance between Flemish and Walloon claims and leadership. But, despite these differences, the national unions are centralized in both federations. Both the Socialist and—even more— the Catholic confederation offices are strong. In the CSC, strike funds are administered not by the national unions, but by the confederation.

Note that in France a national union is called—to transliterate the French word—a "federation," while in Belgium it is a "central."

Pluralism has been accepted in trade-unionism, as in so many phases of Belgian life. Americans do not easily comprehend union pluralism. It was perhaps inevitable in Belgium, given the profundity of the cleavages between Socialists and Catholics, that it came about. It has some positive advantages in keeping union leadership more responsive to membership needs and wishes. And, given the ramifications of a century's other cleavages, union pluralism probably means, on balance, less friction at all levels from the shop to the confederation than there would be if some miracle brought all organized workers under the roof of a single "house of labor."

*Socialist Labor Movement*

Socialists were the first to build a network of trade-unions, consumer cooperatives, and friendly societies allied with their political party. "The future belongs to the class which builds its own institutions," said the Socialist leader Emile Vandervelde. But classes do not build, people build. And people have other loyalties as well as class loyalties. The Belgian workers built as Socialists and as Catholics and as Liberals.

The vision of the future changed as the institutions grew. Edouard Anseele, one of the founders of the embattled Socialist cooperative *Vooruit* (of Ghent) said, "Our cooperatives are the citadel from which we shall bombard capitalist society with sacks of potatoes and four-pound loaves of bread." But how long can the heroic period of a movement last? Less than a generation, if it meets with some success. In the years to come, Anseele and his comrades became more concerned with tending the grocery than bombarding the enemy. The Belgian workers built their institutions, but the institutions integrated them into their society.

As for the political party, it was one of the most solidly organized and labor-based of all Socialist parties.[2] The unions, at first subordinate to the party in the structure of Socialist workers' organizations, went on to achieve equality of power with the party. The consumer cooperatives, at first lively and influential in the movement for workers' emancipation, gradually became rather somnolent. The friendly societies lost their crusading spirit as they became large-scale business organizations performing their mutual insurance functions as part of a universalized social security system. The dynamic wings of the movement now are the party and the unions, or rather small groups within each.

Until World War II, most Socialists had organic ties with the party only through the collective affiliations of their unions, co-ops, and friendly societies. In 1945 the Socialist party dropped collective affiliation and became a party of individual affiliation only. Most of the union members who consider themselves Socialist and vote Socialist do not take the trouble to join the party despite its modest dues. Party membership, of all social categories, is less than a fifth of the total of FGTB membership alone.

A few years after the war, Socialists again established a coordinating mechanism among their various organizations, but one far looser than collective affiliation. This is the Common Action which brings together representatives of the old quadrivium—party, unions, co-ops and friendly societies—at national, regional, and local levels. It serves now chiefly to assess the other organizations' contributions to the party campaign funds. And anyone seeking a place on the Socialist primary ballot must prove his membership or activity in relation to various Socialist organizations: union, co-op, friendly society, and Socialist press. Interlocking directorates and informal contacts are more vital than the formal mechanisms of the Common Action, however. Thus, of the 22 members of the FGTB executive board in 1957, seven were Socialist members of parliament, and the head of the FGTB, who was also a deputy, was one of the three or four men who ran the Party.

The Socialist party and unions in France never attained a clear, overt relationship, originally because the Socialist parties were so divided among themselves (five different "national" parties at the turn of the century), and then because the Syndicalists and Anarchists denied the validity of all political party action. The so-called "a-political" Syndicalists' refusal to recognize the reality of politics prevented the development of a division of labor and a mutual regard between unions and the Socialist party in France, such as Belgium and other advanced western European countries developed.

*Catholic Labor*

In Belgium, even more than in France, the Roman Catholic hierarchy was slow to become aware of that divorce between workers and the church of their forefathers which Pius XI was to name "the greatest scandal of the nineteenth century." Finally moved by the inroads of a militantly anti-clerical socialism, priests led Catholic workers in setting up a network of social organizations paralleling and by now equalling in numbers those of the Socialists.

The Catholic labor organizations have gone on increasing in "the divine poetry of numbers," to quote Pius XI again, and in influence within the Catholic community and within the nation. In the 1920's the Belgian Catholic Workers Youth organization, the JOC (Jeunesse Ouvrière Chré-tienne[3]), was firmly established in its present form, and soon spread to France. This specialized form of the Catholic Action movement helped reinvigorate Catholicism among Belgian workers and train a lay leadership which no longer needed to lean upon the priests' aid in the work of labor organization. In France too, the JOC has helped to train leadership and develop self-confidence among Catholic boys and girls of the working class. But in France after World War II, for a time, many of this élite of the JOC were pulled by the tides of working-class extremism into the Communist stream. In Belgium there was no such attraction, because communism

147

was weak and gradualist forms of action were accepted as legitimate by the working class, Catholic and non-Catholic.

The Catholic schools in Belgium are one major element in the complex of Catholic strength. They enroll more students at every level, from kindergarten to university, than the public educational system. The Catholic vocational schools offer a natural terrain for the recruitment of Catholic unionism.

Church, schools, unions, co-ops, friendly societies, workers' youth groups, men's and women's organizations—all these form even more of a special world than the Socialist world. As Mgr. Brys, the chaplain of the Christian Workers' movement (Mouvement Ouvrier Chrétien, or MOC), which loosely federates unions, co-ops, friendly societies, and workers' youth organizations, recently declared:

A triple idea governs the structure of our great Christian labor organization: that of totality, of complexity, and of unity . . . Our movement must embrace the whole person of the worker, the whole of the worker's life, the whole family of the worker, all workers' needs, and the whole working class. We want the working man and woman, youth and adult, in coming into our movement, to find everything there.

The Catholic labor organizations now maintain formal independence of the political party of Belgian Catholicism. They require that an official resign from his union post if he is elected to political office of more than minor concern —e.g., member of Parliament. But this refusal to have union officials double in political brass is a sign of the closeness of the CSC to the Catholic political party, not of remoteness from it. (The FGTB, however, after World War II settled a long debate on the compatibility of union and political officeholding the other way, although a FGTB few unions have their own rules of incompatibility.)

The Catholic unions had to fight long for the recognition they now get in Catholic political action. Between the wars the Catholic party was a federation of often-quarreling labor, farm, and middle-class organizations (along with the old political clubs, chiefly bourgeois and aristocratic). After the Second World War, Catholics (like the Socialists) reorganized and renamed their party. Now called the Christian Social party, the PSC (Parti Social Chrétien), it was put on a basis of individual, not collective, affiliation. In its decision-making organs and its choice of candidates, however, the PSC gives formal representation to the various organized social interests of the Catholic community: labor, employer, farmer, and middle-class organizations.

The representation of these organized "estates"—to translate the appropriate Flemish term ("standen") of medieval flavor—is facilitated by the electoral system of multi-member constituencies for both houses of Parliament. A slate may be built-up recognizing all the "standen" in almost every electoral district.

The MOC usually represents the labor interest in intra-party negotiation and decision. Within the PSC, labor is the most dynamic element in matters of social policy—or, to the irritation of conservative Catholics, a Left Wing as close to socialism as most of the Socialist party.

The alignments of Belgian politics have been almost constant since equal universal manhood suffrage in 1919. This rigidity is quite different from the changes—both long-run shifts and swings from one election to another—which have characterized the politics of the French nation and its working class. The Catholic party (now the PSC) has been the leading party, the Socialist party a close second, the Liberal party a poor third, and the Communists a much smaller minority in all the national elections since universal equal suffrage after World War I.

Most Catholic workers feel they have little choice even when they are dissatisfied with the PSC. Sitting out the election is not an alternative, for compulsory voting brings everyone out to the polls (and comparatively few people cast blank or spoiled ballots). The Socialist party is hardly more social on most issues than the PSC, and if it is in alliance with the Liberals (as from 1954 to 1958) its economic policy is especially tame. Most Socialist leaders and activists have continued the nineteenth-century fight, not only against the Church's role in politics, but against Catholicism and religion. The Liberal party, historically anti-clerical and long primarily a party of business interests, holds little interest for working-class Catholic voters.

## Liberal and Neutral Unions

The Liberal trade-unions, now reduced in membership to less than a tenth of that of either the Socialist or Catholic unions, are something of an anomaly. Other members of the conservative, business-oriented Liberal party do not hesitate to say as much in the presence of their union associates. Yet these unions remain of some importance on the national scene and in some areas of employment, notably among civil servants and white-collar employees in the private sector. Unlike the two leading confederations, however, the General Center of Liberal Unions does not have well-developed constituent national unions; its one real center is in the confederation.

The Liberal unions are dependent on the party in a way which differs sharply from the pattern of FGTB-Socialist party or CSC-PSC relations. Despite the general acceptance of union pluralism, the CSC and FGTB have contested the Liberal unions' rights to take part in the industry-wide joint commissions and in various agencies of government consultation. Their stronger rivals point out the Liberal unions' small membership and their skeleton or paper development of specific-industry unions, and in some cases question their *bona fides*. But during the late 1950's, the Liberals' participation in successive government coalitions with the Socialists and the PSC won their unions seats at the official bargaining tables in most industries of the private sector and in all areas of public employment. At the top or confederal level, the Liberal union representatives are recognized along with those of the FGTB and the CSC in discussions with the peak employer associations and the government.

The friendly societies associated with the Liberal party are considerably stronger than the unions. They are known as efficient organizations in a field of comparatively little direct ideological interest. Since everyone normally joins a Socialist, Catholic, or Liberal friendly society to get health insurance

150

coverage, the Liberal societies attract people outside the Liberal political orbit.

Consumer cooperatives—the third of the tripod of labor's social organizations—have not been sponsored by the Liberals, with their considerable storekeeper constituency.

Some politically neutral unions exist. But they are of no consequence, except for a minor role in a few branches of government employment.

*The Communists*

In Belgium, for reasons I shall for the most part discuss later—the Communist party achieved little strength before World War II, even at the depth of the depression and the height of popular front movements elsewhere. There was no attraction of Communist strength among the electorate as a whole or among workers to move the Socialists toward a popular front in the mid-1930's. Instead, the Socialists in 1935 joined in a "national union" coalition government with the other two "national" parties, the Catholics and the Liberals, to combat the depression. At its inter-war electoral high, the CP received only six per cent of the popular vote (in 1936).

As elsewhere, the Communists gained strength and prestige after 1941. At the liberation, they led unions of considerable importance. But the other parties postponed the nation's first post-war elections until 1946. The Communists then achieved their all-time high of 12 per cent of the vote— similar to their percentage in other northern countries. But after that their following dropped sharply, and for a time steadily. In the merger of their unions with those of Socialist or semi-Syndicalist leadership, the Communist minority was gradually enveloped by a concerted Socialist drive through the Common Action of unions, co-ops, and friendly societies. Condemned to work within the Socialist-led network of socio-economic organizations, the Communists saw their influence dwindle to the point where, by the 1950's, they no longer held any major union posts. In the 1958 national elections, they mustered a mere two per cent of the popular vote. Most unlike France, revolutionary claims and leftism for its own sake have not held any special fascination for class-conscious workers. And equally unlike France, in Belgium the Communists' influence among intellectuals has always been faint.

## Collective Bargaining

Belgium has a tightly-organized web of national industry-wide collective agreements, many with the government seal on them. After World War I, the government pressured employers in some industries into sitting down with unions in national industry-wide joint commissions ("commissions paritaires"), under government officials as non-voting chairmen. The flowering of both collective bargaining and social welfare came after the Second World War. Personal contacts between labor and management leaders in Nazi-occupied Belgium had resulted in their signing a "pact of social solidarity." This was implemented by a sweeping advance in social security immediately upon liberation, and an early return to freedom of collective bargaining, now for the first time widely and fully accepted by employers.

Under the umbrella of early post-war prosperity, Belgium for the first time became (by European standards) a high-wage economy. The increase in real over prewar wages was the greatest experienced by any of the European democracies.

Basic decisions on labor market policy and the transition to the welfare state were made by representatives of the labor confederations, the peak employer associations, and the government. Continual collective bargaining was carried on by the joint commissions, by now extended to every industry. Agreements reached in these commissions could be —and generally were—recommended to the government for approval, which gives them the force of binding public regulation.

Union and management representatives assumed wide powers in a number of quasi-public agencies administering social security and social welfare programs. A large number of consultative economic and social agencies also brought together labor and management representatives, in joint bodies or with representatives of other organized interests in the economy, as in the newly created Central Economic Council.

So extensive have been the powers delegated to management and union representatives in some of these agencies, so well organized are the groups internally and in their bargaining relations, and so important are their pressures in political and administrative life, that some Belgians have indignantly called their system "corporatist." But that term could be used, if at all, only in innocence of either of state or party dictation to economic groups or of the economic groups' dictation to government or their own members. Moreover, there is no regimentation of individual participation in unions, employer organizations, or other socio-economic organizations. Freedom of membership or non-membership and the pluralism which runs through the society and most of the economy leave the individual free of the constraints associated with corporatism.

In the industry-wide *commissions paritaires* and in collective relations at lower levels, Socialist and Catholic unionists work reasonably well together. Even when their respective political friends are on different sides of the government-opposition fence, the unions' competition is— for the most part—far more restrained than that of the French unions or that of some American unions with overlapping jurisdictional claims. At the national level, the relations between the two big labor confederations and the major employer group, the Federation of Belgian Industries (the FIB, Fédération des Industries Belges) have been rather good. A number of big wheels in the FGTB, the CSC, and the FIB are on sufficiently close terms of personal familiarity to decide some important issues outside of any formal institutions, government-sponsored or otherwise.

At the base, the shop level, union power and industrial democracy are less impressive. Formal mechanisms of representation are not lacking. The law provides for elected safety and health committees and elected consultative plant committees. A national over-all agreement between the unions and the peak employer associations calls for elected committees of shop stewards in the larger plants (over 150 employees). These committees are in each case elected by the vote of all employees, usually from competing slates of the various unions. But all the weight of collective relations is still at the national level. And the national agreements are skimpy on the role of local committees and the handling of grievances. If the unions find qualified representatives in most industries at the national level, they find far fewer at the shop level.

On legal paper, the possibilities of the French system of collective bargaining are not so different from the Belgian. The French have an imposing legal framework of collective bargaining from the national level down. But most different are the content and the spirit of labor relations in the two nations: the balance of power between the bargaining parties and their sentiments toward each other; the relationships of the unions among themselves and toward their members; the unions' attitudes toward government. The French unions are weak and divided among themselves. Most workers' gains have come from government action and employer concessions; almost no innovations have been made by collective bargaining. What are signed as collective agreements are more often the outcome of employer decision than of the play of bargaining power.

In the decade since free collective bargaining was made possible again by law (in 1950) in France, there have been phenomenal modernizations of economic life, enormous increases in productivity, and—with full employment—great surges in the output of industry and of agriculture. Despite the strains of the Indo-Chinese and Algerian wars, there have been sharp rises in real wages and dramatic and expansive changes in the consumption of working-class families.

Strikes have fallen to negligible figures in France since 1953. This is not because of fruitful industrial relations or high morale among workers, but because of union impotence and worker apathy toward the competing unions. For this has been a decade of frustration for the unions and for that minority among management people who would like to see the realities of collective bargaining in practice. Communism is one cause of this frustration, but it is itself also a symptom of other maladies.

Belgium too has experienced large increases in production since the war (although since 1954 less marked than in France) and similar changes in patterns of consumption, despite unemployment which has been relatively high (as compared to France, not to the United States). There have been almost no major economic strikes since the liberation. Unlike France, collective relationships in the labor market have been highly institutionalized, and workers' expectations have been reasonable (perhaps too modest) since the immediate post-war wage increases. The unions have generally gone along with government policies which stressed price stability and the avoidance of inflation, even at the expense of employment and economic growth in the newer sectors of the economy.

### Unions and the State

In Belgium the unions have created power centers which, although strengthened by their role in public and quasi-public organisms, are nevertheless independent. Union leaders are on terms of familiarity with government. They use it, but they stand on their own feet.

In France the unions have long been dependent on the state for the very conditions of existence and functioning. Too weak and divided to confront the employers alone, they resent the state on which they must lean.

Relations among the Belgian unions and toward the government largely follow the rules of the game. One of the rules is that that you are more militant if your political friends are in the opposition, more restrained if they are in the government. But militancy is a far cry from the French union irresponsibility that goes with lack of power. As the Belgian Socialists and Catholics alternate in government coalitions with the Liberals and with each other, there is real pressure not to scrap the rules of the game.

Although identifying themselves with national goals as

generally understood by all classes, the unions, like Belgians generally, retain a wholesome skepticism of the state. If Paul Finet called the French unions too political, his old colleagues in the Belgian labor movement call the Dutch unions too "governmental." Once again, as in so many aspects of life, Belgium lies between France and Holland.

*Unions and Their Members*

Leadership is stable and solidly established in most Belgian unions, as in successful unions everywhere. The "iron law of oligarchy" which Michels formulated has not been suspended in Belgium, but there is a lower ferrous content to its working than in France. The base and the top leadership are physically and psychologically closer to each other because of the small size of the country and the comparative satisfaction of members with the social order.

The competition and potential competition of rival unions help keep all of them more alert to members' feelings than unions enjoying recognition and security might otherwise be. There is the possibility of "voting with the feet" for some dissenting members, but only for "some," although the choice is always there in principle. In practice the social pressures of a Catholic Flemish village or of a predominantly Socialist workplace in Wallonia can be almost as compelling as a union shop.

In France the worker also has a choice among unions. But choice is confused by the myth of working-class unity and by the long-dominant position of the CGT as "the" labor union confederation. The origins of Force Ouvrière as a breakaway movement left many politically indifferent and even some anti-Communist workers within the "old house" of the CGT. Relations between the leadership and the membership have been falsified by the ambiguity about the nature of leaders' ties to the Communist party, even when the fact of Communist affiliation is known (as it generally is), and by the key role of the party in the selection of CGT leadership and changes of policy and style of the organization.

## Why the Differences?

In the course of all too brief description, I hope I have managed to suggest a few reasons for the differences between the countries to the north and to the south of a man-made frontier. Now I should like to consider a series of factors one by one, of which none by itself is decisive, but which taken together may explain many of those differences in the destinies of Belgian and French labor.

## Economic Development

The first country on the Continent to industrialize, Belgium was (and is even now) ahead of France in the changes from a pre-industrial to an industrial society. Its industrial sector loomed much larger in the national economy than did the French, it was more urban, and a larger proportion of its people worked for wages and salaries. Belgians knew earlier and in more overpowering form what Beatrice Webb called "the discipline of great industry." There was, to be sure, a moment of undisciplined fierce protest in the 1880's, when conservatives "first saw the social problem by the light of burning châteaux." Then workers came to accept the imperatives of a capitalist industrialism as French workers—at least their élite—did not. Those imperatives, for the Belgians, included the wage system and the need for self-organization.

Some effects of early industrialization may be seen in similarities between Belgium and the adjacent region of northern France. In the complex of coal, steel, and textiles around Lille and Valenciennes, an early center of French industry, trade-unions and consumer cooperatives have much of the same spirit as those of the Belgian industrial centers of the valleys of the Sambre and the Meuse.

The uprooting of men and women from traditional communities shook the Catholic attachments of the new working classes in both lands. But the Catholic government of Belgium, in a small country with the densest rail network, subsidized "workers' trains" to enable men of the crowded

Flemish villages and small cities to continue living at home in their Catholic communities while earning a living in the mines or mills of "dechristianized" Wallonia. In the few large cities of Flanders where modern industry and transport developed, notably Ghent and Antwerp, however, the disaffection of workers from the Church was almost as deep as in Wallonia or in France.

The differences in material levels of well-being cannot explain the differences in labor attitudes and behavior. Interesting as those differences may be for close study of some of the factors of economic change, they are not the radical differences of different types of development. And they are less significant than the differences among regions within each country, between, for example, Lille and Toulouse in France or between west Flanders and Liège in Belgium.

With the high rate of population growth in Belgium, especially Flanders, and unemployment and underemployment a scourge of the Flemish countryside, per capita shares of the products of industrialization were modest, even if we disregard the manifest inequities in distribution. So, many Flemings went to France for jobs in agriculture or industry as seasonal migrants or as daily or weekly commuters. Between the wars, France sloughed off the worst of its unemployment problem by dispensing with its immigrant workers; Belgium had no such recourse.

After the liberation from German occupation in 1944, Belgium, almost undamaged, and with reverse lend-lease balances from wartime, was in a far better material position than a battered France. A vigorous compression of the currency (which France did not even attempt) helped Belgium curb inflation, while it profited from booming sales to a world short of many goods. This was the material basis for its welfare state and new high-wage economy. In France, inflation and black markets deepened workers' sense of injustice in these years. The French economy did recover rapidly, however, and by 1953 went on to more rapid advances in production than the Belgian economy. Now real wages in the two countries average about the same. But it is too soon for these new relationships to alter the patterns of trade-union life or labor's political action in a France whose public life has been dominated by the liquidation of its colonial heritage.

Within Belgium, recent differences of economic development have revivified and reslanted old regional-cultural conflicts. In the last decade or so, the older industries of Wallonia that paced Belgium's nineteenth-century industrial progress have experienced a decline (the coal mines are the hardest hit). Meanwhile new investments in the most modern branches of industry have gone almost entirely to Flanders. This disparity has made the "Walloon problem" an acute one, while creating new dimensions for the old "Flemish problem." Socialist unionists are in the forefront of Walloon regional claims, out of hope for economic reforms and protest against the economic stagnation which threatens their region, as well as for sentimental reasons. In Wallonia, then, relative economic decline has sharpened labor's combativity.

*Employer Behavior*

In the formative years of labor organization, before the First World War, Belgian employers were no more enlightened, and even less welfare-minded, than the French. They paid lower wages, successfully opposed most social legislation, and avoided collective bargaining. Universal primary public education was postponed for a generation after its establishment in France, and universal equal manhood suffrage even longer. But after the First World War, the unions grew and employer respect came gradually with union strength and government pressures, until the dramatic amplification and intensification of collective relations which we have seen after World War II.

In France, collective relations developed by fits and starts, and almost always as the relations between victors and vanquished, with the rancor of the vanquished. The Popular Front and the sitdowns, compulsory arbitration and the 1938 general strike, the Vichy regime, the liberation, and the Communists' power in the CGT, then their 1947 general strike, the split in the CGT, and the falling away of union membership—all these have been so many episodes in a history of discontinuities and inequality of bargaining power.

The Nazi occupation in Belgium brought labor and employer leaders together in the "pact of social solidarity," of symbolic and practical importance as a charter of post-war social progress. In France, the Vichy regime deepened social antagonisms and left political booby traps for later years.

In the critical years right after liberation, there was a rush of social legislation in both countries. In Belgium it was carried out in consultation with employers and their political spokesmen. In France it was carried out by the parties of the Left, without participation of the dazed parties of the Right, and with little consultation of the employers, who were just coming out of their storm cellars after the upheavals of the liberation.

### Structure of Labor Organization

The structures of the labor movements in the two countries have influenced their philosophies, as well as their possibilities, of action. In Belgium, the tightly meshed organizations of the Socialist world supported each other. The co-ops supported strikes; friendly societies and unions together gave workers their mutual insurance benefits, and all three economic organizations supported the party press and electoral campaigns.

This solid armature of Socialist organization of workers' interests was built before the Communists came on the scene. It resisted communism in a way which was impossible for the weakly structured French unions, with almost no buttressing socio-economic organizations and no organic or working relations with the Socialist party.

### Size of the Countries

Some of the differences in the labor movements stem from the differences in scale of the two nations. France is not a large country in the American or Russian sense of vast spaces and turbulent internal expansion. But, among the

160

nations of Europe, Frenchmen could long feel that theirs was a large, populous, and powerful nation. The French could therefore be intoxicated by political myths, and be extreme in their responses when disabused of their illusions.

Belgians have had the feeling of being a small nation in a world of great states. Their economy, they know, is dependent on exports and the transit trade. The Belgians have none of the myths of national grandeur in the sense of military or diplomatic power; they could not hope to hold colonial empire by force, as the French once thought they could. When they are disabused, the Belgians' shock takes a less extreme form than that of Frenchmen (although there have been some ugly manifestations of xenophobia since the Congo disaster). Belgians cannot nourish the illusions of freedom in foreign policy or in colonial policy which have divided Frenchmen and French labor in recent years and made them vulnerable to neutralism and communism.

The small dimensions of Belgium made for greater responsibility in the unions' relations with the nation, in balancing their demands against those of economic and financial stability, and the nation's international competitive position. "We must save *our* franc," said the Socialist unionists when they urged the party into the government in 1925; the sentiment is still there.

Smallness, of course, is not decisive in itself, for it may enlarge qualities or defects in a people. It enhances the decent qualities of a Denmark or a Norway. But if a country lacks educational attainment, economic development, independence and a sane political tradition, smallness aggravates internal conflict, bitterness toward the world, and the tendency to look inward and backward.

*Catholicism*

Roman Catholicism, for all its universality, takes institutional form in a congeries of national churches. The differences between French and Belgian Catholicism have conditioned political and social life in the two countries.

Belgian Catholics joined the Liberals to make the national revolution of 1830, and the Church agreed to a liberal bill of rights for the people in return for a unique combination of state financial support and freedom from state control. As a constitutional force, supporting a constitutional political party, it could play an integrating role—as well as a divisive role. It has provided one force and one framework for compromise among different classes in Belgium. The play of Catholicism and anti-Catholicism [4] prevented the formation of a single set of working-class organizations. But it also prevented the polarization of conservative elements. And the Catholic party, while its existence may have sharpened religious conflict, provided one structure for reconciling the political demands of labor and employers and other competing social groups.

In France, Catholicism long denied itself that integrating role, by fighting the battles of the French Revolution for over a century after the fall of the Bastille. Thus it made for neither a responsible conservative party within the constitutional framework of the Third Republic, nor for any compromising of the political demands of Catholic workers and employers, and other social categories.

*Political Factors and Political Events*

For all French problems except the care of the Renault Dauphine, we must go back to the French Revolution. It created not only the legend of *the* Revolution, but also—as Denis Brogan and David Thomson have shown—the myth of revolution as a method of change. That myth was kept alive, and the cleavages of the Great Revolution itself were perpetuated by a series of revolutions and constitutional upheavals in the following century. For many workers and intellectuals, the idea of revolution had a legitimacy which the political regime, after 15 constitutions in 80 years, did not have.

French socialism and anarchism were born in the era of revolutions, and never quite recovered from what David Thomson has called "the fascination of the revolution that might have been." This myth the Communists were able to exploit, posing as the heirs of 1789, of the June Days of 1848, and of the Paris Commune, and as the representatives of a "workers' revolution" (in Russia) that, unlike the French attempts, had come off.

Belgian workers for the most part never doubted the legitimacy of the "republican monarchy" which the national revolution of 1830 and the constitution of 1831 created. Like the Americans, the Belgians admired the work of their wise founding fathers, which had indeed been in advance of the time, and which has survived with scarcely any formal amendment since its adoption. The labor movement never entertained the myth of violent revolution as the method of political and social change.

The French received universal suffrage before any other nation in Europe, and their working-class élite soon thought too little of it because of their disappointment with the meager content of social legislation. Belgian workers had to fight for universal suffrage. An equally meager social legislation made them, on the contrary, esteem all the more the full suffrage rights they were denied until 1919. The suffrage fight, moreover, induced the Belgian Socialists into alliance with the progressive wing of the Liberal party, rather than electoral or parliamentary intransigence. That alliance set the Socialist party and the unions firmly on the path of political moderation. They were kept on it by the events of the First World War.

In France, the war interrupted a trend toward moderation in the CGT and in the Socialist party. The labor movement, as in the other major continental belligerents, was torn by revolutionary defeatism and by the postwar recriminations over Socialist and union support of the war. These struggles gave the Communists the opportunity to split the Socialist party (in 1920) and the CGT (in 1921–1922) and take with them their most militant industrial workers. From these splits, the French non-Communist Left has never recovered.

Revolutionary defeatism in the labor movement would have been absurd in Belgium. The neutral little nation, overrun by the Kaiser's armies, was "driven to heroism," as its King Albert said. No one could after the war successfully attack the Socialist party for having joined in the wartime cabinet of national union. The Communists were denied their great entering wedge.

The Belgian Socialists, moreover, joined in a new "national union" coalition after the war, and got it to enact labor's chief immediate political and social demands. In France, on the contrary (where the Socialists had left the government during the war), the immediate aftermath of war was a political swing to the right, disillusionment even among the reformist labor leaders, and the catastrophic general strike of 1920.

As the Second World War approached, international politics once again split the French labor movement (briefly reunited in the Popular Front). The Vichy regime caused another split, this time among the non-Communists, fragmenting the forces which might otherwise have made a more effective stand against Communism at the liberation.

Hitler gave the Communists the opportunity to be patriots in the resistance of both countries, and to emerge stronger than ever at the liberation. But the Belgian Socialists carried out a trade-union unification without the euphoria about labor unity that confused the French. And it was even André Renard, *enfant terrible* of the FGTB and a man with a fondness for syndicalism, who moved the motion in the metal workers union, making membership in the Communist party incompatible with union office.

There remains the general strike which Finet and his friends had just won at the time I met him walking along the Quai des Augustins in Paris in 1950. The French were the great theorists of the revolutionary general strike. They made a cult of the general strike, but a failure of every attempt except the great demonstration of February 12, 1934. And that was not a revolutionary proletarian strike, but a defense of the bourgeois republic threatened by the "fascist leagues."

The Belgians spun no theories of the general strike, but used it in the generation before the First World War to persuade undemocratically elected parliaments to widen the suffrage. The 1950 general strike was called to force the abdication of Leopold III, but it was not directed against the monarchy as an institution or against parliamentary democracy. Wise or unwise, it was a massing of Socialist labor strength for a clear political purpose. Legal or extra-legal, it ended a long period of constitutional and political confusion. It imposed a hard solution upon a monarch and a government wise enough to yield before national unity was subjected to unbearable strains. The King departed, but the monarchy remained. A duly constituted cabinet with a parliamentary majority backed down, but parliamentary government resumed its rights.

*National Values*

In no European country were the values of a capitalist society more thoroughly accepted than in Belgium. Its feudal tradition was weaker than that of France; its aristocracy had less of a separate way of life; its intellectuals offered less pervasive criticism of "the only Catholic country where making money did not carry with it a social stigma." In such a climate, trade-unionism could be businesslike under the garments of Socialist and Catholic doctrine.

Nineteenth-century France has been called the bourgeois society par excellence. But the power of its bourgeoisie was more contested than that of Belgium in that formative century. Much of the bourgeoisie itself were drawn by aristocratic values. Capitalist values therefore exerted less attraction upon working-class leaders and their organizations than they did in Belgium.

Belgians set a greater store by solidity than brilliance. They were more pragmatic and less interested in intellectual debate and doctrinal differentiation than the French. They have accorded a high place to voluntary association of every interest from farmers and factory workers to old age pensioners and the ubiquitous pigeon fanciers. (They have formed and joined functional associations to a far greater extent than have Americans.)

At the turn of this century Daniel Halévy suggested that Socialist enthusiasm was French, but Socialist organization was German and Belgian. To be sure, the nation which formed the Napoleonic armies and wrote the Napoleonic code, which created the French national administration and the French national railways, has not lacked a genius for organizing. But it has tended to rely on the government for most of the organization. Voluntary association has had far less place in France than in Belgium, even in the age of interest-group activities.

The principle of class as a basis of organization was in France an ideal which generated enthusiasm and sacrifice. The ideal was never at all close to being realized, but the animosities of class which were the obverse of its hopes have persisted. Conflicts settled into sterile resentments rather than rising to levels of fruitful tension.

Belgium, on the other hand, seemed to find the forms of conflict its social and political systems could support. Workers' organizations, ideologically divided from the start, pursued the tasks of organization within their several spiritual families rather than, as in France, pursuing an endless debate about "the unity of the working class." Along with their own solidarities, the workers' organizations developed a willingness to work with the representatives of other classes. Twenty-five years ago the head of the Socialist party could say—and a Belgian Socialist might have said it earlier—"We are not a party of class; we are a party of government." While projecting other cleavages in the national community, the competing networks of workers' organizations have generally kept conflict at a bearable level and have often bent it to fruitful emulation and quickening competition. The unions have shared in—and helped to shape—the continuities of the nation's social and political life.

## APPENDIX

1. *Belgian Labor and Employer Organizations and Political Parties*. Initials for names in French. (Each organization is, of course, known among Flemish-speaking Belgians under its Flemish name and initials.)

   CSC—Confédération des Syndicats Chrétiens, Confederation of Christian (Catholic) Trade-Unions.

CGSL—Centrale Générale des Syndicats Libéraux, General Center of Liberal Trade-Unions.

FGTB—Fédération Générale du Travail de Belgique, General Federation of Belgian Labor.

FIB—Fédération des Industries Belges, Federation of Belgian Industries.

JOC—Jeunesse Ouvrière Chretienne, Catholic Workers' Youth.

MOC—Mouvement Ouvrier Chrétien, Christian Workers' Movement.

PLB—Parti Libéral Belge, Belgian Liberal Party. In 1961 became Parti de la Liberté et du Progrès (Party of Liberty and Progress).

PSB—Parti Socialiste Belge, Belgian Socialist Party. (Before World War II, Parti Ouvrier Belge, Belgian Labor Party.)

PSC—Parti Social Chrétien, Christian Social Party. (Before World War II, Belgian Catholic Party.)

2. *Relative Strength of Political Parties.* Popular vote for House of Representatives, June 1, 1958:

| | |
|---|---|
| Christian Social Party | 46.5 per cent (of valid ballots) |
| Socialist Party | 37. |
| Liberal Party | 11.9 |
| Flemish Nationalist Party | 2. |
| Communist Party | 1.9 |
| Miscellaneous | .7 |
| | 100. |

## NOTES

1. The Flemish (or Dutch)-speaking areas of Belgium comprise some 54 per cent of the population. The Walloon or French-speaking areas comprise 33 per cent. The Brussels area, which is more or less bilingual, comprises 13 per cent. A tiny minority in the east speaks German.

2. To avoid burdening this essay with too many different names and initials, I shall use the term "Socialist party" for the organization which was originally called the Labor party (Parti Ouvrier Belge) and only in 1945 became the Socialist party

(Parti Socialiste Belge, PSB). For the same reason I shall speak of the Catholic party at various times, although in 1945 it became the Christian Social party. A list of initials and names of organization appears in the appendix.

3. Every Belgian organization that is national in scope has both its French and its Flemish names. For simplicity, I am using only the French names and the initials derived from the French names.

4. Recent Catholic sociological research indicates that about one half of Belgium's population may be considered practicing Catholics.

# 7 Organized Labor and the Bolivian National Revolution

by Robert J. Alexander

*Latin American Unionism: Early Development*

Frank Tannenbaum has argued that the organized labor movement is essentially a conservative influence in the United States and other highly industrialized countries. Whatever one may think of this idea insofar as the economically advanced nations are concerned, it is certainly not correct with regard to the trade-union movements of Latin America, and most particularly, that of Bolivia.

Organized labor is one of the revolutionary forces in the present Latin American scene. It is an integral part of the revolt against the traditional society which is the fundamental fact in Latin America today. It represents a new class, which is part of the modern sector of the economy of these countries, and it presses inevitably for fundamental alterations in the whole of Latin American society.

Organized labor came earlier in the process of economic development in Latin America than in the similar process in Great Britain or the United States. It appeared on the scene when the society of most of the Latin American countries was still largely dominated by a large landholding aristocracy, the heirs of the conquest of America by the people of the Iberian Peninsula. As a result of this fact, its struggle has been directed as much against this old aristocracy as against the employers for whom its members have worked.

Being on the scene early in the process of economic development, the Latin American trade-union movement has experienced a species of schizophrenia which was inherent in its situation. It has quite naturally sought to obtain a better deal for its members, but has also favored the expansion of the modern, and particularly the industrial, sector of the economy. This modern part of the economy can expand best when the returns to the worker are relatively low, and when profits are relatively high and are invested in the expansion of manufacturing and allied activities. We shall note the importance of this schizophrenia particularly in the Bolivian case since the Revolution began ten years ago.

Latin American organized labor shares with other elements in the community a marked spirit of nationalism. Indeed, nationalism has had a particularly significant role in the first phases of the growth of the trade-union movement of the area. Most of the earliest groups of organizable workers were employed by foreign enterprises—mines, railroads, public utilities, some of the early factories. As a result, the struggle of the workers against their employers took on the color of a nationalistic fight against the "foreign exploiters" of the nation. On this basis, the trade-unions were very frequently able to rally wide support among the general public which they certainly would not have enjoyed had they been facing national instead of foreign employers.

Many cases of the importance of this factor in the Latin American labor movement come to mind. One of the earliest was the general strike of banana workers employed by the United Fruit Company in Colombia in 1928, a walkout which won enthusiastic support and gleaned considerable financial assistance from the most diverse segments of the populace. In Chile, the nationalistic flag is run up regularly any time the copper miners have problems with either of the two United States-owned firms which dominate that industry. In the early 1940's Peron used nationalism as a powerful weapon in forcing the packing houses belonging to British and American interests to bargain with their organized employees for the first time.

There are various reasons for the early appearance of an organized labor movement in the Latin American countries. Fundamental, of course, is the fact that the industrialization of Latin America began and is taking place in a world in which organized labor already was an important factor in the societies of the world's most powerful and highly industrialized nations. The ideas of trade-unionism and of radical political activity associated with it in Europe and North

America were brought into Latin America from abroad. More often than not, European immigrants were the actual seed bearers of these ideas.

This process began very early, even before there was any appreciable degree of industrialization in Latin America. Thus, there were sections of the First International of Marx and Bakunin in Argentina, Uruguay, Brazil, Mexico, among others. Immigrants from Spain and Italy were largely responsible for the precociousness of the labor movements of Argentina, Uruguay, and Brazil before World War I. To the north, the influence of United States labor, and curiously enough, particularly the I.W.W., was very important in launching the trade-union movement of Mexico just before the outbreak of the Revolution there in 1910.

In its early phases, organized labor in Latin America was largely under the ideological influence of the Anarchosyndicalists, though the more or less Marxian Socialists also had a certain importance. This was the "heroic" period of Latin American trade-unionism, with a romantic belief in "direct action" of the crudest type dominating the thinking of the workers, and the most violent resistance being offered to the organized labor movement by both the employers and the governments of the area. General strikes, sabotage, massacres of workers, and even assassinations of police chiefs and other officials were more or less the order of the day in most of the countries.

*Latin American Unionism: Current Status*

However, during the last generation or a little more, Anarchosyndicalist influence has declined, and all but disappeared. This is due to two basic reasons, or so it seems. In the first place, the kind of extreme individualism which characterized the anarchists was much more appropriate to the artisans and the workshop industry which characterized the area before World War I. Factory industry, bringing together large numbers of workers under common discipline and with a common employer, began to dominate the scene after World War I.

A second reason for the decline of Anarchosyndicalist influence was the fact that the attitude of governments and of political parties towards the labor movement changed decisively during the last four or five decades. Instead of seeking to stamp out organized labor as "subversive," governments increasingly sought to protect and at the same time domesticate the trade-union movement. Likewise, there appeared on the scene a wide range of political parties which for reasons of ideology or mere political opportunism, began to speak on behalf of or even in the name of the organized workers.

As a result of these trends, Latin American organized labor now occupies a recognized position in the society of the various countries. Virtually every country has laws recognizing the legitimacy of the trade-unions and their aspirations. Some of the countries have intricate and extensive labor protective legislation and social security. And at the same time, the labor movements have become closely associated with—and very frequently dominated by—political parties and governments.

While gaining considerably in respectability during the last few decades, the organized labor movement has remained fundamentally a revolutionary force in Latin American society. It has become part of a wider movement for changing the fundamental structure of this society, to remove from their position of power the traditional landed aristocracy, to bring the great mass of the citizenry fully into the civic life of their respective countries, and to transform their nations into modern states with diversified and prosperous economies.

In one sense, at least, the trade-union movement is probably of greater importance than any other element in the revolutionary coalition. Organized labor represents the first institution to come onto the Latin American scene in 150 years which is capable of challenging the armed forces as the final arbiters of political affairs in these countries. Through the phenomenon of the general strike, the trade-unions are able to thwart attempts by the military to overthrow regimes of which the workers approve, or are able to oust governments of the armed forces of which the workers disapprove. Although the workers only have this power if they are well disciplined and well led, there is little doubt that the power is there. This has been of key importance in a number of the countries of the hemisphere since World War II.

*The Bolivian Case*

The Bolivian labor movement shares many of the features common to organized labor in Latin America as a whole. It has been a revolutionary force, has faced the problem of supporting capital accumulation while fighting for the material interests of its own members, has won support on a nationalistic basis, and has owed its early inception to outside influences. Finally, it has become intimately entwined with the political parties of the country, playing a key role in 1952 in ousting the oligarchical military regime then in power, and during the last ten years has played a key role in maintaining the revolutionary government in power.

The origins of the Bolivian organized labor movement date from before World War I. Argentine and Spanish Socialist and labor periodicals and pamphlets circulated in the country in the pre-1914 period, and were read by the artisans in La Paz and other cities. Likewise, the publications of the Argentine Anarchosyndicalist labor group, the Federación Obrera Regional Argentina were frequently read in Bolivia, and occasionally individuals affiliated with the FORA found their way to the high plateau and entered into personal contact with the Bolivian craftsmen.

However, until the Chaco War of 1932–35, the labor movement in Bolivia was confined largely to the artisan class in La Paz and a few other cities. Groups such as the railroad workers and the tin miners were little influenced by the beginnings of the labor movement. Such unions as existed in the major cities were largely Anarchosyndicalist in their political orientation. However, in the 1920's a more or less Communist influence also began to appear under the leadership of two colorful individuals. One of these was Gustavo Navarro, a former member of the Bolivian diplomatic corps who had acquired radical ideas in Europe, and began to write social tracts and novels of revolt under the name of Tristán Maroff. He acquired an almost legendary fame in these years as the incarnation of revolt—and from the point of view of the powers-that-were, of absolute evil. The other important figure who sought to sow Communist influence was Roberto Hinojosa, who as a student became local representative of the Tass News Agency, formed a small "fraternal" party of the Comintern, and later became an important figure in the regime of the early 1940's led by Major Gualberto Villarroel, alongside of whom he was finally strung up to a lamp post in July, 1946.

It was the Chaco War which finally paved the way for the Bolivian revolutionary movement and for the rise of organized labor to a position of power and prestige in the country. It severely shook the traditional society, lost it the support of the younger intellectuals of the middle and upper classes, and won the sympathy of these young men for the plight of the urban and rural masses of the country. At the same time, it shattered the utter parochialism of many of the members of the lower classes, who were dragged hundreds of miles down into the jungle to fight a hopeless war, and who, upon their return home, had a restlessness and a potential discontent which was a new factor in the country's political life.

The immediate post-Chaco War years were a period of confusion, politically speaking. Two military dominated regimes, those of Colonels Toro and Busch, claimed to be "Socialist" regimes. Both, for the first time in Bolivian history, adopted a friendly attitude towards the labor movement, and took the first hesitating steps towards changing the basic structure of Bolivian society. However, the ideological orientation of these regimes—which came to an end in the middle of 1939—was unclear and undefined.

During this same period there came into existence five political parties which were to be of great importance. One of these was the Partido Socialista Obrero Boliviano, organized by Tristán Maroff, which took the first steps in attempting to organize the tin miners during the government of President Germán Busch. The PSOB later became discredited and disappeared from the scene completely at the time of the 1952 Revolution.

The second party was the Partido Obrero Revolucionario. This is the Trotskyite party of Bolivia which was organized by exiles in Argentina soon after the Chaco War. It was to have a fleeting period of importance during the first months of the 1952 revolution.

The third party was the Partido de la Izquierda Revolucionaria, which claimed to be "independent Marxist" but contained within it those who after 1952 were to organize the Communist party of Bolivia. It was dominant in the labor movement outside of the mining centers throughout most of the 1940's, but as a result of its collaboration with the oligarchical regimes of 1946–52 it was completely discredited, and split into several fragments after the 1952 Revolution.

The fourth party was the Falange Socialista Boliviana, which was organized by exiles in Chile right after the Chaco War. It was frankly Fascist in its ideology, and was of relatively little importance until the 1952 Revolution. However, since then, it has been the principal center around which the opposition to the Revolution has rallied.

Finally, there was the Movimiento Nacionalista Revolucionario. It was organized by a group of young intellectuals, was frankly nationalistic in its outlook, was strongly anti-British and anti-United States in its inception. After 1942 it was able to make contact with the struggling movement of the tin miners, whose organizations it has dominated since that time. After participating in the regime of President Villarroel between 1943 and 1946, it was driven into the political wilderness during the succeeding six years, and only emerged in April, 1952 when it victoriously led the uprising which overthrew the then reigning military oligarchical regime. It has controlled Bolivia since that time.

Each of these parties, except the Falange, has reached out for influence among the organized workers. Each in turn was able to exercise considerable control over much of the trade-union movement. However, as we shall see, it was the MNR which, by leading the movement basically to transform Bolivian society, has become the dominant political force among the nation's trade-unionists.

In the years following the Chaco War, the organized labor movement of Bolivia began to spread beyond the craftsmen of La Paz and a handful of other cities. During the Busch regime of 1937–39, the first serious attempts were made, with the government's blessing, to organize the tin miners. This movement met reverses after the suicide of Busch in the middle of 1939, but became firmly rooted during the two and a half years of the Villarroel government from December, 1943 until July, 1946. Although the miners organizations were severely persecuted during the succeeding six years, they held together, and played a key role in the Revolution of April, 1952.

The railroad workers were also organized during the early 1940's, under the influence of the Partido de la Izquierda Revolucionaria. The PIR also succeeded in winning considerable influence among the artisans and in beginning the organization of the factory workers of La Paz. It brought together all of the labor groups under its control to form the Confederación Sindical de Trabajadores Bolivianos, or CSTB, which became the Bolivian affiliate of the Communist-dominated continental labor group, the CTAL. This was the principal central labor body of the country until the 1952 Revolution. The principal unions outside of it were those controlled by the MNR, and a small group of artisans and a larger group of organized peasants under the influence of the Anarchosyndicalists.

The government of President Gualberto Villarroel between 1943 and 1946 was kind of a first installment of the Revolution which was to take place after April, 1952. It rested on a coalition of young army officers, some of whom were of frankly pro-Nazi tendencies, and the MNR, which was not of this inclination. The importance of this period for the future was that it was marked by the firm organization of the tin miners, the complete assertion of MNR influence over them, and the fact that the regime took hesitating steps towards dealing with the two major headaches of the country: the question of the tin mines, and the integration of the Indians (who make up four-fifths of the population) to the civic life of the nation.

Villarroel was overthrown and killed by rioters in July, 1946. From then until April, 1952 two presidents and a military junta presided over an essentially oligarchic regime dedicated to the defense of the status quo. Profound changes took place in the political influences over the labor movement during this period. The PIR made the fatal error of supporting and even participating in the governments of this period, and since the workers generally looked upon these regimes as being reactionary, the PIR lost virtually all of its influence over the organized workers. As a result, leaders of the railroad workers, factory workers, and even the artisans of La Paz tended to gravitate towards the persecuted MNR. With the success of the MNR-led Revolution in April, 1952, virtually all of the labor leaders who had been affiliated with the PIR switched to the MNR, and the Partido de la Izquierda Revolucionaria disintegrated.

With the victory of the National Revolution in April, 1952, the MNR was dominant in the labor movement. It had the backing of the great majority of the members of the unions, and of most of the rank and file leaders. However, for a few months after the April uprising, the Trotskyite Partido Obrero Revolucionario was able to exert very considerable influence in the ranks of the labor movement.

The case of the meteoric rise and fall of the POR is an interesting one. The Trotskyites owed their influence in the labor movement completely to their close association with Juan Lechín, the MNR miners union leader who had become Executive Secretary of the Miners Federation in 1945, and remained the undisputed chief of the miners for a decade and a half after that.

Lechín was a man without any particular ideological or political training. He was more interested in the problems of organization and actual leadership of the miners than he was in questions of revolutionary theory. The Trotskyites, on the other hand, were experts at drawing up manifestos and statements of principles, after their own manner, and since they had thrown in their lot with the MNR during the Villarroel regime, Lechín was willing during the first years of his leadership of the miners to turn over the drafting of such documents to the members of the POR. The first result of this was the so-called Pulacayo Thesis, approved at the 1945 Congress of the Miners Federation as a statement of the basic principles of the Federation. It was a strictly Trotskyite document, framed in the turgid prose of which they are masters. To this day, Lechín has not been able to live down completely the "Communist" label which was originally fixed on him by his acceptance of the Pulacayo Thesis.

During the six years following the overthrow of the Villarroel regime, the Trotskyites in the Miners Federation, where they had a small but vociferous base, were loyal to Lechín, who remained one of the principal figures in the MNR. In elections of 1946 a Miners bloc was elected to Congress from the tin areas, consisting of Lechín and a Trotskyite as senators, and several MNR and POR members of the Chamber of Deputies. Among the latter was the POR's main ideologue, Guillermo Lora.

During this underground phase of activity, the Trotskyites were able to extend their influence from the Miners Federation to the La Paz factory workers and the White Collar Workers Union of La Paz. After April, 1952 these were their principal bases in the trade-union movement.

One of the first acts of the labor leaders after the April, 1952 Revolution was to organize a new central labor organization, known as the Central Obrera Boliviana. For a couple years this was a rather ad hoc organization, with an executive committee, consisting of delegates from labor groups in various parts of the country. Those union groups outside of La Paz normally named some labor leader in the capital to represent them on the committee, since they were unable to have anyone stationed there permanently to attend the rather frequent meetings of the COB Executive.

It was through this delegate system that the Trotskyites were in the first months of the Revolution able to more or less dominate the COB. Juan Lechín, who was Minister of Mines and Petroleum in the revolutionary government, and other leading MNR trade-unionists were generally too busy with their activities in the government and with reorganizing their own trade-unions to be bothered about collecting representations from provincial union groups. As a result, not infrequently during the early months of the Revolution the Trotskyites, though having only a small minority of the labor movement under their actual control, were able to outvote the MNR delegates to the COB Executive.

A showdown finally came in October, 1952, when the POR pushed through a resolution in the COB denouncing the government's proposed plans for nationalizing the tin mines. The Trotskyites demanded confiscation rather than expropriation and payment for the mines. A few days after they got the COB to adopt their resolution on this subject, Lechín and his associates brought about the replacement of most of the delegated representatives of provincial labor groups, thus taking the control of the COB which was really their right. From that time on the Trotskyite influence in organized labor began to decline.

The position of the POR political leaders was that the MNR president Victor Paz Estenssoro was the Kerensky of the Bolivian Revolution, and that they were the Bolsheviks, who inevitably were going to inherit the Revolution. They thus engaged in an almost childish and exceedingly mechanical interpretation of the Bolivian phenomenon in terms of what occurred in Russia in 1917.

About a year and a half after their defeat in the COB, the Trotskyite trade-union leaders decided that they had had enough of the doctrinaire attitudes of Guillermo Lora and his friends. As a result, they abandoned the POR en masse, and joined the MNR. Several of them were chosen as MNR members of Congress in the 1956 elections. With their desertion of the POR, that party disappeared as a really significant element in Bolivian politics. It is today split into two bitter rival factions, neither of which has any real influence on events.

*Changing Role of Organized Labor in the Revolution*

For six years following the liquidation of the Trotskyites in the labor movement in 1954, the MNR was absolutely dominant in the ranks of organized labor. Only in the last couple years has there begun to emerge a more or less serious challenge to the MNR, this time from the Communist party. Meanwhile, however, the role of organized labor in the revolutionary regime has been slowly but profoundly changing.

During the first five years or more of the MNR government, the labor movement held a virtually dominant position. Officially, the revolutionary regime was a "co-government" of the MNR party and the Central Obrera Boliviana. The COB regularly was given four ministers in the cabinet, whom it was entitled to select itself. The Central Obrera constituted the Left Wing of the MNR, and it considered itself more or less the watchdog of the purity of the Revolution.

At the same time, the economy was largely dominated by the labor movement. A system of workers representation in management was established in the government Mining Corporation. Labor discipline in the mines was at a very low ebb, and the tenure of any superintendent or manager depended upon his keeping in the good graces of the local union leaders. Even in private industry, the union leaders often brought about the dismissal of supervisory personnel.

However, this situation began to change in 1957. By that time the union leaders as a group had begun to become discredited, since it was widely believed, whether true or not, that many of them had used their powerful positions to become personally wealthy. Furthermore, the attempts of Juan Lechín and his immediate supporters, in alliance with the former Trotskyite trade-union leaders now in the MNR, to thwart President Hernán Siles attempt to bridle the fantastic inflation which the government was then suffering found little response among the workers. In a frank showdown between Lechín and Siles in the middle of 1957, the president succeeded in winning over even Lechín's miners to his point of view.

At that point, the hitherto solid trade-union bloc within the MNR split. It largely divided along pre-revolutionary lines, with the ex-PIR trade-union leaders backing Siles, and the ex-POR laborites supporting Lechín. For some time, the COB was split in two, and it appeared as if this division would reamin permanent.

President Siles failed to follow through on the advantage he had gained over Lechín. Siles did not try to bring about a reorganization of both the Miners Federation and the COB. There is little doubt in our mind that he could have done this in 1957, but for his own reasons he apparently preferred not to attempt such a task.

However, although Lechín remained the top man in both the Miners Federation and the COB, and although the threatened split of the COB into two separate organizations failed to materialize, the division which had been opened in the ranks of labor in the 1957 fight remained. It exists to this day. Witness was borne to this fact by Juan Lechín's support of a rival slate to the dominant group of ex-PIRistas who have controlled the Railroad Workers Federation since the Revolution, in elections earlier in 1962.

There is little doubt that this split in the ranks of the labor movement has served to weaken the influence of the urban labor movement in the revolutionary regime. This was shown during the celebration of the 10th Anniversary of the Revolution in April 1962, at which time there was absolutely no discussion of the policy of "co-government." The regime stood forth quite simply as the government of the Movimiento Nacionalista Revolucionario.

There is another factor more important than its internal splits, which has reduced the importance of the organized urban labor movement in the revolutionary government of Bolivia. This is the growing influence of the peasantry.

During the first years of the Revolution the tenure in office of the government depended largely on the armed militia of the miners and the factory workers, the people who had won the three-day battle against the Bolivian Army which had installed the revolutionary regime in power in April, 1952. However, one of the first acts of the Paz Estenssoro regime had been to organize the peasantry into rural unions, into local units of the MNR, and into militia groups. Arms were distributed to these militia.

During the last ten years the most fundamental part of the government's program has been the distribution of land among the peasants. Although this process is far from completed, every peasant family in Bolivia today possesses its own little bit of land. In addition, the government has given the Indian and illiterate peasants the vote, and has made valiant efforts to extend medical services and education to them.

The upshot of all of this is that the peasants are strong supporters of the regime. They are relatively little influenced by the factional fights within the MNR, and tend to support whoever is in the presidential palace, as the leader and representative of the regime which has given them the land and has made them citizens of the republic.

This shift in power is clear from voting patterns in the elections which have been held since 1956. These make it clear that the MNR has lost most of the middle-class support which it had before 1952, and that there is some disaffection also among the urban workers. However, each election has seen an overpowering support for the MNR among the peasants. They vote for the party which they feel has been their benefactor.

Perhaps even more important is the fact that if necessary, the peasants in all probability would also fight militarily for the MNR regime. Were the Left Wing opponents of Paz Estenssoro both inside and outside of the MNR to try to oust the president, there is little doubt that the reaction of the peasants would be immediate and overpowering. It would also in all likelihood be horrendous, unleashing a race war which would be extremely ugly. It is doubtful if the average peasant militia man, who doesn't even speak Spanish, would be able to distinguish between those whites or near whites who had been on "his side" and those who had been against "his" president.

There is one other key piece of evidence indicating the shift of power within the Bolivian revolutionary regime away from the urban workers. This is the relative ease with which the government of Paz Estenssoro has been able to carry out the reorganization of the mining industry. Soon after returning to office in 1960, he entered into the so-called Operacion Triangular, whereby the United States, West Germany and the InterAmerican Bank provide funds for the re-equipment of existing mines and exploration for new ones, in return for which the Bolivian government agreed to seek to re-establish labor discipline in the mines and would cut down the excess number of workers employed in them.

Although the miners at first resisted the government's attempts to rationalize their industry, Paz Estenssoro won a showdown battle with the leaders of the Mine Workers Federation. Since that time, the labor force in the mines has been reduced by almost 25%, while production has started to increase for the first time in more than a decade.

*Labor and the Future of the Bolivian Revolution*

In spite of the shift of power away from the labor movement, it remains a factor of great importance in the Bolivian Revolution. It is possible that its principal leader, Juan Lechín, will be the next president of Bolivia. As this is being written, he seems to be the "natural" candidate, although there is a possibility President Paz Estenssoro may run for relection himself. Although a year must pass before the 1964 election, there is at least a distinct possibility that the titular head of the labor movement will become also titular head of the Revolution.

However, it is dubious whether the ascension of Juan Lechín would alter very fundamentally the position of the labor movement in the Bolivian National Revolution. For the sake of the Revolution itself, emphasis must now be placed on economic development instead of further reforms; and there is little that Lechín could do, even if he wanted to do something, to shift the basic balance of power between the urban labor movement and the peasantry.

Indeed, the advent of Lechín to the presidency might well be disadvantageous to the organized labor movement. This is because the great question facing Bolivian organized labor is whether or not it is to continue as a really independent force, in both the economic and political life of the country, or whether it will follow the path of the Mexican labor movement, and become largely subordinate to the revolutionary government.

The Mexican and Bolivian revolutions have much in common, though they also have important differences, particularly in the labor field. They are both essentially peasant revolutions, designed to bring the rural masses into full participation in the economic, social and political life of their respective countries. They have both had the agrarian reform as the keystone of their policy. They have both undergone a period of destruction of old institutions, followed by the building of new ones and a growing emphasis on economic development as the third phase of the revolution.

However, there are also important differences. Bolivia has not had to undergo a long civil war as did Mexico. The Bolivian Revolution has been led from the beginning by a well-organized political party with an ideology of its own, which has known more or less where it wanted to take the Revolution.

Finally, the Bolivian Revolution has depended, at least in its earlier phase, on the labor movement to a degree which was not so in Mexico. The relative backwardness of the Bolivian Indians and their inability to assume the leadership of the Revolution for some time to come also differentiates the two revolutions.

Because of these factors, the Bolivian labor movement is in an essentially stronger position than was that of Mexico, which, furthermore, was virtually born during the revolution itself. However, one can ask the question of whether or not the ascension of Juan Lechín, the country's principal labor leader, to the presidency of the revolutionary regime might not weaken the power of the organized labor movement to resist absorption by the party and the government. Since it is unlikely that Lechín can or will want to alter the fundamental direction and policies of the revolutionary government, he may well be in a better position than an outsider to get the labor movement to conform more closely and with less resistance to these policies.

# 8

## Japanese Trade-Unionism as a Model in Economic Development

by Solomon B. Levine

I shall attempt to answer four major questions about the contemporary Japanese labor movement:

1. What are the major structural and functional characteristics of Japan's trade-unions?
2. What factors may explain the characteristics?
3. In what ways do they provide a distinctive model of trade-unionism?
4. Are these factors likely to be replicated elsewhere?

My responses obviously will be of a gross nature, subject to exceptions and qualifications which I shall omit. However, let me summarize my observations as follows: The main features of the contemporary labor movement in Japan (now 8.5 million members strong)—despite a dynamic political, economic, and social setting—have congealed. It is a movement which heavily emphasizes both political and economic activity and is likely to continue to do so for some time to come, although the politico-economic mix is apt to undergo shifts. Further, the two emphases are more complementary than conflictual, although conflict within the movement is marked. Finally, this type of complementary relationship is a product of a type of industrial development and social structure that has a high chance of approximation in other newly emerging nations.

### The "Dual" Movement

It is frequently observed that organized labor in Japan comprises two separate movements: One political, the other economic, with little organic connection between the two. The evidence of separation is as follows: When organizing began 15 years ago, it took place at two levels, national and local, but with little coordination between the two. The national movement mainly stressed political objectives and attemped to organize from the top down. The local level was concerned mainly with immediate income security for its members and did not ascend very far above the grass roots. The two drives did not fully join forces. National organizations cannot count heavily on local support. Local units are weakly affiliated among themselves.

The "dual" movement, however, has permitted both economic and political expression, without undue conflict between the two, although there has been some. The major conflicts have been at the political level. National centers were set-up for political purposes, primarily to impress upon the Japanese, especially wage workers, the need to structure a new Japan. With occupation encouragement from the beginning they have been major platforms for ideological exorcism. A wide range of ideological positions, long suppressed in Imperial Japan, could now find ready expression: communism, the various brands of socialism, anarchism, syndicalism, even capitalism.

Two main ideological poles rapidly emerged at the national level: gradualistic socialism stressed by *Sodomei* (now a part of *Zenro Kaigi*), and communism by *Sanbetsu* (now defunct). Ten years of severe ideological competition at this level of the labor movement followed the surrender. Major federations formed, broke up, reformed, each striving with the other to bring under its wing large blocs of uncommitted trade-unionsts at the local level. Even then, until today, almost half of the organized workers have remained neutral, or so divided among themselves as to be unable to commit themselves one way or the other.

Today, the two principal competitors are *Sohyo*, which as the larger (about 4 million members) presents a spectrum of Marxist and non-Marxist Socialist positions, and *Zenro Kaigi*, the smaller (more than one million members), devoted to a type of Fabianism. Their political party affiliations reflect the differences, of course. In the ideological struggle, communism has lost considerable ground, driven from its earlier influential position by the occupation, the government, management, and the trade-union movement itself. Ideological differences between the two major national centers are probably exaggerated. Both the main streams of *Sohyo* and *Zenro* are devoted to the principle of parliamentary socialism and to the separation of trade-unions from political party organizations; they split on details of policy such as the peace treaty, degree of rearmament, type of neutralism, and on strategy and tactics. The differences, of course, are exacerbated by the competition to gain adherents, especially among the unaffiliated part of the movement. However, the basic notion of providing industrial workers with opportunities for political expression remains. The problem has been how to reach down and convince the rank and filer that his interests can be advanced through vigorous political action of both a party and non-party nature.

*National Unions*

To achieve rank and file support, the chief device has been the national industrial union organization. These organs are primarily creations of the national centers, although there are a few notable cases, such as the Seamen, which had been a thriving prewar union, where the national organization was built up from the grass roots. Almost half of the national unions have affiliated with *Sohyo*, a handful with *Zenro* (some through *Sodomei*); but more than a third have thus far joined and quit or remained "neutral." (A few small ones also belong to a third minor national center, *Shinsanbetsu*.) Today there are about 100 such structures, whose purpose is to strengthen the workers' industrial identification with the national center and coordinate industry-wide struggles that will fulfill political aims. Industrial unionism is seen as the tool for stimulating "class consciousness," rather than the instrument for effective collective bargaining.

These national unions are not strictly industrial, just as in the American case, but are rough catch basins for like-situated workers. Government and private industries are separated— for example, the private and public railways. (The law, of course, has influenced this division.) In many cases industrial jurisdictions are blurred, as in the case of textiles and synthetic chemicals. Pure industrial unionism is fairly rare, indicating how the national centers have catered to interests other than product, occupational, or technological commonality.

There are also attempts to coordinate common industrial groupings through joint councils of various types. But they are not powerful agencies as a rule.

The split at the national center level, of course, is reflected in rival unionism at the national union level. *Sohyo* has been successful at preempting most of the government workers unions (which comprise about one-third of the total of organized labor and about one-half or more of *Sohyo's* membership); *Zenro* has confined itself almost entirely to private industry; and until recently disclaimed any great interest in organizing the government sector. This division, of course, has meant differing emphases on political action between the two. Rival unionism abounds in private industry: coal mining, metal mining, chemicals, textiles, electric power, and so forth. Still other neutral national unions exist in these various fields, so that in a given industry there may be three or four separate national organizations, hedged around further by numerous unaffiliated local units.

The national union serves little more than the political purposes of the national federation or center, and has as its primary function the drumming up of support for the national federation's political objectives. This is revealed by the almost complete absence of the national union from the bargaining table. While the national unions serve as debating forums for constituent local level units, they rarely enter negotiations and have virtually no authority to approve contracts, or to withhold strike funds. They also can exercise little discipline over dissident factions, possess small funds, and provide limited research, educational and legal services. There are notable exceptions, such as the *Seamen* and the *Zenro* textile workers (and at one time in coal mining and electric power) whose very success illuminates the general situation. The chief aim of the national unions is to gain the support of the basic union entities, the enterprise unions.

*Enterprise Unionism: Extent of Organization*

Enterprise-wide unionism is the hallmark of the Japanese labor movement. From the outset, enterprise unionism spread like wildfire, and today there are perhaps 20,000 of these units in Japan. (When broken down into their local branches, there are nearly 40,000 basic unit organizations.) Their structure is relatively simple. It follows the lines of managerial control.

Organizing success came immediately. Most were organized within a couple of years following the surrender. In response to the occupation's open encouragement, workers rushed to join; and the enterprise was easily the most convenient organizational base—for reasons I will indicate shortly. Within a short period, virtually all major enterprises in the modern sectors of both public and private industry were thus fully unionized. This is one reason why since about 1950 the rate of unionization has declined somewhat (about 35% today); for as the industrial labor force expanded, the only areas left for organization have been the small and medium-size enterprises, many of which are family affairs without modern production facilities.

Other types of basic union structure have been very limited. Craft or occupational unionism, despite some successful but limited prewar experience, never took hold—indicating the absence of "job consciousness" that we identify with American or British wage earners. Also, as already indicated, industrial unionism has been established only in the formal organization sense; while general unionism has made headway only on a personal and regional basis. Perhaps as many as 90% of all union units are enterprise-wide structures, with as large a percentage of the total union membership.

*Characteristics of Enterprise Unions*

What are the characteristics of the enterprise union?

1. They are self-contained organizations, with weak "outside" alliances and a strong "inward" focus. As such, they tend to resemble the Perlmanian prescription of "job con-

scious" unionism, except that the consciousness—"enterprise consciousness"—is as an entity toward a group of jobs specific to a particular enterprise.

2. The membership is usually "combined," in the sense that everyone who is a permanent employee of the enterprise is a member of the union. This includes both white collar and blue collar. Once permanent status has been gained—and this is determined essentially by management's judgment as to what will constitute the enduring core of the work force—membership in the union is fairly automatic.

3. Temporary workers are not likely to be members of the enterprise union, although they may form their own union. There have been drives to include them in the main unions on various occasions, but so far these have not been widespread, such employees may make up as much as one-fourth of an enterprise's work force and perform jobs identical to those of permanent workers. They are not covered by the enterprise union's collective bargaining agreement and, therefore, are excluded from many of the benefits, and usually receive lower wage rates.

4. It is the enterprise union that bargains with management. Only in a few instances are "outsiders" permitted to participate in the negotiations. Furthermore, where there is a multi-plant unit (which is common among major enterprises), bargaining is carried on at the top, with little delegation of the function to local "branches."

5. Collective bargaining is confined to a small group of select issues, which usually revolve around the traditional wage system with its characteristics of monthly remuneration, base pay and supplements (largely related to length-of-service, but somewhat to educational level and family status), and periodic wage changes (especially seasonal bonuses). Because of the numerous wage components, rounds of negotiations are often endless. Although "equal wages for equal work" has become an important slogan for the trade-union movement, in actuality the traditional wage system has been untouched. Another omission from collective bargaining is the lack of use of the grievance procedure. Individual grievances are not catered to as they are considered disruptive to the main area

of bargaining; and, in fact, given the concern with the enterprise entity as a whole, individuals are not particularly bent on pursuing their own specific complaints.

6. The enterprise union has a fragile militancy. It blows hot and cold. It is torn by diverse interests (such as white *vs.* blue-collar, old *vs.* young). The Japanese themselves describe it as "flip-flop" or schizophrenic unionism. When issues do well-up, the unit can be easily mobilized and there is intense widespread support for the union leadership in its demands. Once settled, the situation returns to quiescence, the degree of apathy appears mockingly high, and management co-optation again sets in.

*Functional Complementarity*

Existence of enterprise unionism corrects any impression that the Japanese trade-union movement is almost wholly political. This is not the case. In fact, I would contend that as the years have gone by, politicalism has declined and economic orientation increased. There are several indications of this. One, the basic units—the enterprise-wide unions— have primarily focused on dealing with the employer in behalf of their own memberships. Collective bargaining has become wider spread; and, as Japan's economy has recovered and gone on to record-breaking heights, there has been increasing latitude for bargaining over wages and working conditions. Also, as experience in collective bargaining has accumulated, bargaining skills have sharpened; planning and information techniques have improved; issues have become more sharply defined. Quasi-public labor relations commissions have been of help in this regard. A whole new generation of labor leaders at these local levels has emerged in the last dozen years, experienced for the first time with collective bargaining.

Second, the national leadership has veered gradually from a major, almost sole, emphasis on political action. Well-publicized events like the "riots" of June, 1960 camouflage these developments. The national leadership realizes that revolutionary strategy has little appeal for the rank and file, that communism is weak (despite the student movement), and that the day of Socialist government is still far off. Also, they have become disillusioned with the Japanese political tendency—especially on the Left—to split into increasing numbers of factions. The ideological and political differences —minute though they may seem—generate such intense factionalism that unity is often fragmented over narrow political issues.

Political emphasis, however, still takes precedence at this level because the national unions have been shut out from economic leadership by the enterprise unions. The latter, in fact, still expect that if the national leadership is to play any role at all, it will be largely political. But, as the Japanese economy undergoes expansion and change, as automation, for example, breaks down traditional labor market arrangements, and as the industrial structure is transformed, the enterprise unions are likely to look for increasing guidance in their economic functions.

Thus, I reach the conclusions that the Japanese movement is not "dual" in the sense that the national leaders are always operating at cross purposes with the enterprise unions. Instead, organized labor in Japan has made room for both political and economic action rather than one or the other. The enterprise form of organization was perhaps the most efficacious base upon which to wrest advances at the work level. This could not have been effectively achieved through national organizations, for each enterprise unit possessed its own special characteristics of work and job hierarchy, not likely to be duplicated in any other enterprise. National organizations could not acquire the expertise necessary to carry on the parochial bargaining needed under such a system.

On the other hand, given their inward orientation, little could be expected of the enterprise unit to carry on the mass political activity needed to make any major onslaught on the underlying set of political, social, and economic relationships that grips Japan. It is the national units which serve the function of expressing the political aspirations of Japanese workmen. Attempts to transfer this function to the enterprise level have met with spectacular and abject failures. Enterprise unions often split into two when ideological and political issues become paramount.

Despite the limitations at each level taken alone, the separate functions converge together. With enterprise unions pressuring employees to live up to their traditional responsibilities and with the national organizations appealing to the need for a new egalitarianism, the two, when applied simultaneously, strongly challenge managerial policy makers. Thus, mass demonstrations and short walkouts occur frequently on this complementary basis. The problem is how to sustain the challenge in the face of restrictive political, economic, and social conditions, rather than to change it into a wholly political or economic drive.

*Underlying Factors: Political, Economic, Social*

As we well know, only foreign intervention—a war and military occupation—threw off Japan's tightly centralized political control that had patterned the large part of her economic development, her educational system, and her overriding nationalistic ideology. Historically, the Japanese political system was dominated by a set of ruling cliques— the *zaibatsu* industrialists, the military, the government bureaucrats, and the landlords. A political party system that grew up after the Meiji Restoration primarily reflected the jockeying of these narrow groups for power. Until the militarists gained overriding ascendancy in the 1930's, the political system was a delicate balancing of these elite groups, unified by a strong ultranationalistic drive and capped by the Emperor System—a device conveniently manufactured to legitimize the role of these four major political groupings in dominating the nation and warding off Western infiltration. Each in essence was a separate barony that built its own bureaucratic structure to retain allegiance of its members and to enhance its own survival. There was no room in this scheme either for a labor movement or even a substantial middle class of merchants, artisans, farmers, etc.

War, of course, brought the entire structure tumbling down. The problem for the Occupation was how to pick up the pieces and make room for new competing groups of a much more democratic combination. The military was effectively destroyed; the landlords were shunted out of the way by an effective land reform. However, less of an impact was made upon the industrialists, and almost none upon the governmental bureaucracy—they remained symbols of the old order.

In calling for a new political system that would bring forth wide democratic participation, the occupation urged every group, other than the ultranationalists, to make a claim upon the citizen's attention. Thus, the floodgates were opened wide for a variety of ideological appeals, and special efforts were made to offer a party structure that could accommodate these appeals. Both the Socialist parties (as well as the Communists between 1945 and 1949) and the labor movement became major vehicles for voicing protest against the previously established order in this feverish attempt to prevent the old forces from re-emerging. There were really no other channels available for this purpose. This meant that there would be a close alliance between the parties of the Left and the trade-unions, although at the same time they would be open to many competing ideas and programs that would prove divisive especially in the atmosphere of the Cold War. This protest, incidentally, had been the very function of the prewar labor movement, so that occupation policy merely continued with gusto this trade-union role.

Trade-unions have provided the most convenient locale for carrying on the drive. The Left political parties are still embryonic and weakly organized at the grass roots level, while the readily organized unions furnished immediate forums for discussion and competition and thus became the mainstay support for these parties. Moreover, it is at the modern workplace that the most serious challenges to the traditional system of human relationships may be made. Here, the Japanese industrial worker is most beset by the tug-of-war between the old order and the new and thus is responsive to proposals at the political level which would attempt to relieve the tensions that have resulted.

Still another reason why unions have become a political

locale is the role of the two major intellectual groups that greatly overlap: the government employees and the white-collar workers. As for the first group, the labor laws are structured so as to impell political action. Fairly centralized government, concerned with tight control over a presumably free enterprise economy, also invites this emphasis. Here, moreover, because of slow acting governmental budgetary processes, are the groups which are most likely to feel aggrieved at falling behind in their economic status. Moreover, they are easily organized into large units, for the government ministry or bureau also takes on the entity concept identified with private enterprise.

As for the second, we should note that white-collar workers provided much of the leadership in establishing the present system of organization. While, more recently, their leadership has tended to be replaced by production workers, nonetheless their influence has remained strong. In the drive to rescue enterprises from the wartime disaster, the white-collar employees took the lead as it was readily recognized that they possessed the knowledge of enterprise operations and had access to the most vital information. Also, many were intellectually trained and were particularly receptive to ideological and political action. Finally, they felt the sting of status loss as management prestige crumbled and incomes were reduced by inflation.

However, although these factors make for a vociferously political labor movement, it is not yet necessarily a successful political force. The Socialist parties have failed to make any appreciable gains among the voters for almost ten years, and their prospects for improvement do not seem too bright, even at this moment. Japan's rising living standards aided by success in expanding world markets still are identified with the Conservatives. The sense of economic desperation has declined under Conservative rule. The Socialists, divided among themselves, have not put forth a program that has caught the voters' imagination, but rather have dwelt on negative slogans of anti-rearmament, anti-peace treaty, anti-military bases, anti-West, anti-police, teacher law revision, and anti-labor law amendments. Their positive programs are vague, although calling for nationalization, a shift from heavy to consumption industry, and expansion of social security and state welfare services. The Conservatives have whittled away Socialist offerings by co-opting many of their programs, especially in the welfare field, leading the latter to take a position as distinctly opposite as possible.

However, for the trade-unions to give up their political emphasis may be tantamount to committing institutional suicide. The political strand accomplishes several things: (1) it keeps alive a national movement, (2) it makes the conservative government and party responsive to wage earner problems and demands for autonomy, (3) it pressures management into maintaining responsibilities toward workers, (4) it keeps awake rank and file consciousness of the importance of the state in Japanese economic and social affairs, (5) it represents one of the only ways in which frontal attack can be made against the traditional, quasi-feudal, quasi-bureaucratic mode of Japanese life. Moreover, without this activity—however divorced it may get from the grass roots—what economic action there is is likely to be feeble and hemmed in.

On economic grounds, one cannot expect the Japanese labor movement for some time to become highly cohesive. The history of Japanese economic development has seen to this. If political appeal has given some hope for unity to the movement, economic factors have worked in the opposite direction, but allow the movement to be widespread. As I have indicated, enterprise unionism in Japan has been largely a product of the structure of industry and the structure of labor markets. The dual economy of Japan has meant a huge proliferation of very small industrial enterprises, numbering about 3 or 4 million, alongside a handful of highly complex, huge modern establishments (less than 1,800 with more than 500 employees each). In the background is a large set of farms, relatively tiny, about 6 million in number, manned largely on an individual family basis.

Modern Japanese industrialization was a jerry-built, highly dovetailed development. Capital has always been extremely scarce, and only a high rate of internal savings (formerly coupled with overseas conquest) and successful trade balances provided the basis for industrial expansion. They still do. More recently, of course, American aid has provided the margin for this.

Modern industrial plants were built on top of an agrarian economy, with each enterprise entity coming to play a distinctive role for economic development. Its organization and management was placed largely in the hands of the elite *zaibatsu* enclaves, each of which devised its own subeconomy that cut across a variety of industrial, commercial, and financial activities. For each, a specialized labor force was developed, limited, as was discovered during the war, in its versatility and transferability from one enterprise to another even within a given *zaibatsu* enclave. These workers, of course, were also an elite, privileged to serve as the spearheads of industrialization, at centers where scarce capital was concentrated and where Japan's need for a deflationary economy was precariously balanced.

Industrialization spurred on rapid population growth, the population doubling between 1870 and 1940, and adding almost one-third more since the end of the war. The expanding urban centers became great outlets for the surplus population of the rural areas. Both the emergence of large-scale heavy industry and the burgeoning of urban population meant that markets and materials were available for the growth of small and medium enterprises. These, as I have indicated, grew enormously, serving to absorb perhaps as much as one-half of the labor force (over 42 million today). They were tiny, also manned mainly on a family basis. Their functions were to supply local needs, to share somewhat in meeting overseas demands, and, perhaps, as importantly to serve as subcontractors for major industry as buffers for risky ventures. (Small enterprises have been especially vulnerable to the business cycle.) The status of the workers in these sectors, even if we can call them wage earners, has always contrasted greatly with those in the major industries. But they influenced the pattern of work relationships everywhere by emphasizing the family pattern of organization and averting any growth of class consciousness.

The nature of internal Japanese industrial enterprise or-

197

ganization also had much to do with the type of trade-unions that eventually emerged. At first early Japanese firms suffered a shortage of managerial personnel, so that, as one Japanese observer has pointed out, it was "common practice among employers to relegate the function of worker supervision and control to skilled craftsmen." These master workmen took over the recruitment of workers, payment of wages, supervision of work, and they themselves worked alongside their retainers; but they did not become a nucleus of a strategically important trade-union movement.

Rather, beginning around World War I what might otherwise have been a rough repetition of American experience was thrust aside. Craft or sectional unionism was unable to take hold as it had done so over a long gestation period in the U. S. Instead, Japanese employers, who formerly had had little direct involvement in labor relations, now undertook to challenge the "labor bosses" in their authority and control over labor supplies, supervision, training, and attainment of status within the work force. It was around this time that so-called Japanese paternalism took firm hold, as management themselves assumed direct responsibility for committing workers to their own particularized enterprises. This change evolved wth considerable struggle and protest on the part of the labor bosses, but they were eliminated and driven into the traditional and less modern industrial activity. They were supplanted by an industrial relations system that compartmentalized the labor market, restricted the committed industrial worker to his enterprise, built up a wage structure and a set of wage components that straightjacketed workers to narrow career pursuits, capitalized upon traditional seniority concepts deeply embedded in other Japanese social structures. The contrast with the American experience was that in the U. S. the "autonomous worker," to use Soffer's term, remained autonomous and became the mechanism for forcing the labor markets to remain open and intersectional; in Japan he was early converted to the "organizational man."

The two major economic characteristics—the industrial structure (with its concomitant technology and skill demands) and the labor market structures—patterned the allocation of the work force into tightly compartmentalized entities. The worker was bound to his particular enterprise. Through the enterprise he became integrated into the general Japanese society. Once he had made his entry as an accepted worker, he was fixed for his career, acquired all his training and skill there, and became fully identified with the firm to which he had become permanently attached. All rewards were geared, moreover, to this system. Wage earners worked their way up a career ladder within a given group. With seniority came periodic wage and benefit increases. With retirement came company financed maintenance. The typical wage scale was spread widely, with a tenfold increase to be achieved over a career. If a worker quit or for some henious offense was discharged, he would not be taken on anywhere else in major industry. In return, the permanent worker was permanent: no layoffs. There grew a fierce demarcation of managerial from non-managerial personnel. They were separate in terms of education and often background. There was almost no possibility of interchanging status, in either direction. All this was fortified in the period of the thirties and the war years, when the military took over control from the *zaibatsu*, crushed out of existence what unionism existed, and sponsored the wartime patriotic worker fronts—interestingly, organized almost on the same structural basis that the Japanese unions have today.

The occupation made relatively little impact upon this system. Once GHQ policy shifted back to rehabilitation, the original economic structure re-emerged and has continued to remain pronounced. The only major differences were some of the legal forms: most tenants gained title to their land, the *zaibatsu* enclaves were formally broken up, the military lost all control over production. Although their product mix has changed with shifts in world markets, very few important new enterprises have arisen to take over these markets. The old firms expanded. While new technologies were adopted, again it was mainly the old major enterprises that modernized and revamped. The problem was and is how to utilize the given structure to optimize the flow of imports and exports through Japan's economic sieve.

Thus, in the postwar period, there came into being a trade-union movement without any significant collective bargaining experience, yet with a structure that could overwhelm the employers, which at one point it almost did. Actually, it was the only way to organize, for the whole system of specialized economic entities was on the verge of collapse, and each enterprise-attached group came to the rescue of its own enterprise in order to fortify it against enormous vicissitudes and uncertainty. The local unions were founded to assure enterprise stability and insofar as the union leaders had a quarrel with traditional management on this score made it appear that labor unionism was the same old variety of British and American trade-unionism protesting against the harsh treatment that workers receive in industrialization. But that was only a minor part. Japanese union organization was the means for providing leadership in the operation of the given industrial apparatus at a time when the traditional leadership was eliminated and humiliated. Whereas American unions had always attempted to co-opt some portions of the managerial function in order to survive and be viable, Japanese management now had to co-opt unionism in order to assure its own survival. Thus, there were many concessions made—and many "excesses" committed in the early postwar years.

In sum, economic reasons stressed the entrenchment of the permanent industrial worker. These workers formed tight enclaves within the enterprise enclaves themselves. This was independent trade-union action, but it was *limited* or *confined* economic trade-unionism.

Sociological factors also strengthen the tight compartmentalization of the Japanese trade-union movement. Perhaps the most marked characteristic of Japanese social relations in contrast to the West is the historical absence of individualism—a word which has long been regarded as sin by many Japanese. The lack of individualistic tradition almost meant the lack of the concept of contract as we know it in the West, with obvious implications for the employment relationship. The bureaucratic collectivity has remained the major feature of Japanese social organization with a history of hundreds of years derived from the agricultural system and feudalistic political divisions. A major collectivity has been the "house," or extended family, in which the individual is submerged and performs a function only as related to the prosperity and survival of the house. Religion, marriage, child-rearing, and adoption practices fully illustrate this point. Loyalty and subservience are readily carried over to other units of social organization. Essentially, as Y. S. Matsumoto point out, what has developed in postwar Japan, despite attempts to foster individualistic democracy, has been the transformation of the social structure from one set of collectivities to another.

Such an underlying social-psychology means that attachment to industrial enterprise follows the time-honored family form. Efforts to recruit permanent workers into industrial work stressed the security afforded by the kinship entity. Workers of like background were sought out as members. Commonality of aspirations and goals also meant that personal leadership would receive heavy stress, rather than representative or elective leadership. Thus, for example in the case of the trade-unions, it is often observed that leadersip is highly personal and charismatic. In turn, the members are seen either as blind followers or apathetic. Tenaciousness of collectivity orientations also is reflected in the reward system, with its emphasis on age and length of service within the given enterprise.

Identification with a given collectivity makes it extremely difficult to achieve identification with any other group, occupational, political, or ideological. It is all-inclusive. This means, for example, that workers gave little thought to job opportunities outside the enterprise with which they establish connections—whether they are permanent or temporary workers. It also means that workers are not likely to pay continuing attention to outside organizations that appeal for their support, and that ideological movements among workers are not likely to be long-lasting. These characteristics profoundly shape the type of trade-unionism that has emerged. If the family is declining as the key social unit, the work group and enterprise has been taking its place. There is a minimum of individual aspiration and achievement and a maximum of group aspiration and achievement. Thus, the union promotes security within a given status structure; it does not seriously challenge the structure itself. It does not deal with the relationship of one occupation to another. From this point of view, craft unionism is as revolutionary as industrial unionism.

On the other hand, the strength of collectivities is so great that enterprise unions in most cases are sure of rank and file support when the union challenges managerial authority. These challenges have become legitimate in economic areas when there are questions of the equitable distribution of wages and the application of welfare services such as old age pensions and retirement benefits. They are occurring with increasing frequency as management has been faced with more and more complex technology and pressure to rationalize. At the same time, union protest has been encouraged by both legal and international influences, as the workers themselves have gradually awakened to a need for self-determination. Within this context, however, extremism easily occurs. For when protest arises, it is readily directed at the entire system and, therefore, may take on an "extreme" political form. But these protests prove ephemeral because as a rule there is basically no commitment to revolutionary ideology. Japanese-style compromises are worked out.

*A Distinctive Model?*

While the Japanese variant may not be distinct in combining emphasis on both political and economic action, the way in which it combines the functions appears different from Western species. That the division, moreover, is not as conflictual as may be assumed is also an important distinctive characteristic. Although the politicalism of the national organs restrains the economic orientation of the enterprise units and vice versa, it is doubtful that one could exist without the other. There is a complementary relation between the economic and political activities that gives the movement functional unity.

Enterprise unions perform an economic function for which the national organizations are poorly equipped to handle.

National unions furnish an outlet to enterprise unions for expressing political protest which the latter by themselves are not structured to mobilize. Without the enterprise union base, national unions would find a highly fragmented audience. Without the national union superstructure, enterprise unions would doubt their own legitimacy. Failure of the enterprise unions to perform even their limited economic role might easily lead to extreme political stress by the national unions and invitation of state controls. Failure of the national unions to express forceful ideological positions could mean that enterprise unions would succumb to employer domination.

This model of a labor movement has emerged because of the peculiar set of circumstances associated with the rise of industrialism in Japan. A highly structured, centralized controlled, modern economic apparatus was rapidly set upon a traditionally diffused, family-oriented, but homogeneous agrarian culture. For a labor movement to make any impact upon the rigid system of power under these conditions, even with the most favoring of circumstances (such as an occupation deliberately attempting to smash the traditional power complex), required a varied broad-scale attack.

But there was the pull of the old, as well as the push of the new. Workers sought to protect themselves in the way they knew best—within the given industrial structure through the device of enterprise unionism. At the same time, they responded to appeals that questioned the entire structure— voiced by the national unions. In the minds of the Japanese workmen, these were not necessarily contradictory responses. The eclectic Japanese for centuries have successfully managed to embrace divergent ideas and to blend them into an integral whole.

## Will the Model be Replicated Elsewhere?

One of the major problems of the newly emerging nations—especially those that aspire to democratic societies— is how to institute democratic industrialism without destroying their own distinctive cultural bases. In a sense, this has been the mission of postwar Japan, although considerably delayed by perhaps 50 years or more; and, as a result, the Japanese trade-union movement may be a "distortion." However, because of the basic dilemma, it offers an alternative that in its main features may well prove viable.

Among undeveloped free nations, priority of industrialization has meant that labor relations must not be permitted to interfere unduly with this goal. Ideological struggle at the operating levels of production and development would play havoc with the attempt to achieve industrialization. Yet, if democracy is to be achieved, some leeway must be given to worker participation in vital decisions at both the level of goal formation and program execution. The Japanese formula of dividing the political and economic functions may well prove the way out, however unpalatable it may seem to Western trade-unionists. This does not mean that Japan has found the "perfect" combination, for I am afraid there is no such thing. However, like Japan, the emerging nations are likely to develop dual economies, and dual societies, for some time to come. Such structures, in order to afford the expression of labor aspirations, will also need several levels for such expression; one level may not suffice. The exact combination, of course, will vary with the nature and extent of the superimposed industrialism, the rate at which it takes place, and the strength of traditional forms of social organization. At any rate, while new labor movements will have much to learn from the West, it may well be that Japan offers, at least in the earlier stages of industrial development, a model as relevant as any, if not more so.

# The Role of Trade Unions in the Newly Independent Countries of Africa

9

by Stephen Low

The rapid pace of political development in Africa has drawn world attention to that continent. In the realm of labor affairs we are becoming aware of African trade-unions, most of which have come into existence within the last 20 years. In the latter part of this period the membership and importance of these organizations have grown far more rapidly that any economic or industrial development would appear to warrant. Awareness of this fact has led many European and American labor specialists to approach African trade-unionism with caution. Unfortunately little has been written on the subject and few have had extensive experience with it. Events, however, demand some sort of analytical framework within which to approach trade-unionism in Africa and particularly in the newly independent countries of the continent which present the West with such a challenge.

This paper will approach the role of trade-unions in these areas by examining first the nature and character of trade-union organizations in order to determine the dominant forces operating within them. It will then note the peculiar historical heritage of the colonial period and the factors which have created the predominantly political character of these unions. The significant changes resulting from political independence will then be discussed. The conclusions indicate that the trade-union in newly independent African nations may at least for the time being perform a very different role in its society than has been the case in Europe and America.

*Nature of Trade-Union Organizations*

The organizations with which this paper deals can best be described as economic groups which combine for social purposes. They have in common one significant thing only— they are organizations of workers. Included within this definition are organizations of agricultural (chiefly plantation) workers, white-collar workers, and factory employees. Their purpose for combining includes the betterment of the economic condition of their membership, but it is by no means limited to this. Both the number of persons and subjects covered are broader. It is the assertion of the political and social demands of the entire society which are often involved. When the national federation of unions in the Ivory Coast (*Union Nacionale des Travailleurs de la Cote d'Ivoire*) recently demanded that French employers cease employing the familiar "tutoyer" form in addressing workers, it was performing a broadly social function. The assistance given by virtually every African trade-union to the independence movement within its own and other countries is a better known demonstration of this fact.

The potential organizable labor force is remarkably small. It is estimated that not more than five per cent of the total population in tropical Africa belongs to the wage earning group.[1] Of this, less than half and perhaps not more than 10 per cent (varying from territory to territory) of the wage earners are organized in trade-unions.[2] Drawing its membership from such a small base, it is surprising that the trade-union movement has gained the importance that it has.

Even among wage earners, the stable regular workers form only a small proportion. In the former territory of French West Africa only half the wage earners can probably be classified as belonging to the permanent labor force.[3] The rest are either migrant or seasonal workers for whom wages are neither the sole nor in many cases the main source of income. They or their families have cultivations on which they raise subsistence and cash crops. Among wage earners, whether permanently employed or not, only a small number are skilled. It is estimated that in French West Africa only about one-third of the total number of wage earners worked on jobs requiring any skill whatsoever.[4]

Trade-unions in this area have two rather unusual characteristics in terms of Western experience. In the first place a majority of their membership is made up of government workers, and in the second place white-collar workers form over half the membership. In the former territories of French West Africa, 60 per cent of total union membership are government workers, and over half of the remaining 40 per cent are white-collar.[5] It can be assumed that a substantial proportion of the government workers are white-collar, although many may be manual. The same is probably true of many of the former and present British colonies. Most of these workers are clerical staff of the government or private business establishments.

Not only are a majority of the members white-collar workers, but virtually every major union leader comes from this group. To name just a few of the most prominent, Sékou Touré, President of *Union Generale des Travailleurs d'Afrique Nord* (UGTAN), was a postal clerk; Tom Mboya of the Kenya Federation of Labour, was a sanitary inspector; John Tettegah, Secretary General of the Ghana Trade-Union Council, was a clerical worker; Rashidi Kawawa, Secretary General of the Tanganyika Federation of Labour, was a government clerical worker; and Laurence Katalungu was headmaster of a school before becoming a clerk for the mining company and head of the Northern Rhodesian African Mineworkers' Union. Most of the leadership received a secondary education and started to work in clerical, teaching or lower supervisory positions.

The significant point is a sociological one. It is the small number of persons in these African societies, totally committed to the modern economy, who form the leadership and core of the trade-union movements. This group which is deracinated from tribal life, educated to Western concepts of freedom, equality, and democracy, and within reach of Western levels of living, provides the impetus to the revolutionary process of modernization being undertaken with increasing vigor in these countries. There are two social organizations which express their aspirations: the political party and the trade-union. Because the latter is organized according to employment patterns, economic demands receive first but not sole attention. This group is indispensable to the processes of change now taking place.

*External Impetus to the Formation of Unions; Colonial Heritage*

Most trade-unions in tropical Africa have come into existence within the last 20 years. They were organized partly as a result of the local conditions and desires of workers and partly owing to external factors. The controversy which has taken place over the relative importance of these two influences seems resolvable in terms of time. That there was a spontaneous desire on the part of many African workers to combine to improve their working conditions, as Hodgkin claims, is undeniable.[6] African railway workers in the Sudan and French West Africa, mineworkers in Ghana and Northern Rhodesia, transport and dockworkers in a number of countries early formed unions meeting genuine industrial needs. However, it seems likely that the expansion from these rather isolated examples into the creation of militant and integrated national trade-union movements was largely a result of forces which were in many cases external to Africa and in all cases external to the industrial or labor relations requirements of the situation.[7]

Perhaps the greatest external stimulus came from the metropolitan countries. Beginning with the despatch of Lord Passfield (Sidney Webb), Secretary of State for the Colonies, in September 1930, the British colonies were urged to enact legislation legalizing trade-unions and to afford them sympathetic supervision and guidance. More important, the Colonial Development and Welfare Act of 1940 provided funds for development projects in colonial territories contingent on the satisfaction of the Secretary of State that the law of the colony gave reasonable facility for the formation of trade-unions. Shortly after that the first British trade-unionists assigned to the colonial governments arrived in Africa to assist and advise the young trade-unions, as well as employers and governments.

Full-scale participation of Africans in the trade-union movements in the territories of French Africa followed the Decree of August 7, 1944, which abolished the educational requirements for simple membership in unions. While the French Government itself was perhaps a less active promoter of trade-union organization than was the British, French metropolitan unions took a more direct and active part in organizing and running trade-unions in French Africa than did the Trade-Union Congress (TUC) in British Africa. Immediately following the War and enactment of the 1944 Decree, organizers of the *Confederation Generale du Travail* (CGT) followed shortly by the *Confederation Francaise des Travailleurs Chretiens* (CFTC) and later by the *Force Ouvriere* (FO), sent organizers to Africa to establish branches of the parent organization. Cooperation between membership in the two areas was extremely close for a 10-year period and included training in France of a large number of African trade-unionists, constant presence in Africa of French leaders and advisers, frequent exchanges for conferences in one or the other place and financial and material help from the parent organization.

In British areas, trade-unions were organized on a national, or more often a plant basis entirely unconnected with the TUC or British national unions. However, the TUC did provide office equipment, libraries and scholarships to unions in the dependencies. The International Confederation of Free Trade-Unions (ICFTU) has played something of a role, particularly in British territories, and the World Federation of Trade-Unions (WFTU) in the former territories of French Africa.

Inside Africa the organizational drive of the trade-union movement received assistance from political forces in Guinea and Ghana and perhaps in some of the territories of East Africa during the drives for independence. This has also been the case in both Morocco and Tunisia in North Africa.

In sum, Britain and France, the major metropolitan powers, were convinced on the basis of their own experience that a free trade-union movement was an inevitable and desirable element in the development of a modern democratic state. They therefore set about to facilitate the establishment of such a movement and influence its growth along responsible and democratic lines organized in patterns similar to their own. Increasing world attention to the situation in Africa, whether brought on by the International Labor Organization (ILO) or ICFTU interest or by quickening political activity, reinforced this determination. The Cold War added a further motivating force to these activities not alone on the part of the metropolitan countries but of other organizations and nations as well. It is probably fair to say that the major initiative in the formation of employees organizations came from abroad and that it was motivated by essentially political factors largely unrelated to the local situation.

*Special Advantages of Unions in Colonial Areas*

In his excellent discussion of labor problems in French West Africa before its recent breakup into autonomous territories and independent states, Elliot Berg discusses three factors inherent in the colonial relationship which strengthened the bargaining power of unions.[8] These levers can roughly be described as political, social or racial, and economic.

1. *Political.* In French West Africa unions were able to use the French desire to hold the territories within the French community as a political weapon with which to back wage demands. The threat of all-out and disruptive strikes, aimed no longer at wage increases but instead at revising the ties which bound the territories to France, succeeded in securing a significant wage increase in 1953. In British areas, however, the lack of geographical or territorial labor organizations or, put another way, the multiplicity of small plant or company locals made the threat of political strikes for economic ends more difficult though not unknown. Here the strike was used more often for political purposes and was generally organized by political leaders. An example was the abortive "positive action" strike led by Nkrumah in 1950 in the Gold Coast.

2. *Social or Racial.* Not only in French West Africa but all over tropical Africa the demand for racial equality was used as a weapon to raise African wages to the higher level enjoyed by European expatriots. Because of their sensitivity to the charge of racial discrimination, colonial administrations in some cases unified their salary scale under such pressure, but adopted an allowance structure which restored many of the financial advantages to expatriots. Gradually, African demands have chipped away at these allowances, though substantial differentials remain.

3. *Economic.* Two economic restraints which directly or indirectly may cause employers to hold out against demands for wage increases were to some degree absent in French West Africa. The inflationary pressure created by the increased purchasing power flowing from higher wages was funneled off in increased purchases of imported goods. Thus the government had no reason to put pressure on employers to oppose wage increases because of the inflationary pressure they might generate. The second restraint which was relieved was the need, for competitive reasons, to keep prices of colonial products down. The special preferences given by France to products from its colonies allowed employers in the export sector of the dependencies to pass wage increases on to the consumer in the metropole. Although the first of these two economic factors acted in more or less the same degree throughout tropical Africa, the second did not. Britain did not create the same protected market for colonial products that France did. The advantages arising from membership in the sterling block did, however, provide some benefits for colonial producers.

The colonial relationship produced unique and artificial conditions which influenced trade-union development. Factors external to the local situation encouraged their growth, and special conditions gave them artificial advantages. This "hot house" climate had a number of results. In the first place, mass movements were created in a relatively short space of time. Nominal membership of unions in tropical Africa increased from approximately 200,000 at the end of the forties to a figure which was probably over a million at the end of the fifties.[9] Membership, however, is a poor measure of union strength in this part of the world. A union with a handful of members has been known to bring out 30,000 workers on strike for over a month. A better statement might be that the potential of the movement was immeasurably increased.

A second result was almost inevitable. Lack of discipline and poor organization characterized many unions in countries approaching self-government all over Africa. The chief exceptions were mostly the unions which had sprung up in response to local needs. For the rest it is probable that conditions inimical to the formation of unions might still have outweighed those favoring their formation had it not been for the special colonial conditions. Tribalism, illiteracy, migrancy, lack of urbanization, lacks of skills, poor transportation and communication facilities, and the ever-present alternative of cash or subsistence farming all would have acted to thwart the creation of unions of any kind, much less well-organized or disciplined ones.

A final result of the colonial situation was the creation of an atmosphere of irresponsibility. The government and metropolitan trade-unions appeared willing to assist African labor organizations for reasons different from the latters' needs or performance. African unions felt little community of association with government or employers as long as they remained foreign and consequently felt little purpose in exercising restraint. In short, the consequences of their actions appeared to hold few long-term economic, political, or social penalties for them.

*Political Orientation*

As a result of the particular political and social structure of the United States, the current of the American labor movement which developed into its main stream found it expedient to exert its influence on political affairs as a sort of pressure group rather than by means of direct involvement. This experience has now become a tradition. This pattern was based upon conditions unique to the American scene. However, the situation in many African areas appears to call for a somewhat different approach which is based upon two broad categories of conditions.

## The Predominance of Government

It has already been noted that the majority of trade-union members in most of the areas concerned here are government employees. This condition reflects the basic predominance of government as an employer throughout the region. Not only does government employ the great majority of clerical workers, but also a large number of manual employees. In virtually the entire area, the railways are government owned. Government has at least a partial interest in the mining industry in Nigeria, and an indirect interest in Uganda mining, for instance. A large part of all road construction and maintenance and a great share of other construction is the work of government employees. In most British areas, the Public Works Department has the largest single payroll in the country.

So pervasive is the role of government as an employer that it is able virtually to establish the going wage rate. In East Africa the Public Works Department monthly wage rate for common laborers is generally accepted by private employers. Where a tradition exists of a higher wage level for government workers, the differential is recognized and fixed, and acts in the same influential pattern. In both English and French areas, government has the responsibility for setting minimum wage rates. When one considers that over half and perhaps as many as two-thirds of the wage earners are unskilled common laborers earning little, if any, more than the minimum rate, the importance of this power becomes evident.

Beyond the pattern of wage rates, the government regulates a wide range of affairs relating to labor through legislation. Partly as a result of the virtual commitment of the metropolitan powers to apply to their dependencies ILO conventions to which they have become a party, and partly owing to the feeling that a self-governing state should start off with a modern labor code, elaborate and progressive labor legislation has been adopted, closely patterned after that of the metropoles.

The domination of government in the field of labor relations is part of the pattern of extreme concentration of power in the hands of the ruler which has characterized African society from well before the coming of the European. It gives rise, quite naturally, to the attitude that change can only be secured through application to the government. In other words, the government was not only economically dominant but its political power put it in such a position as to make other institutions appear almost as its instrument.

*Economic Weaknesses of African Unions*

The advantages which the unions derived from the special colonial situation were more helpful in strengthening them vis-a-vis governments than individual, private employers. The threat of disorder, demands for self-government, racial equality, and absence of restraint imposed by danger of inflation brought on by wage increases, were all effective levers on governments, but were of little use in disputes with private firms. They provided more of a political than economic advantage. Furthermore, except for the last mentioned, these advantages can best be supported by means of the one kind of action the unions are well organized to undertake—the one- or two-day demonstration strike, short general strike, or mass demonstration. This kind of agitation, on the other hand, is of little effect in dealing with private employers.

In fact, the structure of the unions and the economic position in which they operate render them extremely weak in struggles with individual employers.[10] In the first place, the ready availability of alternative employment makes it very difficult for an organization of workers to develop a disciplined and militant attitude among its membership concerning demands. The absence of serious land pressure and the closeness to tribal life make return to the family cultivation a relatively easy and not unpleasant alternative. Since many wage earners are simultaneously deriving income from these land holdings where their families are adequately provided

214

for, their wages are not necessary "to keep body and soul together." It is sometimes difficult, therefore, to get workers sufficiently excited to want to strike on a purely wage issue. On the other hand, the same lack of absolute dependence on the income from wage employment or on any one job can lead to a very volatile labor situation where a small slight to a worker's dignity, for instance, can cause the entire force to walk out on a moment's notice. As a matter of fact, the wildcat, unorganized, short-term strike is a great deal more common throughout Africa than the deliberate walk-out to back priority demands after exhaustion of negotiation. Whether its membership is overly docile or volatile, a union is handicapped in its dealings with the individual employer.

A second weakness of unions with regard to individual employers springs from the low-skill level of the majority of workers. Because the labor force is easily replaceable, it is unable to put really effective pressure on the employer. It is not unusual for an employer to fire his entire force and have a new one at work within a few days. In the same period the first group has disappeared from the lodging and even town in which they were living.

Third, even in the case of strikes by relatively skilled and urbanized workers, the financial position of the union is such that very little if any assistance can be given striking workers. Organized picketing for any length of time is rare. The best that can be expected is help to strikers from relatives and friends. Except in these few cases where the checkoff has been bargained [11] or legislated,[12] dues payments are made by a fraction of the membership at irregular intervals.

It is clear that under these conditions union leadership which directed its members in a series of ruinous struggles against private employers rather than attempting to secure its demands in demonstrations against the government, would neither be adequately representing its members' interests nor would it long remain in power. The latter type of activity, however, must be coordinated closely with political parties. By acting together, maximum pressure is brought to bear, and both economic and political demands may be achieved.

The above situation has sometimes proved difficult for

those raised in the Western tradition to understand, either because of ideological inflexibility or because of personal involvement on the side of the metropolitan powers. It did not prove so to the Africans, however. With the possible exception of the African Mine Workers Union in Northern Rhodesia and some of the Nigerian unions, virtually every major union throughout Africa has developed intimate ties with the political party in the vanguard of the nationalist movement of its area. In Tunisia the *Union General des Travailleurs Tunisiene* (UGTT) worked closely with the Neo-Destour; in French West Africa the *Confederation Generale des Travailleurs d'Afrique* was created in no small part as a result of efforts of the *Rassemblement Democratique Africain*; in Ghana Nkrumah's Convention Peoples Party (CPP) relied heavily on the Ghana Trade-Union Congress (GTUC); in Tanganyika the Tanganyika Federation of Labor leadership has a major voice in the Tanganykian African National Union (TANU); and in Kenya Mboya directed both the Kenya Federation of Labor and the Nairobi Convention People's Party. These relationships were no accident. They reflected the realities of a political and social climate which is very different from our own experience.

*Independence*

Self-government brings with it radical changes in the situation described above. The fundamental difference is a psychological one. The attitude that the direction of events is in alien hands exercised for alien purposes is replaced by the exuberant belief that at last Africans have acceded to responsibility and power and that their destiny is in their own hands. A newly independent government may attempt to avoid some of this responsibility by conjuring up the continuing opposition of "neoimperialism," but eventually it will have to accept its responsibilities and in the interval it may dampen the enthusiasm for the national effort which comes with newfound self-government. For the positive forces released by independence are great. With few exceptions, the new governments received virtually unanimous support from their people. They accepted responsibility and mounted ambitious national programs. Though they differed widely in detail, all these programs were based on two general appeals: national unity and economic development.

Although virtually every government in every country calls for national unity when it first assumes power, the appeal expresses somewhat different meanings. Among the newly independent countries of Africa, the emotion whipped up in the process of achieving independence and exhilaration of its first years has forced the burying of all differences in the interest of self-government, and the assertion of nationality. It is not unfair to say that where strong and popular governments are in power, national unity has meant that open or public opposition is scarcely tolerated. Where opposition attempted to assert itself, it has been labeled disloyal and treated accordingly. The flush of new nationalism in these areas has so far shown only limited comprehension of the sophisticated, Western notion of a loyal opposition. Since the opportunities to practice this concept were of short duration during the colonial period, it would have been surprising if the commitment to it were great.

In terms of labor organization, the appeal of national unity has prevailed in the thinking of virtually every important leader, whether Socialist or Marxist, over the dogma of class warfare. Sékou-Touré, Nkrumah, and Bourguiba have all made clear statements rejecting the latter. In spite of the fact that Tunisian conditions differ somewhat from those described above occurring in tropical Africa, the Tunisian premier has perhaps best articulated this feeling and some of his statements are worth quoting here. In the fall of 1959, Bourguiba said in a speech at Metaloui that "class warfare is inconceivable. To attack an employer, to treat him as an enemy, or to sabotage his business will lead to the ruin of all."

On the positive side, national unity is conceived of as a partnership of all national elements. The close political involvement of unions during the colonial period, therefore, cannot help but continue. Addressing the UGTT annual congress on April 1, 1960, Bourguiba said:

The Party and UGTT are merely two different aspects of the same popular movement, which is profoundly united be-

217

cause of mutual confidence . . . Between party and UGTT it cannot be said there is cooperation, truce, compromise, or even peaceful coexistence. There is only unity. The UGTT Secretary General is a leading member of the Party and is in a position to defend UGTT interests.

The second general appeal made by every leader is for an all-out effort towards economic development. This is essentially a productionist directive and inevitably conflicts with the basically consumptionist function of the trade-union. Sturmthal has quite correctly pointed out that this apparent contradiction is not necessarily irreconcilable; that social service functions can help maintain trade-unions; and that moderate wage pressure from unions can under certain circumstances assist development.[13] Nevertheless, in real terms, the conflict exists. It presents the unions with a situation in which their national political interest finds itself opposed to their particular economic interest. This places them in the new and unfamiliar position of having to apply self-restraint and discipline to themselves and their demands. The delicate balance between the national development program which calls for restraining consumption in order to accumulate investment funds and legitimate worker demands will inevitably be maintained by government. Few new governments in Africa are likely to be willing to entrust such an important function to the private negotiations of employer and union, even if either of these two parties were prepared to arrive at a settlement without it.

The transition from colonial status to independence involves fundamental changes in the outlook of trade-unions. Overnight they are being required to revise their attitude from one of irresponsibility to responsibility, from lack of discipline to discipline, from opposition to partnership, from consumption to self-denial, and from avoidance of full-work commitment to a wholehearted effort for production. The only change in the external situation is in the psychological climate. The positive forces released by the culmination of the nationalist movement in independence are great. But great demands will be placed on them.

*The New Shape of Trade-Unionism*

What kind of trade-unionism seems likely to emerge in the newly independent countries of Africa? From the discussion that has preceded, it is clear that it will have a very different shape and position from the industrial trade-unionism with which we are familiar.

At least in the immediate future there seems to be little prospect for large scale use of the technique of collective bargaining as it is known in Europe and America. It has been seen that union strength is better organized to place pressure on government than private employers. But the new atmosphere of unity would hardly tolerate large scale, public demonstrations of political opposition. Even in the case where a well-organized union of permanent, skilled workers felt itself in a position to bargain with a private employer, the interests of the development program might well force government to intervene in the settlement of a wage dispute. In these highly centralized economies one wage increase could cause wide-scale unrest if government were not prepared to follow through in granting similar increases across the board, and budgetary demands present a major obstacle to such increases.

One important modification of this picture appears necessary. In countries like Morocco and perhaps Nigeria, where no single leader backed by a powerful party has been able to assert himself, appeals to national unity have somewhat less force, and as opposition appears, public demonstrations dramatizing workers' demands may become possible. It is notable, however, that even in Morocco where one government has followed another and the strength of the central administration has been limited, the powerful Union Marocaine de Travail has frequently restrained its demands, particularly on Moroccan employers, and directed most of its efforts toward attempts to build power against the governments or rival trade-unions. Here, too, severe restrictions are placed on traditional collective bargaining.

How are wage decisions to be made in the absence of the

machinery of collective bargaining? Although the machinery may be different, the fundamentals are the same. Wages will be determined by bargaining at the locus of industrial power. For the time being the extreme centralization of power in the newly independent African states places this locus, together with all other power, in the councils of the political party. When Bourguiba says that the UGTT Secretary General will defend the union's interest in his capacity as a leading Party member and then on another occasion that, "The Government will intercede with the companies to see that workers receive as high salaries as possible and will represent their interest before the employers," [14] he is making this point. Government, as he describes it, is acting as the instrument of Party policy. All decisions affecting an area of potential conflict or important economic functions are in the final analysis political decisions and must be dealt with by the highest political body, the Party. But if the major industrial relations decisions are made here, it is vital to the worker and union that its strongest representation be here.

The right of participation on the highest level of the party is granted on the basis of the trade-union leader's loyalty to the party and the position of power and influence which he brings to it. His bargaining strength depends on his power base. Providing he exercises control over organized labor, including as it does the group most intimately involved in the modernization revolution, he will carry considerable weight within the party. He must transmit party decisions to workers' organizations which more often than not involve him in attempting to enforce wage-restraint policies. In order to do so, he must be in a strong position within his organization. The party is the exchange point where workers' demands are weighed together with those of employers and the economy at large. It is here that the decisions are made, whether or not labor leaders are present.

A large number of African trade-unionists have already achieved high party and governmental positions. Rachidi Kawawa in Tanganyika, Cyril Adoula in the Congo, and Sékou Touré in Guinea have each moved from leadership of the trade-union movement to head of government. Mboya in

Kenya, Tlili in Tunisia, and Tettegah in Ghana are all men of considerable political influence as well as being trade-union leaders. In most of the countries of French-speaking Africa, the Ministers of Labor are former trade-unionists. In Senegal, Ibrahima Sarr, former head of the powerful Railway Workers Union, is Minister of Labor and a Secretary on the Executive Bureau of the ruling party specifically charged with "liaison with trade-unions."

Labor representation in party councils is not necessarily confined to the highest levels. Trade-union members of plant, neighborhood, section, and county party units is the best way of assuring that labor's demands are put before committee meetings and party congresses.

Nevertheless, there will inevitably be a large number of questions which the party has neither the time nor the technical qualifications to consider. It seems unlikely, however, that it will be willing to abandon a voice in their resolution. As the new governments develop, new institutions will appear to perform this function. Various kinds of tripartite bodies of representatives of labor, management, and government (party) will be formed, if they have not already been, to deal with these questions. African trade-unionists are already aware of the importance of these "intermediary bodies"— economic and social councils, national planning councils, etc. —and are demanding that they be established with organized labor given an important voice in them. Means must be found, they say, to institutionalize a "permanent dialogue" between governments and trade-unions.[15]

## NOTES

1. Hodgkin, Thomas L., *Nationalism in Colonial Africa*, New York: New York University Press (1957), pp. 118–119.
2. Ibid., p. 133.
3. Berg, Elliot, "French West Africa," p. 200, Chapter 5, in *Labor and Economic Development*, ed. by Walter Galenson, New York: John Wiley & Sons (1959).
4. Ibid., pp. 199–200.
5. Hodgkin, op. cit., pp. 126–127.

6. Ibid.
7. The primary importance of external factors is stressed by such writers as Lord Hailey, *An African Survey*, p. 1446; Davison, R. B., "Labor Relations in Ghana," and Bowen, Walter, *Colonial Trade-Unions*. The Fitzgerald Commission investigating the disorders in Nigeria which took place in 1949 went so far as to state that, ". . . trade-unionism in Nigeria was not a native growth. It was deliberately planted on the people by the British administration as part of the industrial system." Great Britain, Colonial Office, *Report of the Commission of Enquiry*, p. 13.
8. Berg, op. cit., pp. 230–241.
9. *Presence Africaine*, "Note sur le Syndicalisme en Afrique Noire." The more recent figure is my own estimate.
10. See Berg, op. cit., pp. 225–226.
11. Northern Rhodesia Mine Workers; some Nigerian Unions.
12. As in the Ghana Industrial Relations Act of 1959.
13. Sturmthal, Adolf, "Unions and Economic Development," *Economic Development and Cultural Change*, Jan., 1960.
14. Speech at Metaloui, Fall, 1959.
15. *Report to the Political, Economic and Social Committee of the Dakar Trade-Union Conference*, January 9–14, 1962.

*PART III*

# 10

## Unions in the New and Developing Countries

by Everett M. Kassalow

A good starting point for a comparative analysis of unions in the developing countries is a quick survey of the key characteristics and tendencies of the developed Western labor movements today. Of course I shall be touching only the most common generalizations here.

To begin with, one of the important features common to all of these Western union movements is their insistence and reliance upon independent freedom of action. Even under Socialist governments, Western trade-unions jealously continue to guard their independent industrial functions—they are the active representatives of the workers in industrial life. While they may moderate their direct collective bargaining activities and demands when a Socialist labor government is in power, they do this on a voluntary and cooperative basis, always from a jealously guarded independent base of operations.

Collective bargaining in all of these Western countries has far-reaching economic importance. Strikes, for the most part today, in these same countries, are part of the collective bargaining process and are generally employed only in that context (exceptions, of course, should be noted especially in France and Italy where the demonstration and political types of strikes still persist; from time to time Belgium, too, is an exception to this general rule on strikes). While all of these Western movements may in varying degrees look to the government for some help in regulating wages, hours and working conditions, they basically depend upon independent union action and collective bargaining in this sphere. Again while governments exercise some initiative in regulating wages and working conditions, outside of special emergency situations, governments, too, tend to leave a wide area of

225

freedom for unions and managements in collective bargaining.

In every case, the Western union movements have their own independent methods and means of financing their operations. There is a strong tradition against relying upon the government in this respect.

In most instances, as we shall see, these characteristics tend to be lacking or are only of minor importance as we come to study the trade-union movements in the new, developing countries.

Many of the generalizations I will hereafter make apply to nearly all of the labor movements in the newly independent or developing countries. However, these generalizations and trends apply with special force to the developing labor movements of Asia and Africa and to a lesser extent to Latin America. Most of the Latin American countries won their independence over 100 years ago, and as a consequence their political and social structures and development in some ways resemble the Western countries more than they do the new countries in Asia and Africa. On the other hand, the common struggle against what is loosely called "colonialism" and the great emphasis being placed upon rapid economic development tend to place most of the Latin American countries and their labor movements at a state more like those of the new countries of Asia and Africa than like the West.

Finally to complete this preface, I must note that since I am dealing with such a vast area, I shall in many cases only be able to mention briefly any number of problems and issues, all of which really deserve lengthier treatment.

*Labor Movements in New Countries Not Primarily a Product of Capitalism*

In any case, turning now to these movements themselves, perhaps the first and most significant thing that must be understood is that in many instances they are springing into existence and developing against a social and economic background which is different from that which shaped the movements in Western countries. The Western unions arose as a reaction to, or, if you prefer, as part of the development of capitalism in Europe and the United States and particularly industrial capitalism from the end of the eighteenth century and early nineteenth century onward. It was this rise of capitalism which shaped the society and the labor movements in it.

This broad shaping force doesn't have the same central role in many of the new countries; where capitalist forces do exist, their role is often rather limited in importance. In most of these countries what is going on first and foremost is a different kind of social and political revolution—a struggle for independence from a colonial mother country and/or a struggle to eliminate the vestiges of colonialism and feudalism in the new independent countries. This struggle is bringing on to the scene all kinds of new groups in these colonial and ex-colonial countries, including the native middle classes and the free professions, new military leaders, urban workers, and peasants.

Almost simultaneously with this struggle for social and political independence many of these same countries are caught up in programs of intensive economic development. This economic development, however, is generally being led and directed by central state authorities and, in many ways, is quite different from the "simple" capitalist revolution which served as background for the emergence of labor movements in western Europe and the U. S.

As a last general background point, one must always have in mind the almost constant pressure which Communist political and labor forces are exerting upon the new countries and the labor movements therein. In so many instances the new country movements must conduct an almost constant defensive battle against Communist labor appeals and groups.[1]

*Political Importance of Urban Working Class in New Countries*

Where do the labor movements fit into this developing pattern in the new countries? It must be first appreciated that there is only a relatively small working class and indeed a very small urban population in most of these new countries. The

227

greater part of economic activity is agricultural in character and very often it is agricultural for local use only, with little relationship to the market economy.

Although this working class is relatively small, the very nature of what is going on in these countries tends to make it important politically. It is one of the few urban groups in the population and as such it is more mobile and perhaps I should say more "mobilizable." And when you are in the midst of a revolutionary process, be it struggling for independence or trying to transform an old colonial order, you look for "mobilizable" allies.

This urban working class is one of the few groups which is breaking from the eternal, unchanging cycle of life, the thralldom which characterizes a traditional society.

I was forcefully struck with this fact when I had occasion recently to see the wonderful trilogy of Indian movies, Pather Panchali, which dealt with the life of Apu, the Indian village boy, as he moves from the staid isolated life of a rural village into an urban setting. In one scene Apu is led by his sister from his small village across a great meadow to have his first look at a railway train. As he steps forth from the meadow after an all-day journey the train suddenly bursts in front of him. The enormous effect of this encounter with one of the symbols of a modern industrial civilization gave me some sense at least of what is involved in the transition from the routine of a village life which has gone unchanged for hundreds of years to the dynamism an urban civilization can produce. It is, I think, difficult for most of us, brought up and taking for granted the kind of modern industrial civilization such as we have in America to comprehend fully the explosive effects of modern urban life upon the minds and attitudes of new, industrial workers in these new countries.

The very act of coming to live in an urban setting or taking a job in an industrial type of activity makes a sharp break with the past traditional life. Inevitably those who undergo this experience are more prepared for additional changes and activities than other members of the society. The emancipating character of urban life in many emerging societies is comparable to the role played by the cities in freeing merchants and craftsmen from some of the restrictions of feudalism in the later middle ages of European history.

Let me add that the working class, too, has been assigned a key role in the thinking and programs of practically all modern revolutionaries, especially those under Marxist influence. It is almost inevitable, then, that when political leaders set out on a course of independence and development in these new countries, a course with truly revolutionary consequences, they should look to the urban working class as one of the forces they must stir into action. Needless to say, it also becomes one of the forces these same leaders can use as a base of power.

*Developing Social and Political Revolution and Workers' Citizenship Needs*

As the revolutionary, nationalistic process, both political and economic, gets under way, the needs and drives of the working class in these new countries draw them into the process. It is by participating in this upheaval that, for example, they can gain full citizenship rights, voting rights, the right to hold office. Immediately they begin to feel the compulsion for education themselves and educational opportunities for their children. They want the right to move and change jobs —rights which have previously been forbidden them in a colonially dominated society. They demand that all jobs be open to them and that the kind of racial limitations on different jobs so characteristic, for example, of many parts of Africa, be eliminated. Often all of these things are lumped together under the heading of putting an end to colonialism.

It should not be surprising, therefore, that some unions will enter with enthusiasm into this revolutionary political process. Surely there are no more important rights to be won in a modern society than the ones I have just outlined. In a sense this is much the way the American working class operated in the United States in the second, third and fourth decades in the 19th century. Recall the great emphasis given to political action by the labor movement at that time and its relationship to the Jacksonian struggle to achieve full citizenship in the developing American society. Voting rights, free-

229

dom from debt imprisonment and free public education were in the absolute forefront of the unions' demands in those decades.

The way in which this revolutionary force sweeps all groups and cracks open all kinds of opportunities has been described in a novel about the Mexican Revolution which Hirschman has recently quoted. In this novel a successful businessman, the son of a peon, in defending the Mexican Revolution to a young intellectual, admits that there is still much poverty and injustice in Mexico, but he adds:

There are also millions who could go to the schools which we, the revolution, built for them, millions who found jobs in urban industries, millions who without 1910 would have been peons and are now skilled workers, who would have been domestic servants and are now typists with good salaries, millions who in twenty years have passed from the lower to the middle class, who have cars and use toothpaste and spend five days a year in Telcolutla or Acapulco . . . These people are the only concrete achievement of the Revolution and this was our achievement . . .[2]

*Unions and the Dominant Nationalist Party Movement*

Under these circumstances, as you can see, the government, and, as often as not, the central nationalist revolutionary political party tends to become the greatest center of power and indeed almost a total center of power in the new emerging society. In many countries the nationalist party movement becomes almost a do-all and end-all of what is going on. Within this party many factions and groups contend and jockey for position and influence.

Colin Legum, a leading British expert on Africa, in reviewing a book on Nkrumah of Ghana quotes him as saying, "The party is the state." Legum adds: "Everything revolves around it, the trade-union congress, the United Ghana Farmer's Council, the National Cooperative Council and the National Council of Ghana Women." [3]

The trade-union movement is frequently one of the important networks of institutions making up the central nationalist party.

Hans Tutsch describes Bourguiba's Tunisian nationalist party in the following terms:

The Liberal Constitutional party has established a large network of organizations which embrace practically the whole population. It controls the trade-unions, which have a stronger organization in Tunisia than in any other Arab country. It also has a youth organization, student groups, women's league and professional associations of farmers, tradesmen and manufacturers. The Association of Trade-Unions exercises an important function: it devotes itself to raising the standard of living of its members but it also powerfully supports Bourguiba's stabilization policy. With its help the government has succeeded in putting a brake on the turns of the inflationary spiral but the recent refusal to increase wages has caused perceptible tension in the trade-unions, which the Communists are trying to exploit in their propaganda. No other Arab leader besides Bourguiba has at his disposal such a modern 'capillary' organization and power machine. But it all stands and falls with the leader.[4]

I think Tutsch's phrase, "a modern capillary" organization, is a rather good one.

Within this political party, of course, what goes on is what Stephen Low has described as a "head-knocking" process.[5] Here labor operates as a force within the party struggling for such things as education, housing, and health facilities as opposed to emphasis upon purely industrial ventures. With the more extensive government ownership or operation of different services or industries in the new countries, key wage policy decisions may also center in the government sector. It becomes pretty obvious if labor is to operate and share in the surging new power of the developing society, it must have a role in these political councils.

In a sense the plural party system which we look to as a necessary safeguard of democracy in the West has a partial counterpart in the struggles between different groups in the same party in the new countries. As Legum notes of Ghana, "The Opposition party, although considerably weakened, still battles on. But the real political life is carried on within the [government] party. It is here that political argument is fierce and open."

231

Of course, the pattern I have described here is not everywhere the same. In India, for example, although the dominant Congress party and the Indian Trade-Union Congress —the party's arm in the labor field—are in something of a similar relationship, there are other parties and other labor movements. Yet much of the activity and struggles of the working class in India are concentrated in the political and governmental spheres.

The existence of several parties and several competing union movements is more common in a number of Asian countries. It reflects the pressure of international forces (the Communist party) as well as the emergence of different ideological groups early in the independence struggles. In some of the Asian countries we find the "old" problem of plural unionism as a factor in the labor picture. Competing labor federations, each usually tied to a different political party, are vying for the workers' support. This pluralism often operates, as in France and Italy, to weaken the collective bargaining side of unionism and it leads the unions toward greater dependence upon politics and government.

On the other hand, the single dominant party-union operation, described above in Bourguiba's Tunisia, is in many respects similar to the role played by the central, revolutionary political parties in Mexico and Bolivia. In these two countries the union movement has been a key factor in the "mission" of the party and the revolution, and they are best understood as one of the great forces within the revolution.

Finally, in a handful of the emerging countries the trade-union movement has taken a clear-cut stand separating itself from political parties. Generally, this separation has occurred in former British colonies where the influences of the British Trade-Union Congress and/or a former colonial labor officer were significant. Generally, too, this has occurred in countries where the legal recognition of the trade-union movement predated recognition of native political parties. As we shall indicate below, after independence is achieved it becomes increasingly difficult for unions to stand clear of the political forces.

232

*Economic Origins of Unions in the New Countries*

At this point I should like to turn to the economic origins and early functions of the labor unions in the new societies, keeping in mind the general milieu and framework in which they are operating. Obviously, of course, even during the colonial period when political channels were often not available or not fully open, the impact of urban life and industrial development alone was a force for bringing unions into existence. Unions at this stage tend to concentrate in the public service and transport, early industries of employment concentration.

In Africa where mining was a key industry in colonial economic development, unions also came into existence. Petroleum plays a similar role in parts of Latin America and Asia. In Latin America and the Far East, where colonial capital flows into plantation type of agricultural development and the mass employment of agricultural labor takes place, we find plantation worker unions emerging at a relatively early period.

Since foreign (colonial) capital tends to predominate in these major industrial and agricultural ventures, the union movement takes on a kind of anti-foreign, political character as well as an economic one. Indeed, even "routine" economic action against a corporation which is controlled by foreign or colonial capital inevitably has political overtones.

*Social and Economic Complications: Excess Population, Migratory Labor, Tribalism and Communalism*

During the colonial period and even after freedom is obtained, the great excess labor force, the enormous unemployment and under-employment which one finds in so many of these societies conditions and limits the purely industrial effectiveness of these unions. This is in contrast, by and large, with the absence of such vast population surpluses when most of the Western labor movements were developing in Europe and the United States.

The migratory character of the labor force in many of these

countries—the continuation of ties between village and tribe on the one hand and urban worker on the other—also makes it difficult for effective unionism to emerge. So many workers, at least in the early years of their urban lives, continue to have tribal ties and they look upon their stay in the cities and industries as a temporary affair.

In the words of a group of African workers, who were studying at the Kampala labor college run by the International Confederation of Free Trade-Unions, the migratory "worker who expects to stay in any given place only a short time has no incentive to strive for higher wages and better working conditions . . . The result of being on the move is frustration, sweated labor and insecurity . . . The migrant laborer has no interest in joining trade-unions: The workers consider regular payment of union dues a waste of money, because they expect to be going back to the reserves or to move into another district. They are also scared of taking part in strikes for fear of losing their precarious jobs . . ." [6]

Curiously enough, in parts of Africa labor mobility has sometimes been restricted or forbidden to achieve the same object of keeping labor low paid and controllable.

Tribal influence in the lives of the workers in Africa often makes it difficult for unions to reach and hold them. A report of the International Confederation of Free Trade-Unions on the *Particular Problems Facing the Trade-Unions* (in Africa) states: "Relations between employers and their workers are often maintained, on works committees and in less organized forms, through tribal elders, thus cutting the ground from underneath the trade-unions . . ."

Even in a case where a union was operating in Kenya, tribal pressures contrived to elect a new General Secretary who had "no trade-union experience at all," but did belong to the dominant tribe.

Again understanding a force like tribalism is difficult for someone born and bred in the modern West. I am impressed with some brilliant passages from Peter Abrahams' (the South African novelist) book about *Udomo* the prototype of the new African revolutionary leader. Udomo has led his country to independence and finds himself thereupon confronted with other obstacles, as he seeks to modernize his nation. He analyzes these in a passionate dialogue with some of his traditionalist enemies: "As I say, our country has three enemies. First there is the white man. Then there is poverty. Then there is the past. Those are the three enemies.

"When I first came back I recognized only one of the three: the white man. But the moment I defeated him I saw the others, and they were greater and more dangerous than the white man. Beside these two the white man was easy, almost an ally. Well, I turned him into an ally against poverty. He works for us now, builds for us so that those who come after us will have bread and homes. There are schools and hospitals in the land. The young men and women are waking up. Why do you think I spent so much money sending them abroad? I'll tell you. Because I need them as allies to fight our third enemy, the worst enemy we have: the past. I've paid lip service to the ritual of ju-ju and blood ceremonies and worshipping at the shrines of our ancestors. Now I don't have to any more. There are enough liberated young people now for me to defy all that is ugly and evil in our past. We can defeat it now. And you, Selina, and you, Ade, whom I once loved as a brother: you are the past. I'm going to defeat you! It is you who now stand in the way of Africa's greatness. Go on: fight me at the party conference and see who wins! You're too late, my friends. You're too late . . ." [7]

In parts of Asia the force of communalism which works for particular castes or religious communities as opposed to the general welfare can operate in a way as similarly divisive as tribalism. It can hinder the development of an effective general labor movement.

In some areas, on the other hand, unions occasionally grow on tribal or communal foundations. The union leader is looked upon as a kind of headman who looks after "his" people. Here the union may serve as a transition institution easing the worker from a traditional to a more modern status. The plantation workers union in Ceylon, for example, is essentially a Tamil organization and has, consequently, a communal cast about it.

*Commitment of the Labor Force*

The persistence of village ties, tribalism or communalism also hinder what some writers have called the full commitment of workers to an industrial way of life. "Industrialization requires not only the recruitment and training of an industrial labor force but also its commitment to an industrial, as opposed to an agricultural, way of life. As an economically underdeveloped nation moves toward industrialization, some part of the rural labor force is either pushed or pulled toward the growing industrial cities. But ties with the village and the land may remain strong. The development of a labor force which accepts the discipline of factory work and the conditions of urban living is much slower than the initial recruitment of enough workers to man the mills and factories." [8]

*Sources of Trade-Union Leadership*

Again, recall that the Western unions developed at a relatively slow pace, during a hundred or more years of industrial expansion, nearly always under or against repressive opposition of employers and government. This hardening industrial and social process tended to produce a stalwart, deeply experienced union leadership.

Repression was certainly not absent from the development process in most of the new countries; but the time periods of social and economic development are being telescoped together more closely. Even before independence in some of these countries (especially in the British colonies) colonial administrators intervened to help some unions come into existence. In any event, as independence is won, government sympathy for and encouragement of unions often becomes the policy of the day. In a sense, then, opportunities to build unions exist before the working class has gone through the same sort of grim maturing process it underwent in the West.

It is not surprising that many of the unions in the new countries are often created by "outside" leaders—i.e., leaders who do not come from the jobs or industries where the unions are formed. Many forces operate to bring this about.

In many of the Western countries the first unions were

usually formed and led by skilled workers, who were often quite literate. The lack of opportunities to fill many of the skilled jobs, and outright exclusion from such jobs on racial (as in Africa) or political grounds has severely limited the number of native skilled workers in many of the colonial countries.

Frequently the first labor unions are created directly by political parties and political leaders. This tended to be true in the countries like India and Ceylon where at a relatively early date British colonial rule yielded some form of parliamentary institutions to the native population. The leaders of parliamentary political groups found it advantageous to create trade-unions as a base for political following. I should add that these political leaders were also motivated often enough by humanitarian factors. Moreover, given the low level of literacy in the working population and the fact that most of them didn't even have command of the language of the ruling class, namely English or French, it was almost a "natural" development for the unions to be led by "outside" as opposed to rank and file worker leaders.

The low level of literacy and the lack of any broadening experience of the bulk of the working population continues to handicap unions after they are organized. There are constant complaints about poor administration and loose handling of funds.

Let me note that a somewhat different pattern emerges in some parts of Africa so far as leadership is concerned. In important parts of Central and Eastern Africa where "white" economic interests and settlers were deeply embedded, neither British nor Belgium rule yielded parliamentary institutions which gave sufficient scope to indigenous forces. Native *political* leadership consequently often was slower in developing in these countries. On the other hand, "liberal" colonial administrators often permitted trade-unions to develop among the native workers. In some countries, therefore, native leadership tended to develop first in the trade-union field. Later some of the leaders switched over to the political field as the independence process got more fully under way. I shall merely mention to you such names as Mboya in Kenya, Touré in Guinea, or Adoula in the Congo as outstanding examples of political leaders who gained their first, basic experience in the union movement.

In any event regardless of whether the labor movement develops first or is created later by political forces, in most countries once independence is won, the political process tends to take over as the prime moving force, and the labor movement finds it must relate itself to this central political force.

Since the political force is of such major importance, it frequently happens that the best labor leaders are drawn off from the unions into political roles.

One can sympathize with the almost plaintive cry of one of the leaders of the Nyasaland Trade-Union Federation on this hemorrhaging process confronting the labor movement in so many of these new countries.

Perhaps the biggest problem of all facing the Nyasaland trade-unions today is that of leadership. We are under no illusion that the present trade-union leadership is the best the country has to offer. But here we come up against the phenomenon that so many educated people are being canalised into the political movement at the expense of the labour movement. It is unfortunately true that to many Nyasas an easy way into the legislative council is more important than the interest of the workers.[9]

I have heard the same complaint from other trade-unionists coming from the new countries.

In 1958, according to Hodgkin, "trade-union leaders held portfolios in the governments of seven out of the eight territories of French West Africa . . ."[10]

In a society where the sources of experienced leadership are still extremely limited, it is perhaps inevitable that trade-union leaders will continue to be drawn off into other activities. A number of the developing country labor movements have come to the conclusion that the only way to "meet" this drain is to concentrate on their own training programs so that there can be a steady upward stream of new young leaders making their way into the movement.

*Forms of Unionsim*

As might be expected under the conditions we have been describing, the forms of trade-unionism in these newly developing countries are frequently different from those we have normally come to expect in the Western world. The lack of industrial development, and the lack of communications mean there is an absence of the force that normally produces *national* industrial or occupational types of unions which are the key units of labor in the Western world. It becomes far more feasible to organize the Singapore *general workers'* union (to use a hypothetical case), taking in all of the occupations in one area than to try to form a textile federation or a steel federation. General workers unions, in turn, can in some cases hinder the development of effective collective bargaining. In Gambia, West Africa, where there is an important general workers union, "the lack of specialized unions has hindered the growth of trade-union negotiating machinery and made necessary the use of statutory methods in labour matters." [11]

There is a tendency to form geographically-based unions under the impulse of the political needs of the day. Where unions are created or led by political leaders, these leaders prefer to reign over geographical groupings since these are more viable and effective for political purposes. Political leaders often lack interest in the more industrial side of unionism. A report on British Guiana in 1949 noted:

In British Guiana, as in the rest of the West Indies, politics are the all absorbing concern of the people and trade unionsim there has reversed the natural pattern by developing the political before the industrial aspects of industrial organization. There have thus been examples of 'personalities' founding unions more with an eye to political gain . . . than to the real benefit of the worker . . . [12]

The other side of this problem has been well stated by the great Indian Leader, J. P. Narayan, who relates what happened in the 1920's, when the Congress party made an alliance with the All India Trade-Union Congress and many Party leaders served as officers of the AITUC: "While it must be admitted that the trade-union work done then by Party members was not much to boast of, it should be remembered that the claims of the freedom movement were so heavy and most of us were so intimately connected with it that there was little time to attend to other work." [13]

A further complication is the tendency to form a large number of small unions. In many cases unions confine themselves to just the one work place at which they originate. A Fabian Society pamphlet on *Colonial Trade-Unions*, notes that in the various British colonies "many examples could be given of a multiplication of unions and unions with a membership so small that it is impossible for them to be of any service to their members." The same pamphlet goes on to prescribe amalgamation to overcome their weakness.

As industry develops and deepens, national industrial or occupational unions (mainly industrial, however) begin to emerge but it is a long time before they can challenge the power of city or regional groupings. India, for example, seems to be somewhere in the middle of this process with some national industrial unions emerging, but with the basis of power continuing to be largely geographical. Often political leaders resist the formation of national industrial unions which they fear will "threaten the power and prestige" they enjoy over more or less isolated, geographical types of unions.[14]

Union forms generally reflect the changing needs of workers and their movements. This has been true in the United States and in other Western labor movements as first political then more purely industrial needs seem to be more important. One can probably anticipate similar shifts from general and political to more industrial forms of unionism once basic political rights are established.[15]

### Collective Bargaining and Government Intervention

In the face of the presently existing types of union structure, it is not surprising that unions depend much less on collective bargaining and look to government more to help solve their problems. It is not that there is an absence of collective bargaining, but it hardly occupies the position of central thrust that it does in the Western labor movements.

As independence is gained, many of the new national governments, having struggled against colonial despotism, seek to identify themselves as progressive and they embody the rights of unions and collective bargaining in their new constitutions. Often they subscribe to ILO Conventions on Freedom of Association and the like.[16]

In a few new countries the system of extending collective agreements, first developed in some European countries, has also been established. Under this system an agreement negotiated with one or a group of employers can be extended by the government so that its terms control wages and related conditions in an entire industry or geographic area regardless of the state of unionism.

In a sense, however, all this legislation is too advanced for the weak unions to take advantage of it. Lacking industrial experience, lacking seasoned leadership, dominated by political forces, the unions are often not able to move ahead with collective bargaining. "Excessive" government largesse combines with other forces to ease the unions down the path of depending more upon government action than upon collective bargaining.

The relative weaknesses of the unions often lead them, at an early stage, to an acceptance and, indeed, an advocacy of systems of government intervention and arbitration as the prime means to resolve major issues in industrial relations. Such, for example, tends to be the basic policy of the Indian Trade-Union Congress. On the other hand, as the new governments turn increasingly to rapid economic development plans, they are often more than satisfied to prevent strikes and substitute government arbitration for them.

This process can go pretty far, with the unions becoming virtually the wards of the government, as seems to be the tendency in Ghana, where there now exists a virtual "concordat between organized labor and government. On the one hand, the trade-unions [have] conceded the principle of compulsory arbitration and relieved the government of anxiety about strikes. On the other hand, the government [has] provided legislation designed to increase the organizational and financial strength of the union." [17]

It comes as no surprise, therefore, to find the government rebuking the TUC of Ghana, during a session of the Parliament, for not identifying itself closely enough with the Convention People's party, and for trying to raise union dues from two to four shillings a month.[18]

In Mexico, after World War I, the labor movement was virtually "created out of whole cloth by a governing regime . . . In the ensuing decades, labor prospered under a friendly government and, at the same time, provided the ruling regime with its principal organizational strength . . ."; but according to one study, this movement now appears to be "passing into a stage where unions are seeking freedom from the dictates of government and are stressing collective bargaining and related activities . . ." [19]

Developments like those in Ghana, however, raise the question as to when does a union organization cease being a genuine movement, and when does it become a mere arm of the government with no real representation function on behalf of the workers. The distinction between a labor movement which has some real functional representational role and one which is purely a manipulated arm of the State is a critical one, though sometimes hard to make in some of these new societies. After all, if this distinction has no meaning here, then there is no line of distinction between unions in Soviet-totalitarian countries and Western democratic societies. I shall return to this problem at the conclusion of the chapter.

Like our own unions, these bodies, I might say, are changing affairs. To mention one interesting aspect of change, in some countries the unions served as a prime power point during the struggle for independence. The were frequently called into the streets to demonstrate against the colonial rulers or to paralyze the colonial economy. This is a heady sort of diet and not calculated to produce the king of "responsible unionism" we are more accustomed to.

Indeed, this is such a heady sort of diet that it can be something of a strain once independence is achieved and the new national government has taken power. Now these kinds of demonstrations and political strikes are frowned upon and, indeed, in some countries are quickly outlawed. This is particularly true as the new regimes undertake intensive economic development programs.

### Unions and Economic Development

As previously suggested one of the major forces operating in most of the new countries are their governments' bold and far-reaching efforts at intensive economic development. They are determined to pass quickly from their predominately agricultural status to a more advanced industrial existence. This is being done under the direction of central planning authorities.

Where do the unions fit into this program? Since this process of development always involves a strong effort for capital accumulation, it almost inevitably makes for some collision with union efforts at winning immediate gains for their members.

Confronted with these conflicting pressures, Asoka Mehta, leading Indian Socialist and one time trade-union official, has formulated what I would call the classic non-consumptionist sacrifice prescription for unions in the new countries. I believe this is worth quoting from at some length.[20] Mehta begins by noting that trade-unionism as practiced in the West, with its emphasis upon raising wages and protecting the workers against employers is not possible in the developing countries. (He also rejects the use of unions as *purely* political party adjuncts as in the case of the Communists or Socialists. Our concern here is with his critique of the usual economic role of unions.) "In underdeveloped countries . . . the chief problem is economic growth, and, therefore, the major question for unions is subordination of immediate wage gains and similar considerations to the development of the country." Unlike the developed countries where the unions' desire "to share in the high industrial profits is understandable," in underdeveloped countries "no such bases exist for such legitimate claims."

Capital accumulation and the development of industry are

the order of the day. Unions should cooperate with the State in such a production effort, particularly in view of the fact that a great part of the development will be in the public or socialized sector. Unions should act to increase "the labor productivity through propaganda," educate "their members to give up extra-spendthrift habits of the labor class" and encourage "small-savings among the classes," etc.

Mehta adds: "The economic implications of such trade-union behavior are twofold: (1) to restrict consumption and (2) to bring about an increase in the desired levels of production . . . any attempt to increase consumption of the population is likely to generate inflationary pressure . . ."

In addition to campaigning among and educating workers on the importance of the development plans, Mehta believes the union can play an important role in cushioning the shock of urbanization. They can help the new worker adjust to urban and industrial life; help him with his housing problems; help him to form cooperatives; provide training programs, etc.

Mehta has posed a stark form of unionism, but it is probably typical of the way in which economic planners look upon the labor function in a newly developing society. All thought of economic gain from industry must be sacrificed on the altar of capital accumulation and economic development.

Let me first comment that this kind of medicine in this stark form could only work in an authoritarian or totalitarian society, or for a relatively brief period of emotional involvement in the early days of a popular revolution. Labor reaction to industrialization in a democratic setting simply can't be canalized this way. Labor protest and labor demands are an inevitable reaction to industrialization and one should start out accepting this inevitability, and be concerned to see that such reactions take a constructive channel and not try to wish or do them away.

The net result of pursuing the non-consumptionist total sacrifice pattern to the hilt could be the sacrifice of the legitimate social and economic needs of the workers. In addition, it would weaken the free labor movement to the gain of a Communist-led labor movement. To some extent this has

244

already occurred in some of the new societies where the Communist labor unions have taken the lead in agitating for workers' gains here and now.

Several years back I was struck by the rather sad state a union could fall into if it allows the Communists to steal the lead entirely in agitating for gains from an employer. In one of the "new" countries, in a textile mill, rival unions, one Communist and one non-Communist were struggling. The non-Communist union opposed the agitation of the Communists, but it also noted that productivity in the plant had risen "as high as 90 per cent." One of the leaders of the non-Communist union thereupon addressed the management:

> I hope the management, which I believe is a progressive one, would not want for the workers to agitate for the fulfillment of their demands, but will anticipate the same and meet them before they are made . . . the management will not be justified in continuing to treat labor so niggardly particularly when they have shown better efficiency and their wages are extremely low. The management must realize that the only way to keep up the level of efficiency is to strive and secure a satisfied labor force.

One can only wonder how long a union like this so lacking in militance would continue to command support from the workers in the plant.

### Workers Needs and Social Overhead

In a sense the formulation of the problem of unionism in the developing countries as a case of a production versus a consumption function is not a fair one. Actually, many of the most pressing needs of workers in these societies tend to be in the field of social-overhead, viz: decent housing in the new urban areas, decent health facilities, or educational opportunities for themselves and their families, as opposed to a purely wage emphasis.

Given the pressures of modern life and communications, it is doubtful that any viable non-totalitarian industrial society can be built by ignoring these social-capital needs. To do otherwise would jeopardize sound industrial development and also play into the hands of Communist trade-union groups.

A fairer statement of this problem might, in the words of one African union leader, go something like this:

There must be equal opportunity for everyone in the community to participate in economic development and to enter into and rise to the highest levels in any branch of economic activity. While the chief emphasis in economic development plans is likely to be on industrialization, the trade-unions should ensure that social development is not neglected. Social measures, including proper care for public health and education as well as the provision of decent housing for workers, should occupy an important place in development programs. *The peoples of the newly developing countries must be saved from the worst effects of the industrial revolution as they were felt in the older countries. Trade-unions, for their part, should be ready to cooperate in measures to increase national production* and this should not be in conflict with their defense of employment opportunities, trade-union rights or living standards and working conditions and insistence that the benefits flow, in part at least, to the workers.[21]

A black and white, consumption versus capital-accumulation formulation is also unrealistic in other respects. Economic planning is never so tight and so perfect as to justify the kind of total abnegation which some call for on the part of labor. I can recall a conversation I had with the personnel director of an Indian textile plant—one plant of a large, privately owned industrial complex. He thought it absurd to talk of the unions foregoing their regular function of pressing for wage gains for the workers. It was clear to him that even in the face of the country's development plan, private profits were being made and fortunes accumulated. For the unions to ignore these facts would be absurd.

Important unions like the plantation workers in Malaya or Ceylon, the dockworkers in many African and Asian countries—these and many other examples can be cited where ordinary private companies continue to operate and where more or less traditional bargaining can and must go forward. In Latin America, of course, the structure of the economy is even more privately oriented and traditional union-management bargaining has developed.

But some caution must be injected here. The growing, world-wide desire for more rapid economic development is apt to lead to more and more emphasis upon state planning and the accumulation of capital in many new states. What will be called for, if democratic forms and institutions are to have a chance of survival and growth, is a sophisticated degree of cooperation between the unions and the planners. All-out repression of wages in favor of capital accumulation can probably be pursued only in a totalitarian society.

Direction of the economy by government planners provides no guarantee that worker dissatisfaction with economic inequalities won't boil up. Behind the wave of strikes and demonstrations in Ghana during the past two years appears to lie the workers' feeling that "officials and Government Ministers [were] becoming wealthier while the workers suffered," as well as "anger about the arrogance of party leaders who sit in large new buildings, drive about in new cars and who have lost touch with the rank and file." [22]

In a sense, the revolutionary struggle going on in many of these new countries is the familiar pattern of the double revolution. Thus, even as independence is being won, conflict between social groups in the nation's society itself begins to develop. The experience in Ghana seems to have a parallel in the Congo, where the Leopoldville Courrier d'Afrique criticized the government for "threatening the trade-unions" who were protesting against "injustices." Rather than criticize the unions, the newspaper declared: "The one gesture that everybody is waiting for from the 'big shots' is that instead of preaching austerity—for others—they should start by agreeing to a reduction of their own remuneration, which is excessive." [23]

### Unions' Inflationary Impact May Be Exaggerated

Paul Fisher has suggested that the inflationary threat which unions in the new countries pose is probably exaggerated. "In view of the relatively small proportion of the labor force in the less-developed countries which is affected by successful union efforts to raise the wage level, it would seem rash to credit labor unions necessarily with the ability to increase substantially the general consumption level . . . Dual economies persist in less developed countries. In many cases, in the midst of oversupply of unskilled labor, labor markets achieve . . . a degree of isolation which reserves wage gains for the permanent privileged members . . ." Again: "Most union wage drives are devoted to restoring the workers' wage eroded by inflation . . ." and unions, thus, don't actually lead on the inflation side.[24] As previously mentioned, the great pressure of over population is also a highly limiting factor on union collective bargaining efforts.

In any event, to repeat what was said earlier, the wage "drive" as such may not be as immediately critical for some unions in the developing countries for a number of reasons. The very act of transferring from a stagnant rural economy to any type of modern industrial job will probably mean, to begin with, a substantial "economic" gain for a worker; the shortcomings in this worker's life are apt to be in the field of housing, the newly stimulated desire for educational opportunities, and the like. Moreover, the weakness of their industrial thrust is apt to temper the collective bargaining wage drives of unions, anyway.

What would appear to be dangerous is any program which rules out completely the industrial bargaining demand side of unionism in the new countries. Attempts to smother demands and social protest entirely will only end up by diverting it into destructive channels.

## CONCLUSION: UNION PROSPECTS IN THE NEW COUNTRIES

Finally, I should like to consider some key long-run problems, tendencies and implications of trade-union development in new countries. Western experience seems to suggest that the essence of lasting, successful unionism lies in building effective representation forms for workers in industrial life.[25] This is true whether or not a separate and additional political arm is also created by the labor movement. Moreover, while it is common enough to find Western union movements underwriting the costs of political parties, especially labor and Socialist parties, the reverse situation of party supporting unions financially is virtually unknown in the West today. Again, although some of the European Socialist parties reserve a certain number of places on the party executive for trade-union nominees, the reverse situation of party representation on the union executive is quite rare.

Will, can, or should the union movements in the new countries anticipate the emergence of a similar clear-cut independent industrial status and function for unions in their societies?

The twin issues of independence from outside forces and the relationship to political parties may be the most crucial long-run issues confronting trade-unions in most of the developing countries. These issues, which in a sense are really one and the same, come up persistently in conversations with union and political party leaders from new countries. The same issues also crop up in the training schools which the ICFTU and the Israeli Histadrut conduct for unionists from the new countries.

In the face of great divisive forces such as tribalism, communalism, regionalism, and the vestiges of colonialism, as well as the necessity for rapid economic development, the notion of a fundamental line of separation between unions and parties, or unions and governments, seems inconceivable to political leaders in many of the new countries. Julius Nyerere, the leading political figure of Tanganyika, has stated with great force the case against the Western type of trade-union independence in the emerging countries of Africa. Nyerere insists:

. . . the Trade-Union movement was, and is part and parcel of the whole Nationalist movement. In the early days when a trade-union went on strike, for instance, and its members were in dire need of funds to keep them going, we saw no doctrine which would be abrogated by our giving financial support from the political wing to the industrial wing of the same Nationalist movement. It was simply a case of the right hand helping the left hand, or vice versa. It would clearly have been ridiculous to preach an imported doctrine of 'independence' . . .
This cooperation between the various organizations forming a Nationalist movement is not only desirable but logical. It springs from the very premises of nationalism. For example, if I try to walk from point A to point B, by the very definition of 'walking' my two legs will cooperate in taking me

there; I do not have to appeal to logic even. Still less do I have to worry about whether the independence of my right, or my left leg is being undermined by its need to seek the cooperation of the other. Either both legs are mine, or they are not. If both are mine, they must cooperate; to contemplate anything else is to contemplate an absurdity . . .

Similarly, either the trade-unions and the political organizations are prongs, or 'legs' of the same Nationalist movement, or they are not. If they *are*, then the question of whether they should or should not cooperate in getting the country from point A to point B does not arise . . .[26]

It was partially in response to positions such as Nyerere's that Omer Becu, General Secretary of the International Confederation of Free Trade-Unions, set forth a very thoughtful presentation of the case for the independence of trade-unions. Becu notes that the International Labour Organization has already resolved that even when trade-unions, "decide to establish relations with a political party or to undertake constitutional political action as a means towards the advancement of their economic and social objectives, such political relations or action should not be of such a nature as to compromise the continuance of the trade-union movement or its social and economic functions irrespective of political changes in the country."

Becu agrees with this general proposition, and adds that, "In the same manner, the free trade-union movement holds that trade-unions have a primary responsibility toward their members in the service of whom they have a continuous and fundamental task to perform. They have the specific obligation to prove their effectiveness in the field with which they are most directly concerned, that of collective bargaining. If the trade-unions are to accomplish their broader tasks they must command the allegiance of the workers and must be able to maintain that allegiance, in the first place by effective action to improve the wages and other conditions of the people they represent. Free and voluntary cooperation with other progressive forces is necessary for the common weal, but no political party, however close its affinities with the trade-union movement may be, is in a position to carry out the everyday activities of the trade-unions." [27]

# UNIONS IN THE NEW COUNTRIES

Obviously, it is difficult to forecast the actual lines of development which the labor movements in the new countries will take. The basic social economic and political forms in these countries will differ in many ways from what we have known in the past, and one must expect differences in union forms. One thing that can be safely said is that any effort on the part of Western unionists and students of labor to make a simple prescription of present Western union forms for all the countries is likely to be self-defeating. Present Western union forms themselves are the result of more than one hundred years of evolution and adaptation.

Nevertheless, the problem that Becu and others have raised is a real one. Unless unions achieve some independent industrial status, they will run the danger of losing influence in their own societies. Merely to be part of a political grouping without some independent industrial base can lead to a loss of special identity and influence on the part of the unions. The path to such independence is, however, very likely to be a very difficult and slow one in many of the new countries. Perhaps the most sensible prescription one can make is to ancitipate and, indeed, encourage a continuing dialogue between Western and new country trade-unionists, both of whom, after all, are now caught up in a world of constant change.

## NOTES

1. For a detailed treatment of the programs and tactics of the Communist labor forces in the developing countries of Asia and Africa, see the paper by George Lichtblau in this volume.
2. *Latin American Issues, Essays and Comments*, edited by Albert D. Hirschman, Twentieth Century Fund, New York (1961), p. 31.
3. *The Observer*, (London) July 2, 1961.
4. "Bourguiba's Tunisia: The Man and the Party," January 30, 1960, *Forum-Service*, London.
5. See Stephen Low, The Role of Trade-Unions in the Newly Independent Countries of Africa.
6. *Free Labour World* (April, 1960), pp. 151–2.

7. *Wreath for Udomo*, New York (1956), p. 348.
8. Myers, Charles, "India," in *Labor and Economic Development*, ed. by Walter Galenson, New York: John Wiley & Sons (1959), p. 26. Myers and other members of the Inter-University project have stressed this problem of commitment of the labor force in the context of the economic development of the new countries. It is possible, however, that this problem can be exaggerated, especially in the face of the vast population surpluses in most Asian and African nations—these surpluses tend to create competition among workers for the relatively few industrial jobs. See, for instance, Morris, M. D., "The Labor Market in India," in *Labor Commitment and Social Change in Developing Areas*, ed. by W. E. Moore and A. S. Feldman, Social Science Research Council, New York, 1960.
9. *Free Labour World*, April, 1961.
10. Hodgkin, Thomas, *African Political Parties*, London: Penguin Books, African Series WA12 (1961), p. 119.
11. Roper, J. I., *Labour Problems in West Africa*, London: Penguin Books (1958), p. 20.
12. Quoted in Bowen, Walter, *Colonial Trade-Unions*, Fabian Colonial Bureau Pamphlet (1954), p. 7.
13. Rose, Saul, *Socialism in Southern Asia*, New York: Oxford Univ. Press (1959), p. 20.
14. Ghose, S., *Trade-Unionism in Underdeveloped Countries*, Calcutta: Bookland Private, Ltd. (1960), p. 89.
15. See Sturmthal, Adolf, "Unions and Economic Development," *Economic Development and Cultural Change*, Jan. 1960.
16. Time prevents my discussing the external influence exerted by the trade-union movements of the developed areas upon the movements in the new countries. In spite of intense nationalism, it is interesting how many of the new country movements value and seek assistance from the Western movements. One reason why the Communists are encouraging "neutralist" federations in Africa and elsewhere is to help cut off "Western" influence and contacts.
17. Rimmer, Douglas, "The New Industrial Relations in Ghana," *Industrial and Labor Relations Review* (January, 1961), p. 216. A rash of strikes in Ghana in the past two years suggests, however, that all is not quite so set, as Rimmer implies.
18. *Labor Developments Abroad*, U. S. Dept. of Labor (June, 1961), p. 13.
19. Troncoso, M. P., and Burnett, B. G., *The Rise of the Latin American Labor Movement*, New York: Bookman Associates (1960), pp. 150–2.

20. Mehta, Asoka, "The Mediating Role of the Trade-Union in Underdeveloped Countries," *Economic Development and Cultural Change* (Oct. 1957), pp. 16–23.
21. Tom Mboya addressing 1959 ICFTU Congress, *Free Labor World*, Jan.–Feb. 1960, p. 31, emphasis in the original.
22. *The Observer*, Aug. 28, 1960, and the *Washington Post*, Oct. 1, 1961.
23. Quoted in *African Forum*, News and Comments (London), Aug. 26, 1961.
24. Fisher, Paul, *Unions in the Less Developed Countries, a Reappraisal of Their Economic Role*, in this volume.
25. See Clegg, H. A., *A New Approach to Industrial Democracy*, Oxford: Basil Blackwell (1960), p. 131.
26. Nyerere, Julius, *The African Trade-Unions*, Dar Es Salaam, Tanganyika, Dec., 1960.
27. *Free Labour World* (July, 1961), pp. 278–9.

# NOTES ON THE CONTRIBUTORS

*Everett M. Kassalow*

Since 1957, Director of Research, Industrial Union Department, AFL-CIO; also since 1959, Director of Special Research Seminar on Comparative Labor Movements, sponsored by the National Institute of Labor Education; also since 1960, special lecturer on international labor problems, American University. He has also served with the United Automobile Workers and the United Rubber Workers in research capacities in the past. From 1955 to 1957 he was Labor Adviser to the International Cooperation Administration, Paris, France. His earlier service included work with the National Security Resources Board and the U. S. Department of Labor. His publications include numerous articles on domestic and international labor problems in various published volumes as well as the *Monthly Labor Review*, *The New Republic*, and the *Harvard Business Review*. He is currently serving as member of the Executive Board of the Industrial Relations Research Association.

*David J. Saposs*

David J. Saposs is presently Adjunct Professor, School for International Service, American University. In the past few years he has also served as Visiting Professor, Industrial Relations Institute, University of Illinois, and at the Industrial Relations Center, University of Hawaii. He has had a long career in government, including service as Labor Adviser with the Office of Military Government for Germany, Labor Adviser and Coordinator for InterAmerican Affairs and Labor Adviser of the U. S. Aid Mission to Europe. He has also served as Chief Economist, National Labor Relations Board and Assistant to the Commissioner, Bureau of Labor Statistics, U. S. Department of Labor. Saposs is the author of numerous works, including *Left-Wing Unionism*, *The Labor Movement of Postwar France*, *Communism in American Unions*, and *Communism in American Politics*.

*Arnold Leslie Steinbach*

Arnold L. Steinbach received his Doctor's degree in law, economics, and politics from the University of Vienna in 1918 and a diploma from the same university in actuarial statistics in 1919. Before his arrival in the U. S. in 1935 he was Executive

# NOTES ON THE CONTRIBUTORS

Director of the Labor Market Agency in Vienna. In 1947 he joined the Office of International Labor Affairs, U. S. Department of Labor and since 1949 he has been Chief of the Division of International Trade-Union Organizations. He has traveled extensively, mainly in Europe.

## George E. Lichtblau

George E. Lichtblau is a specialist on international labor affairs in the Department of State. He has lectured in his field and published a number of articles on the activities of the trade-union internationals, the politics of trade-union leadership in the underdeveloped countries, and a critique of Socialist developments in southern Asia.

## Paul Fisher

Paul Fisher is Social Development Advisor, Agency for International Development, and Adjunct Professor of Economics, The American University, Washington, D. C. Born 1908, he was educated at the Universities of Paris, and Vienna. He has taught at various colleges and universities (Clark, Minnesota, Dartmouth), and is a contributor to economic journals on national and international labor issues. He is listed in *American Men of Science*, and *Who's Who in Southeast*.

## Bruce H. Millen

Millen is currently serving as Labor Attache in the American Embassy, New Delhi, India. He formerly served as Labor Adviser in the Bureau of Near East and South Asian Affairs, U. S. Department of State in Washington, D. C. Mr. Millen was on leave from the government service in 1961 during which time he completed research on a volume to be published by Brookings Institution, *The Political Role of Labor in Developing Countries*, to be released early in 1963. Mr. Millen has also served as Labor Attaché in Norway and as Assistant Labor Attaché in Italy. During the '40's Mr. Millen worked for the CIO both in its political action and organizing work.

## Val R. Lorwin

Val R. Lorwin is professor of history at the University of Oregon. He has served in federal government agencies dealing with labor and consumer problems and international labor affairs, and as an adviser to United States delegations to the International Labour Organization, the United Nations General Assembly, and the Economic and Social Council. He is the author of *The French Labor Movement* (Harvard University Press, 1954), and articles (in symposium volumes, economic and historical and labor relation journals, and the *Encyclopedia Britannica*) on French and American labor history and international labor problems. For some years he has been working on a study of Belgian political life.

*Robert J. Alexander*

Associate professor of economics, Rutgers University, Robert Alexander is the author of *The Peron Era* (1951); *Communism in Latin America* (1957); *The Bolivian National Revolution* (1958); and *The Struggle for Democracy in Latin America* (1961). He has worked with the Office of Inter-American Affairs and the International Cooperation Administration.

*Solomon B. Levine*

Solomon B. Levine is a professor of labor and industrial relations in the Institute of Labor and Industrial Relations at the University of Illinois. For the academic year 1962–63 he is serving as a visiting professor of industrial relations at Massachusetts Institute of Technology. He was a Fulbright research scholar in Japan in 1953–54 and a Fulbright lecturer in Japan in 1959. He has also served as a consultant to the Ford Foundation and Asia Foundation in various projects concerning industrial relations in Japan. He is the author of *Industrial Relations in Post War Japan* (University of Illinois Press, 1958). He holds a B.A. and M.B.A. from Harvard University and Ph.D. in economics at M.I.T.

*Stephen Low*

Stephen Low is a Foreign Service officer who has served in Kampala, Uganda, and Dakar, Senegal. Between these two assignments he spent a year studying the problems and theory of labor organization during which he developed the ideas contained in the paper included in this collection. Prior to entering the Foreign Service, Mr. Low received a BA from Yale University and Ph.D. from the Fletcher School of Law and Diplomacy.